The NEW RULES
of SALES
and SERVICE

Also by David Meerman Scott

The New Rules of Marketing & PR: How to Use Social Media, Online Video, Mobile Applications, Blogs, News Releases, and Viral Marketing to Reach Buyers Directly

Marketing the Moon: The Selling of the Apollo Lunar Program (with Richard Jurek)

Real-Time Marketing & PR: How to Instantly Engage Your Market, Connect with Customers, and Create Products That Grow Your Business Now

Marketing Lessons from the Grateful Dead: What Every Business Can Learn from the Most Iconic Band in History (with Brian Halligan)

Newsjacking: How to Inject Your Ideas into a Breaking News Story and Generate Tons of Media Coverage

World Wide Rave: Creating Triggers That Get Millions of People to Spread Your Ideas and Share Your Stories

Tuned In: Uncover the Extraordinary Opportunities That Lead to Business Breakthroughs (with Craig Stull and Phil Myers)

Cashing In with Content: How Innovative Marketers Use Digital Information to Turn Browsers into Buyers

Eyeball Wars: A Novel of Dot-Com Intrigue

The NEW RULES
of SALES
and SERVICE

HOW TO USE AGILE SELLING, REAL-TIME CUSTOMER ENGAGEMENT, BIG DATA, CONTENT, AND STORYTELLING TO GROW YOUR BUSINESS

REVISED AND EXPANDED

DAVID MEERMAN SCOTT

WILEY

Published by John Wiley & Sons, Inc., Hoboken, New Jersey.
Published simultaneously in Canada.

For general information about our other products and services, please contact our Customer Care Department within the United States at (800) 762-2974, outside the United States at (317) 572-3993 or fax (317) 572-4002.

Wiley publishes in a variety of print and electronic formats and by print-on-demand. Some material included with standard print versions of this book may not be included in e-books or in print-on-demand. If this book refers to media such as a CD or DVD that is not included in the version you purchased, you may download this material at http://booksupport.wiley.com. For more information about Wiley products, visit www.wiley.com.

Library of Congress Cataloging-in-Publication Data:
Names: Scott, David Meerman, author.
Title: The new rules of sales and service : how to use agile selling,
    real-time customer engagement, big data, content, and storytelling to grow
    your business / David Meerman Scott.
Description: Revised Edition. | Hoboken : Wiley, 2016. | Revised edition of
    the author's The new rules of sales and service, 2014. | Includes index.
Identifiers: LCCN 2016012015 (print) | LCCN 2016022539 (ebook) | ISBN
    9781119272427 (paperback) | ISBN 9781119272434 (epdf) | ISBN 9781119272441 (epub)
Subjects: LCSH: Selling. | Customer services. | Internet marketing. | Big
    data. | BISAC: BUSINESS & ECONOMICS / Sales & Selling. | BUSINESS &
    ECONOMICS / Marketing / General.
Classification: LCC HF5438.25 .S347 2016 (print) | LCC HF5438.25 (ebook) |
    DDC 658.8—dc23
LC record available at https://lccn.loc.gov/2016012015

Printed in the United States of America

*This book, my 10th, is dedicated
to my grandmother Dorothy Miller Jones (1905–1996).
When I was a child, Grandma Jones taught me that
if you want to receive letters, you've got to write letters.
I wish I could share with her that
the same thing is true today about
social networking and customer engagement;
you have to give to get.*

Contents

Introduction

Are you old enough to remember when travel agents were an essential part of your life? To book a vacation you had to go to a travel agent. There was no other choice. Every town had at least one, and in the big cities travel agencies were on every corner.

First, before you set foot in the travel agency, you might do a little research about the sort of vacation you had in mind. Warm weather at a beach? Or perhaps a week of skiing? Maybe a cruise? Did you want to go somewhere exotic and far away? Or nearby within driving distance?

Doing the research was really, really difficult.

You would ask friends for recommendations, but they knew only so much. You could read a travel magazine, but with only a limited number of pages in each issue, it was hardly comprehensive. Guidebooks helped, but because of the book publication cycles, they were inevitably dated. If you wanted to compare different destinations, you needed more than one guidebook. And by definition, a book is just one person's opinion—the author's. No matter how much research you did, it was never enough to get a total picture of a potential holiday location.

Sooner or later you had to go into that travel agency, and that's when you surrendered control of the already imperfect process: You had to put yourself at the mercy of a salesperson. As she sat behind a terminal, she tossed out destination options, quoted prices for flights and rental cars, and suggested hotels. Perhaps she loaded you up with a bunch of brochures to look through.

The best travel agents were adept at matching destinations, experiences, and properties to a traveler's needs. They built a loyal following and made a good living via repeat business and word-of-mouth referrals.

But too often, agents weren't very good and just sold what was most convenient. They would steer clients to the easy sale in Florida instead of the more complicated booking at a small resort on an obscure island in the

French-speaking part of the Caribbean. Worse, unscrupulous agents would sell crappy cruises simply because they earned additional commissions from low-end operators desperate to fill their ships.

The bottom line in booking a vacation 20 years ago was simple: The travel agent was in charge of the sales process because she had the information. The unfortunate traveler was limited to her recommendations and her prices.

And it wasn't just travel. This was the case for nearly every sales situation one transacted.

It's a new world now. The way we book travel today is so utterly different from being tied to agents as to be unrecognizable.

Recently my wife and I went on a 10-day expedition to Antarctica. Since I was a kid I'd dreamed of seeing giant blue-green icebergs up close and encountering penguins and whales in the most remote continent on earth.

We began our independent research on the web more than a year before our expedition.

We used Google to find the results for such phrases as "Antarctica travel," "Antarctica expedition," and "visit Antarctica." Our searches led us to about a dozen expedition outfitters, and we carefully checked out each of them via their sites. We also found personal blogs written by people who had undertaken such an expedition. These offered great information about what we needed to consider. There were independent reviews of operators and expedition ships. We found articles profiling Antarctica travel on newspaper and magazine websites. We even landed on the site of the International Association of Antarctica Tour Operators, and while it is a trade organization, we learned a lot more there.

Unlike booking travel 20 years ago, we were in charge of the buying process. We had information from experienced experts to aid us when making our decisions. We could learn from those who had gone before us on their social networks. And we could book directly with our choice of outfitter.

> Now, buyers are in charge of relationships with companies they choose to do business with.

Smart companies understand this new world and build a buying process around the realities of independent research. Instead of generic information dreamed up by an advertising agency, they tell authentic stories that interest their customers. Instead of selling, they educate through online content. Instead of ignoring those who have already made a purchase, they deliver information at precisely the moment customers need it.

As my wife and I evaluated the various expedition outfitters, we quickly narrowed our choice to several, based on the content on their websites. We explored information about the wildlife we were likely to observe such as chinstrap penguins, gentoo penguins, elephant seals, leopard seals, minke whales, and humpback whales. We viewed amazing photographs of icebergs and watched videos of birds unique to the harsh climate. We explored ways to combat seasickness during the two-day voyage from southern Argentina to the Antarctic continent. We learned about the ships and we could virtually meet the expedition leaders. And yes, we could compare pricing of the various travel options.

We were finally ready and chose to book a 10-day adventure with Quark Expeditions, a Canada-based polar travel outfitter operating a fleet of six ice-strengthened expedition ships. The information provided by Quark served to guide us from our initial research phase to the decisive moment when we felt sufficiently educated and ready to reserve our cabin.

Quark Expeditions tells a compelling story to customers contemplating an Antarctic adventure. The informative content that Quark freely provides—stories of amazing encounters with wildlife and stunning scenic vistas, about expedition staff who are leaders in their specialties and eager to help guests learn, and detailing the professional experience that ensures a safe and enjoyable trip—leads buyers like me to the point when they are ready to take the next step.

The Quark story comes from the top. Its president and CEO, Hans Lagerweij, leads their communications efforts and tweets regularly about polar travel via @hanslagerweij. As part of our research process, I tweeted Lagerweij, and he got back to me quickly. Unlike most CEOs who care more about the financials than about their customers, Lagerweij is in the thick of communications and sets the tone for what his entire team delivers, from the expedition experience itself to how that experience is sold to potential travelers.

When I placed a call to Quark Expeditions, I reached Paul, a "polar travel advisor." I knew exactly what I wanted: which expedition ship (the *Ocean Diamond*), the dates of travel, and the type of cabin. Paul didn't need to sell me, because the online content had already done that! And here's the important point: Paul knew this. Unlike the sales process a decade ago, Paul's job was 95 percent done by the time he answered my call. The actual transaction was simple and was completed quickly.

Once we had booked our expedition, the online storytelling didn't stop. At this point, Paul became a content curator, digging into Quark's information library to send me what we needed to make our trip more enjoyable.

Paul sent us content on optional Antarctica activities: camping, cross-country skiing, kayaking, snowshoeing, and yes, even a polar plunge into near-freezing water! (Gotta do it, right?!) All of these options were presented to us at the right moment in the buying process (after we booked the trip but well before departure). We also received information on an optional trekking and canoeing trip in Tierra del Fuego National Park near Ushuaia, Argentina, the southernmost city in the world and the departure point for our expedition.

Later, as the date of our trip neared and as we began to plan what we needed to pack, we received a PDF checklist of essential and suggested gear. We also watched a video of Quark's merchandise coordinator, Jaymie MacAulay, answering commonly asked questions about the best clothing to pack when traveling to the polar regions. There was information on cameras, binoculars, and video equipment. We learned about sunscreen (it's bright in Antarctica in the near 24-hour December sun). Of particular importance, we got information on antiseasickness remedies for the notorious Drake Passage in the form of a post on the Quark Expeditions blog and a video on their YouTube channel, and we were given ideas about medicine to bring.

In short, through the provision of online content, Quark led us from the initial Google search through to closing a sale, and then continued the virtual relationship all the way to our expedition departure date.

The storytelling and content delivery didn't stop there.

Among the staff of our expedition were several professional photographers, including the amazing Sue Flood, a wildlife photographer, author, and filmmaker. (She was associate producer on the award-winning series *The Blue Planet*.) A personalized copy of Sue's beautiful photography book *Cold Places* now sits on our living room table. The photographers on board the *Ocean Diamond* delivered lectures during the Drake Passage crossing and were available in the evenings after we finished each day's exploration. They offered advice about how best to photograph the amazing wildlife and scenery we were experiencing. When we went out on the Zodiac (a rigid inflatable boat), they were there as well and came with us when we landed to explore. While shooting their own photographs, the photographic experts were also available and eager to answer questions or offer advice.

During each night's expedition recap, passengers were encouraged to upload their own photographs. The best of the photos submitted by passengers as well as those from the professionals were then collected into a Quark Expeditions Photographic Journal chronicling our voyage, which each of us was given on the last day of the expedition.

This is an ingenious sales move by Quark. Once we got home, we had a collection of hundreds of photos by which to remember our journey. The stunning images were sure to spark curiosity about Quark among our envious friends (and possibly implant the idea that we might actually do it again). Other expedition outfitters don't bother to share photos, or when they do they usually sell them to their customers. Quark Expeditions sees the value of making them free.

Many of us had epic photos included in the disk that had been shot by Quark staff members, and these could be easily shared via social media. This, of course, serves as free promotion for Quark Expeditions voyages. For example, one of the several shots of me doing my polar plunge that were taken from a Zodiac near the *Ocean Diamond* was perfect to share on Facebook. Last I checked, there were 153 likes and 47 comments on this photo, the most I've ever gotten on a Facebook post. And each person who sees my photo is a potential customer for a Quark voyage in the future.

We continue to receive information from Quark Expeditions via email about its expeditions, including a trip to the North Pole on a nuclear-powered icebreaker.

These are the New Rules of Sales and Service at work. And they are completely different from booking travel a few decades ago. Sadly, many in the travel business haven't figured this out. And it's the same story in every industry.

> We live in the era of a buying process controlled by consumers, not a sales situation stacked against us. The good news is this means that people who understand the new realities can make their business fantastically successful.

The Time Is NOW

Because of the biggest communications revolution in human history, your marketplace has changed. The vast majority of human beings, more than five billion of us, are connected instantly to each other via web-based and mobile communications devices. In this technology-driven life, we crave humanity. Information about products and services is available to buyers everywhere, 24/7, and for free, and anyone can generate attention by publishing valuable content. With the expense of publishing essentially free, customers have a (loud) voice through social networks and review sites.

Therefore it is time for the New Rules of Sales and Service: **Authentic storytelling** sets the tone with **content** as the link between companies and customers. **Big data** enables a more scientific approach to sales and service. **Agile selling** brings new business to your company, and **real-time engagement** keeps customers happy.

Of course, it's not just the travel market that has changed. Every business is going through transition. Consumer products, business-to-business products and services, healthcare, nonprofit organizations in search of donations, politicians eager for votes . . . everything. Buyers are now in charge. We have instant access to virtually unlimited information. Winning companies are no longer determined by the salespeople with the best closing technique. Now success belongs to organizations that tell their buyers the best stories, companies with the best content, and those whose information aligns perfectly with buyer needs.

In *The New Rules of Sales and Service*, we will look at how people buy in today's world of always-on 24/7 information and what that means for sellers and for those who service existing customers.

I'll share how authentic and effective stories are created and how those stories are aligned with the needs of the buyer. If employees are infused with a coherent and compelling story—a corporate narrative that is defined by the CEO and has a cascade effect on all staff members such as Hans Lagerweij's stewardship at Quark Expeditions—then those employees have the means and the understanding to engage their customers instantly. Once the beat is laid down by the CEO, the employees work together like a tight rock band with the notes coming from each player to make music.

We'll focus on how real-time engagement with customers by service staff and agile sales techniques rule the day, and the importance of clear and effective content that drives people to be eager to do business with you.

I will show you how you too can make the transformation from the old ways of selling and servicing clients to the new realities now defining how people buy and do business. And I'll offer many examples of success like Quark Expeditions so you can learn from those who have mastered the new approach.

Living in the Past: The Old School of Sales and Service

Quick. What do you think of when I say "sales"?

Unless they are salespeople themselves, most people tell me they think of a slick car salesman in an ill-fitting suit, spouting a line like: "What would it take to put you into this car today?"

When people think sales, they associate it with being hustled and taken advantage of. They think of dealing with a salesperson as an adversarial relationship. The very word *sales* can prompt sleazy connotations, and people become automatically defensive in order not to be taken advantage of.

If they are of a certain age, some people think of the hustling character played by Alec Baldwin in *Glengarry Glen Ross* and lines like: "Coffee is for closers." That's the movie adapted from David Mamet's 1984 Pulitzer Prize– and Tony award–winning play in which sales guys fight for a Cadillac El Dorado (first prize) or a set of steak knives (second prize). Third prize is getting fired. In such a testosterone-fueled environment, the hapless customer is just a mark. *Glengarry Glen Ross* is so iconic in American sales circles that many salespeople quote from it liberally. I've seen clips from the movie at several companies' sales conferences. And it's no surprise that it powerfully reinforces the average customer's unease with salespeople.

How about when I say "customer service"? What comes to mind?

Many people describe the experience of calling a toll-free telephone line, only to be told "Your call is important to us" and then being forced to endure a frustratingly long wait "due to higher than average call volume." When an actual person picks up on the other end of the line, it may be difficult to understand the accent of the outsourced representative in a far-off foreign land.

Or if it is a face-to-face encounter with someone in customer support—an airline ticket counter, say—the majority of people tell me they anticipate that indifference will prevail, if not outright rudeness.

But in today's always-on world of the web, these old school approaches to sales and service need not be the norm. Modern businesses recognize that buyers have access to real-time information on any product or service that interests them and are thrilled to wait until they are fully educated before finally reaching out to a sales representative at their chosen company.

> Smart companies understand that people have choices of whom to do business with, and they are transforming the way they sell and service customers.

At the same time, the web is a vast supermarket of customer information and intelligence. If a buyer is wondering how to use a product or wants to know if others have experienced the same problem and can suggest a fix, an encyclopedia of firsthand knowledge is easily at hand. People tweet their frustrations with the services they use, providing a perfect opportunity for brands to engage on customers' time. Yet most organizations still force customers to use the antiquated telephone, and make them wait on hold for a representative rather than engaging them with digital tools at the precise moment the customers need help.

The best companies recognize that real-time engagement on social networks like Facebook and Twitter not only makes customers happy because their problems are instantly addressed, but also provides guidance to future customers with the same concerns via the public discussions. Such attention to customers' needs serves to brand those companies as ones that others will want to do business with.

First Marketing and PR, Now Sales and Service

Early in my career, I worked as a sales representative at a Wall Street economic consultancy. Back then the salesperson had the information and therefore the power in the relationship.

If the buyers wanted information about how the product worked, they needed to come to me. If they wanted to negotiate a discount, they had to come through me. If they wanted to speak to a customer to learn about their experience with my company, they had to come through me. If they wanted to talk to the founder of the company, they had to come through me. I was involved from the very beginning of the relationship, and most of the leverage was with me, the sales rep.

But now, because of the wealth of information on the web, the salesperson no longer controls the relationship. Now, the buyers can check you out themselves. They can find your customers and read their blog accounts about what you do. They can reach the founders directly via Twitter and LinkedIn. Buyers actively go around salespeople until the last possible moment and then come into negotiations armed with lots and lots of information. Now it's the buyers who have the leverage.

> Most sales organizations are built and run as if it were still 1989. The sales model is broken.

The New Rules of Marketing and PR Are Now Widely Adopted

For the past decade, I've been evangelizing how marketing and public relations (PR) have changed as a result of the web.

Throughout 2005 and into 2006, I saw the patterns clearly and wrote a book that eventually became *The New Rules of Marketing & PR*, now an international bestseller in its fifth edition and available in over 25 languages from Bulgarian to Vietnamese. The book, which has sold 350,000 copies in English, is about how to use social media, online video, mobile applications, blogs, real-time media, and viral marketing to reach buyers directly. I don't say this to brag, but rather to outline how online content has transformed the way organizations reach buyers. It has made the marketing and PR functions unrecognizable from those of just a few years before.

Prior to the web, generating attention meant buying expensive advertising or convincing the media to write or broadcast about us. But now we've got a better way: generating attention by publishing information on the web so people find it while searching with Google and other search engines, and discover it when they share on social networks.

Since *The New Rules of Marketing & PR* was initially published, the biggest challenge to getting these ideas accepted has been fear. People are reluctant to change. There has been a huge disconnect between what people actually do as consumers and what they focus on as marketers and entrepreneurs.

While many companies are doing a good job generating attention via online content, a number still insist that their target market is "different." Even though nearly everyone turns to search engines when researching products and services and consults one's network of friends, colleagues, and family members for advice through social networks, the fearful marketers who are resistant to change still invest an inordinate amount of time and money on traditional interruption advertising. These holdouts still focus on the traditional method of pitching-based media relations. They are using the old rules to try to generate attention.

During the past several years, hundreds of people have asked me to extend the ideas I wrote about in *The New Rules of Marketing & PR* to sales and service. They've told me how they've transformed their marketing and public relations functions and now they are ready to do the same with their sales and customer service functions. In 2012 I knew I had to begin researching the ideas that are now part of this book, and I started writing the first edition in 2013, which was released in 2014, and worked on this revised edition in 2015 and 2016.

> The marketing and public relations functions have started the transformation due to the advances in real-time technologies of online content and social media; now it is time for sales and service departments to understand the new realities of growing business.

Living Real Time and Mobile Has Changed Everything We Do

The two most important trends not only for marketers and PR pros but for salespeople and customer services types alike is to understand the importance of real time and the rise of mobile.

Real time means that news breaks over minutes, not days. It means that ideas percolate, and then suddenly and unpredictably go viral to a global audience. It's when companies develop (or refine) products or services instantly, based on feedback from customers or events in the marketplace. And it's when a business sees an opportunity and is the first to act upon it. However, too many companies leave themselves fatally exposed by flying blind through this new media environment.

Real-time engagement is about reacting instantly to what's happening in the market, following up on opportunities in seconds, and inserting your company into stories being reported by mainstream media. Those skilled at long-term campaign creation frequently lack the necessary skills of instant engagement. So an understanding of real-time media is essential.

> While marketing is the provision of content to many potential customers, sales and service are now about the provision of content to buyers one at a time based on their needs.

You can engage desktop-computer users when they're at their desks. Sometimes you can engage notebook users at Starbucks. But only when users go mobile can you engage all of the people in real time all of the time. That's why mobile devices are the fastest-growing and most fascinating field in real-time market engagement. We need to understand the ramifications of people being constantly plugged in and looking for information while on the go.

Slowly over nearly a decade, the importance of these ideas has caught on with marketers and public relations people. Today, tens of thousands of organizations around the world have teams who are creating content to publish on their websites, writing blogs, and creating online videos, as well as engaging in social networks like Facebook, LinkedIn, and Twitter. And many are operating in true real-time fashion and understand mobile.

In just a few short years we've gone from skepticism to deployment by many companies, nonprofits, and other outfits.

Why Sales and Service Are Experiencing a Revolutionary Transformation

Today it's up to customers when they want to engage a salesperson. If I'm interested in buying something, I go to the web, I go to Twitter or Facebook or LinkedIn, and I ask my friends and colleagues and family members for advice. I go to a half-dozen websites and do research. When I'm finally good and ready and I've built up my body of knowledge, I reach out, typically electronically through email, and say, "Hey, I'm interested to go to the next step," and almost always the salesperson who calls me assumes I know nothing. Most organizations are still using traditional selling and service models that were developed decades ago. This needs to change, or your organization will suffer.

> Just as online content is the primary driver for successful marketing and public relations, online content is quickly becoming a dominant driver for sales and service as well.

Restoring the Human Touch: The Compelling Power of Authenticity

People want to do business with other people. That's been true since the beginning of time. A hundred years ago our great-grandparents knew the people who sold them hardware or shoes or chickens. There was a personal touch. If there was good service at a fair price and maybe a kind word and a smile, they had a business relationship that lasted for many years.

However, during the past several decades huge companies have been selling identical products to millions of people via mass media advertising on television, and in the process many companies have lost the human touch. Many smaller companies adopted the mass media approach model for their own markets. Advertising agencies were hired to develop "messages." Salespeople memorized scripts. Top executives fretted about financials, but not about customers.

Now, buyers can interact with anyone who is active in social media. They can see what companies are doing. Who is engaged? Who will talk to me? Does anyone care?

We're back to a hundred years ago and the ability to converse with the person who is selling. What can you tell me about this bike? Is this wetsuit good for scuba diving too, or is it appropriate only for surfing? Which Antarctica expedition is best for me?

An authentic encounter with a representative from a company in a sales or service situation humanizes an organization after decades of sameness.

The Importance of Story

The best businesses have an organizational story that underlies everything they do. For these outfits, that story and the resulting culture it builds mean that everybody—from the CEO and the executives to the salespeople and support staff, even the person who answers the telephone—are all delivering the same information.

By story, I don't mean making up a fairy tale. No, rather the narrative should be a real and authentic account of what the organization is all about. People associated with the company should know these stories by heart and be able to convey them easily when the need arises. These might include a compelling account detailing how the company was founded. They could tell about employees who go out of their way to help customers, or could explain how the company's products are the most expensive in the market and the reasons why.

Social Media Is All about Connecting and Sharing

When I was writing the first edition of *The New Rules of Marketing & PR* way back in 2005 and 2006, I felt as if I was the only person who had identified the idea that communicating on the web was fundamentally about understanding your buyers and publishing the valuable information that informs and educates (YouTube videos, blog posts, e-books, and the like). This was a radical idea at the time the book was released in 2007, and it was not without controversy, especially from traditional advertising veterans and public relations professionals.

But then, slowly, an understanding started to build about the power of reaching existing and potential customers on the web. Soon the incredible rise of social networking services like Facebook and Twitter created an environment where millions were exposed to what many were now calling "social media." And then, starting in 2008, the revolution that is web communications went mainstream. The idea of social media entered its full-blown hype mode in recent years, as thousands of instant experts began talking about using social media for growing a business.

Alas, all too often these self-proclaimed gurus spend way too much time talking about the individual tools (such as Twitter) and not enough about the practical aspects of the tools and what they can do as part of a company's overall strategy. And when people hear about Twitter again and again in the same context as social media, no wonder they get a hangover.

So, yes, *social media* is a buzzword that I am sometimes sick of hearing myself.

It seemed to me that most so-called experts were just hyping the tools themselves. Sure Twitter is important. But what's fundamentally more important is how people need to evolve their mind-set to be successful. Creating a Facebook page or jumping onto Twitter won't transform your business. Changing your mind-set to one of understanding buyers and publishing content on the web will.

Content Drives Sales and Service

As buyers move through the sales cycle, they self-select information that will help them. Perhaps they will encounter a blog post here, a webinar there, or maybe an e-book to read on the train ride home, just as Quark Expeditions reached me when I was investigating a visit to Antarctica. Salespeople can't hoard information like they used to, because it's all available on the web. So the smart ones have transformed themselves into a sort of information broker, serving up the perfect content to each buyer at the right time.

On the service side, once someone is signed up as a customer, information delivered at the right moment makes for a happy customer who renews existing services and buys more over time. And happy customers talk up companies on social networks.

We're All in Sales and Service Now

Back in the twentieth century, organizations had sales departments and customer support departments. Most big companies still do, but with the rise of social networking and instant engagement on the web, now we're *all* in sales and service.

Think about it. If you work at a big company and you're on LinkedIn or Twitter, you can instantly engage with your network no matter what department within the company you happen to work in. If you're an accountant at a technology company and somebody you follow on Twitter happens to mention that he or she is researching a technology like the one your company makes, bingo! You can point the person to a video on your company's YouTube channel. Even though you're not formally in the sales department, you're still driving your contacts into the buying process.

> If you run a small company, then you're in sales and service. If you're a doctor or lawyer or accountant, you're in sales and service. Entrepreneurs are in sales and service, too. Everybody who lives by their wits by going independent or starting something new or running an established organization should always be selling and providing support. The good news is that it is much easier to actually handle the sales and service aspects of running a small business.

Online Content That Informs, Entertains . . . and Sells Insurance

With my friend Larry McGlynn, I went to the Nantucket Demolition Derby. It was great to watch car crashes in beautiful autumn weather.

McGlynn is president and CEO of McGlynn, Clinton & Hall Insurance Agencies and is my insurance agent. He is a funny guy, so I'm always thinking of bad insurance humor.

"Larry, there are going to be a bunch of auto policy claims from today," I say, deadpan, as I watch the cars smash into one another.

He laughs. "Yeah, this is the only time an insurance agent can enjoy a car crash."

"Hey, is my rental car covered?" I ask. "Maybe I can take a spin in the next heat!"

That got us to plotting. No, I didn't crash my rental car in the next heat. Rather, we shot a YouTube video.

McGlynn writes the *Massachusetts Family Insurance* blog, so he understands how interesting content can serve as a way to sell for his insurance business. He pulled out his iPhone and shot a few minutes of footage. When he returned home, he had it edited into a fun little video, which he released on YouTube with the title: "When does an insurance agent enjoy a car crash?"

When I speak with entrepreneurs like McGlynn, so many of them push back on content creation. "I'm just a . . . ," they say. (Fill in any occupation—lawyer, doctor, restaurant owner, software entrepreneur, whatever.) "There's nothing interesting about my business that I can write about or show on a video."

Nonsense.

There's always something interesting that offers opportunities for creative content if you keep your mind open.

Have your iPhone ready. Interview a customer. Make a short film about something interesting in your market. Create a Periscope live video stream or shoot an interesting photo and post it on Instagram.

It has never been easier to tell interesting stories to your marketplace. Creating content like the video McGlynn made is virtually free. Ideas for stories are all around you if you just take a look.

McGlynn's publishing efforts generate sales to new customers and also provide service to existing customers, keeping them happy so they continue to do business with his company with annual renewals. Others in his organization follow his lead and will share the content he creates.

"We are all selling," McGlynn says. "We're selling ourselves and everyone is selling their businesses. Today people use the Internet to search for answers to their insurance questions. If I can provide those answers, then people will see me as an expert, and it may lead them to contact me for both advice and service."

McGlynn publishes information on his blog that he knows people are searching for. Recent blog posts have examined what insurance can provide in the event of a laptop computer fire, coverage issues that occur when traveling abroad, and what "replacement cost" means in a homeowners' insurance policy. One of my favorite blog titles is "no txt'g while drv'g!" in which he reviewed the existing laws against distracted driving, and how a violation of those laws can negatively impact any insurance defense in a civil lawsuit.

"Sales coming from my blog posts are indirect," he says. "It's not like I am calling them because I am trying to make a sale. I am giving them some information. I am giving them some knowledge. I am trying to give them something that makes them think about their current status, and then they can make the decision whether to contact me or not." And contact him they do, because McGlynn tracks sales directly to his blog posts.

"One of the biggest problems that insurance agents have always had is that they rarely hear from their existing clients," McGlynn says. In order to keep himself in his clients' minds, he emails links to his blog posts to his list of customers. "I contact my clients on an irregular basis, now and then and not every week because that would be too often. It gives me a chance to make contact and let them know that I am thinking about them. For example, when Hurricane Sandy was making its way up the East Coast, I emailed a post I had written months before just to let people know, hey, be prepared for hurricanes. I sent it when it became apparent that Sandy was coming so all my existing clients could review the post when it was urgent."

McGlynn says he tries to write a new blog post each Wednesday, although he does take some weeks off when he is traveling. "Most of my posts come from listening to people's questions," he says. "Whether it is in our office or in their office, my clients give me the best ideas." For many people, insurance is an unfamiliar and intimidating topic. When the time comes to learn about auto, home, or life insurance, they don't know where to turn. McGlynn realizes this and creates posts to help. He has fun with some of his posts, such as the demolition derby video. Content like this gets shared and has become a new form of referrals.

"Much of our business is word of mouth from our customers. The blog gives our customers something to pass on to their friends and colleagues," McGlynn says. "It's the sort of referral that didn't exist two years ago before I started the blog."

Updates to This Revised Edition

In the past several years since I wrote the first edition of the book, I've seen some people and organizations make great progress in the ways they sell and service their customers. However, the majority of companies I see are still using ineffective approaches. There are lots of organizations struggling because they are living in the past.

As I write this new edition, the United States is in the thick of the 2016 presidential election cycle. The primaries are in full swing and are playing out as a massive case study illustrating what approaches to sales work in the modern world. According to data reported by MSNBC, Republican candidate Jeb Bush spent $38.1 million on advertising in calendar year 2015. That's way more than any other candidate. In contrast, Donald Trump spent just $217,000 on ads in 2015. But Jeb Bush's investment had yielded just 3 percent support from likely Republican primary voters according to a late

December 2015 Fox News poll, and he dropped out of the race in February 2016.

At the same time, Donald Trump is way out in front on real-time connection. He's constantly commenting on the news of the day from the podium at his campaign rallies and talking about the other candidates on his Twitter feed. That same Fox News poll places Trump at 39 percent support. Real-time connection trumps traditional techniques like advertising as a sales tool, a topic I focus on in Chapter 6. I'm not advocating for any particular candidate's politics, nor am I predicting any eventual winner; however, we can all learn from how effectively they sell.

This new edition of the book builds on the first edition with an extensive rewrite. I have checked every fact, figure, and story. But I've also listened. In the past few years, I've met thousands of people like you, people who have shared their stories with me. I have drawn from those experiences and included in these pages new examples of success.

This edition features a discussion on several new agile selling tools, including Periscope, a live video streaming service that some people are using to generate sales and to service customers. The real-time web has sparked a tremendous opportunity for reaching people directly—so I've added to the chapter on agile, real-time social sales, including more on newsjacking, the technique of injecting your ideas into a breaking news story to generate media coverage, get sales leads, and grow business.

Learning from Examples: How the Successes of Others Can Provide Ideas and Options for Your Own Organization

Throughout this book, I'll be sharing examples of success like that of Quark Expeditions and McGlynn, Clinton & Hall Insurance Agencies. I choose large organizations and smaller ones. Some are service businesses and others sell products. I'll talk about a political candidate, several doctors, and a country music star. I profile a nonprofit organization. I have chosen people to learn from in various parts of the world, proving that the New Rules of Sales and Service work in global markets.

As you read the stories, keep in mind that you will learn from them even if they come from a very different market, industry, or type of organization than your own. If you work at a nonprofit, you can learn from the experiences of corporations. Those who work at big companies will find value in what small practitioners are up to. In fact, in my experience, you will learn more by emulating successful ideas from outside your industry than by copying what your peers are doing. Remember, the best thing about new rules is that your competitors probably don't know about them yet.

In Chapter 1, I illustrate how many people are failing to engage their audiences by continuing to apply the old rules in a new age. Their companies are lagging because they fail to see and understand the opportunities. Chapter 2 lays out the basics of the New Rules of Sales and Service so you'll be able to grasp the ideas before I dig into the tools and techniques in later chapters. Chapter 3 focuses on how to create a compelling company narrative and why it is essential that the people at the very top of an organization are involved in this effort. Additional chapters will take deeper dives into buyer personas, the buying cycle, agile sales, and real-time customer service. The last two chapters discuss how you can build your personal brand and your company's business by being social.

In these last several chapters, I'll also address the fears many people feel about plunging into this new environment. I've heard from people at my live events and though social networks and email that they have anxiety about learning a new technology and technical skills. We are long past the time when you needed to learn to code, but many think they will have to go back to school and hit the books to learn. Others relate a fear of losing one's personal life to being always on 24/7 and the requirement to respond to email, monitor websites, and participate on social media. Fear not! While it is human nature to be apprehensive of change, there are many ways to retain control of your life and keep digital access manageable.

Feel free to jump around from chapter to chapter. I write in the style of a blog post, so just like in a blog, you might want to dip into sections on your own timetable rather than follow the linear fashion of the book from cover to cover. While salespeople might want to read only the chapters on sales, I'd encourage you to look into sections on customer service as well. It's important to keep in mind with online content that the lines between what is sales and what is service are blurring, so, for example, those in traditional service roles are building loyalty that drives future sales. It's valuable and essential that everyone now has a working knowledge about how the sales process has changed.

Thank you for your interest in the new rules outlined here. I hope that you too will be successful in implementing these strategies and that your life and work will be made better as a result.

—David Meerman Scott
www.DMS.live
www.WebInkNow.com
@dmscott

1 The Old World of Sales and Service

" **I** 'm fed up, and I won't tolerate this anymore!"
I've heard many variations on this theme in recent years.

We're fed up with unwanted phone calls interrupting us at home and at work. We hate wading through hundreds of unsolicited emails. We've had it with intrusive social media messages. We're tired of poor service from companies that don't treat us with respect or that send us into a phone mail maze that wastes minutes of our time and never connects us with a living person.

> We wonder why there is so little humanity when we interact with the organizations and businesses we patronize.

The Old Sales Model: "Dialing for Dollars"

My first sales job required me to make cold calls to bond traders and convince them to buy economic consulting services. We had lists of names and numbers to contact that came from directories of people who worked in banks, securities companies, savings and loan associations, fund management firms, and government agencies.

My sales colleagues and I would psych ourselves into the right frame of mind each morning by drinking a few cups of coffee, maybe telling each other a few off-color jokes (common in the 1980s testosterone-fueled Wall Street markets portrayed in *The Wolf of Wall Street* book and film), and discussing the latest stories in the *Wall Street Journal*. On a typical day we might set a goal to contact every person overseeing trading at all the savings and loan associations headquartered in Arizona.

It was brutal work. Most people were unaware of our firm. And my call was but one of the many sales intrusions each prospect would receive during a business day.

We hated cold calling—"dialing for dollars."

But the technique was necessary because in the years prior to the World Wide Web there were few other ways a potential client might learn about our company.

Unfortunately, many organizations are still operating as if it were 1986, and they continue to focus massive investments on interrupting people with an army of salespeople making cold calls.

Companies like the one I worked for in the 1980s relied on direct sales efforts that required lots of money. The sales commissions were high. (A big reason I stuck with my sales job even though I hated it was that I made good money for someone who was in his early twenties.)

Indeed, many large organizations have complex and expensive sales training programs with expensive in-house and external experts focused on educating the sales staff in the latest techniques. Complex enterprise software packages are implemented so salespeople can micromanage each sales encounter.

The Voice of Authority: When the Salesperson Was the Expert

Prior to the web, the salesperson needed to be the expert. The buyer didn't have the ability to go online and conduct independent research; an important aspect of the sales process was the buyer's education by the seller.

Prior to launching her own business as a digital consultant and storyteller, Joanne Tombrakos enjoyed a corporate career in sales. She worked 25 years at media companies selling radio advertising and later advertising to cable television networks. She worked at smaller companies like Beasley Broadcast Group and large operators including Time Warner Cable. "When I started selling and for many years after, I was the expert," she says. "I would go to a client and I could tell them everything they wanted to know about radio and television. But when you are selling one medium, you have to know all the other competing media. You need to know print, and when the Internet came into play we had to know that."

Today, in a world in which buyers have the ability to do their own independent research, many customers are more educated than the salespeople they do business with. However, many companies and the salespeople they employ have not adjusted their strategy accordingly. They still rely on cold calls, and they still approach the sales process as if they have the informational upper hand in the relationship.

"That's the biggest shift for salespeople," says Tombrakos. "They're no longer the expert. Today the client knows as much, if not more. The salesperson has to be better prepared. Most salespeople are not using visual tools to help them. Many aren't even doing something as simple as pointing people to the web. I have a lot of friends who are still working in television ad sales, and they continue to dig in their heels. I think many salespeople are blind."

While the sales cycle has transformed into a buying process led by the customers, Tombrakos says that there are many simple things a salesperson can do to remain an expert in the new world of digital information. "When I get a new client, I start following them on Twitter. Salespeople seldom take advantage of opportunities like this, as they are still terrified of the digital world. There are so many new ways that salespeople could use digital tools to establish themselves as an expert. It could be something as simple as sharing information on LinkedIn. If they share information with a client, they are likely to be perceived as an expert in a particular area. They should be the one who informs their customers, 'Hey, I just read this great new book with some fantastic ideas.' They should be making new connections and establishing their credibility, but most companies are not training their people on how to use digital communications. They hear 'social,' and they think it's watercooler chitchat and nothing more."

Fortunately, today we no longer have to rely on the cold call, because buyers are looking for what we have to offer. And they know what they want.

The Salesperson Expert versus the Web-Educated Buyer

To illustrate the point about how salespeople used to hold the power position when they were keepers of information, think about the process of buying a car in 1995. You'd be exposed to television and magazine ads. Perhaps you'd purchase a buyers' guide such as *Consumer Reports*. You could ask friends and coworkers for advice. But to get detailed information on models, options, and pricing required a dreaded visit to the dealership to talk to the salesperson, who was smugly aware he had all the information power.

Today, how do you buy a car? Do you blindly go to visit the dealership to ask the salesperson? Or do you spend hours on the web learning as much as you can and only visit the dealer when you are ready to buy and already know everything you need to get a good deal?

Remarkably, nearly all companies are still operating in a world as if the salesperson is the king of the information kingdom. Companies insist on driving all online interactions to a salesperson.

One manifestation of this behavior is the insistence by most companies that buyers supply personal details—particularly an email address—before they can get information such as a white paper. When I question marketers about this practice, they tell me that they need sales leads and that salespeople follow up on the information requests.

The idea that you shouldn't give information for free predates the web. Requiring an email registration is simply applying what we did in the past to the new realities. This is far less effective than making information freely available to be downloaded and shared. And it risks losing potential customers who are wary of providing their email address out of fear that it will be recycled and sold to data brokers and spammers.

Are you managing your sales and marketing process using 1995 calculus? Do you assume that salespeople are the fonts of all knowledge and all information flows through them? If so, I think you are less successful than you could be.

> Your salespeople should assume that they are the last place a buyer goes, not the first. They must assume that very little of their knowledge is proprietary. They need to facilitate the sale, not control the information.

Think back to buying a car. How do you want the dealer's staff to interact with you when you walk in? Do you want a confrontational relationship where they feel they have the information power? Or do you want the dealer to assume you have already done your research and are ready to close a deal?

It's not just telephone sales and in-store persuasion where companies need to refocus. Consider sales dysfunction at its worst: the business-to-business (B2B) trade show demonstration.

For some markets, the trade show demo is very important. While I was in high school and during the summers of my college years, I worked in a cheese shop. Once a year, I went to New York City to attend the Fancy Foods and Confection Show. Demos were all over the place, many involving tasty treats: cheese, sausage, chocolate, coffee, bread, and more.

Okay, but what about B2B technology companies? Can you imagine anything more boring than a 10-minute screen-by-screen demo by a product manager spouting industry jargon, boring buyers with all the best-of-breed, cutting-edge features of some mission-critical, flexible, and scalable solution that improves business processes using industry-standard technology? Want to scream?

Yes, there are exceptions. But in my experience, the trade show demo is terrible for generating sales and often an excuse fest for both buyers and sellers. The company uses it as an excuse to explain poor sales, and the attendees use it as an excuse to indicate their lack of interest: "Sure, I'll have a free pen, but I'm too busy for your demo."

Nearly all B2B technology company trade show demos are conducted out of laziness. Here's how the dysfunctional process works and why B2B technology demos are so overused. Marketers don't understand their buyers, the problems their buyers face, or how their product could help solve these problems. The simple reason: because they don't get out into the market. Instead these marketers are holed up in their offices where they construct a demo script using reverse-engineered language that they believe the buyer wants to hear based on the product's features, rather than on buyer input. The marketers then recruit salespeople to hang around the trade show booth and lure people in with the promise of a tchotchke or the chance to win an iPad. During the demo the salesperson, under the direction of marketers, goes through each feature while spewing superlative-laden, jargon-sprinkled, gobbledygook-filled hype.

Um . . . This is not effective. It is the old world of sales.

Throughout this book, we'll explore how to move beyond these dusty old paradigms.

Any new initiative should start with buyers and your buyer personas. What problems do your buyers have? How can your company solve those problems with technology? How do your buyers describe the solutions?

Business-to-business companies need to rethink the entire trade show experience, not just the demo. I'd ask a more fundamental question: Do you need to be at the trade show at all? And if so, do you really need a booth? The web is a free 24/7 trade show. Consider refocusing your efforts to blogging or a content-rich website or other online initiatives to reach buyers.

"These Sales Leads Stink!"

Salespeople have traditionally relied on the marketing department to generate sales leads. Sales managers often tell the marketing team: "Get me some good leads! These leads stink! My people can't sell to these!"

And the marketing team responds: "We gave you good leads! Your guys just stink at closing!" Having been in the middle of these discussions at several companies, I've heard them time and time again.

Back in the mid-1990s it was hard to find evidence of love between marketing and sales. At many B2B companies the relationship was downright adversarial. Often, the tension extended all the way up to senior management.

It all stemmed from the sales process involving a "handoff." Marketing generated leads, handed them over to sales, and then the sales team owned them until they closed.

We're in a world now where sales and marketing coexist throughout the entire sales process. Buyers are evaluating offerings throughout the sales process based on what a salesperson says or does and what they see and do on the web and in social media.

Savvy marketing and sales professionals understand that sales and marketing must work together to move prospects through the sales cycle. This is especially important in a complex sale with a long decision-making cycle and multiple buyers, each of whom must be persuaded. The good news is that web content not only can motivate buyers during a lengthy sales cycle but may even shorten the cycle.

Tell the Truth: The Power of Authenticity

Do you believe these claims?

- Lose 20 pounds in a week, no exercise or diet required!

- My husband is the former oil minister, and I want to give you $20 million!

Of course not! Scam artists prey on the one person out of a million who is gullible. Everyone else knows these are lies.

How about these claims?

- And now he's making $30,000 a month from his own website.
- We exceed your expectations.
- The Service Plan covers everything.

Hmm. These statements sound a little fishy too, don't they?
What about these?

- Regular price $100.
- Our products are [pick one] innovative, cutting-edge, world-class.
- Light.
- Deluxe.

It's so easy for salespeople to slip into little lies. You've got to resist those seemingly small exaggerations and half-truths that harm your brand.

Or how about that often-used claim salespeople make, "We're the best in the industry," when referring to their company, products, and services?

Besides being overused and a cliché, there are a number of problems with "the best in the industry."

The phrase forces people to consider what exactly is "the industry"? Oh, it looks like the company is the best in the home electronics and appliance repair industry. Any claim that requires the buyer to infer that there are implied qualifications hiding within the pitch immediately raises skepticism.

The phrase "the best in the industry" forces a comparison that people weren't necessarily making. You instantly divert people's attention to the competition and what they might have to offer. "Oh, so you're the best in the e-cigarette cartridge industry? That probably means there is a cheaper alternative."

- The leading provider of . . .
- Service that's second to none.
- Your call is important to us.

- Due to higher than expected call volume, your wait time is longer than normal.
- We love our customers.
- This is the best price I can offer.

Are you telling the truth? Or making something up in an attempt to sound good while hiding what's really going on?

You know what? Your customers can see through the smoke screen. Anyone who grew up reading *Mad* magazine or watching *The Simpsons* (probably many of you) was trained at a formative age to approach nearly all sales claims with critical and humorous skepticism.

Truth: We're trying to save money by firing customer support reps and therefore average wait time is now over five minutes.

Company claim: Your call is important to us.

I stay at many hotels where there is ample evidence of wasted energy. Some hotels sport massive energy-sucking atriums. Some keep the public areas way too cold in the summer and too hot in the winter.

Yet at these same hotels, you might see a sign in the bathroom or on the bed saying how much they "care about the environment" and inviting you to "save our natural resources" by reusing the towels and sheets rather than having clean ones provided each day.

Here's how the disconnect played out at one hotel I stayed at:

"The Resort features a dramatic, soaring 18-story glass atrium complete with vibrant indoor gardens, flowing waterways, and panoramic vistas of the river."

"One of your shower heads has been turned off in an effort to minimize water usage and protect one of our most precious natural resources."

Do this hotel's owners want to protect the environment? Or do they want an atrium with water fountains and sunlight coming in during the hot day sucking tons of energy? Which story is the truth?

Or maybe this is the truth: Some boneheads convinced the hotel to install these newfangled shower heads, and when the CFO saw the huge increase in water and energy usage, he had a fit and told the boneheads to do something about it, so they made up some hogwash about how they love the environment.

Or this: The hotel owners really want to save the planet but some idiot convinced them that it had to have an atrium and now they are stuck with it.

Your customers can spot hypocrisy a mile away. What are you saying to people? Are you telling the truth?

Customer Disservice: The Little Things That Drive Us Crazy

Alas, sales has no monopoly on the reasons why so many businesses are operating dysfunctionally today.

It's easy to find countless customer service departments still following the old rules.

For one of my several email accounts, I use EarthLink. I've generally had good service and have been using it since about 1996. But the content in the EarthLink customer service messages I received several years ago made me want to scream.

At that time, I had a prepayment plan that allowed me to save money by paying for a year in advance. When the period was near expiration, I got a message with these instructions:

> *** **Your prepayment plan will be expiring soon** ***
> Renew by contacting Customer Service at service@earthlink.net.

So I sent an email as directed, and this is what came back:

> Thank you for contacting EarthLink,
> We received your email, however in order to better serve you EarthLink only accepts replies to outbound email messages or new messages created by completing our online email form. . . . We ask that you resubmit your request using our online email form . . . , or, by inserting the following URL in your web browser:
> http://support.earthlink.net/email
> Using this form will help us direct your email to the right department so that we can provide you with an accurate and timely response.

They told me to email them. When I did, they told me not to. So now, armed with new information, I had to go through a rigmarole with all sorts of drop-down menus, none of which offered me the option to renew my prepayment plan. This after they told me to send them an email, and then said they don't accept email.

Ugh.

Communicating with customers via email is a great way to build loyalty and sell more services. But the content needs to be right. All automatic email messages (as the ones from EarthLink obviously were) need to be checked and rechecked by humans to make certain that the information in them is accurate and makes sense.

Don't ever make your most valuable customers (those who pay up front, in advance, for long-term contracts) jump through hoops to do business with you!

It's not just email support. If you own a car, consider the experience of taking it in for service at the dealership.

You have to call weeks ahead to get an appointment that requires you to miss part of a workday. If the dealership doesn't have a loaner car or courtesy transportation, you need to have your spouse or a friend drive you to work and then back to the dealer.

Inevitably, there's the telephone call with the bad news. Your "rocker arm" or "strut" or some other random part "needs to be replaced" and for some reason this process always seems to cost an extra $800.

Okay, so let's assume the dealer is honest and you really do need the part to be replaced and it really does cost $800. Why phone with the news? Why not email me a PDF document or a link to a video that describes the issue and maybe even includes an educational photo of the actual dodgy part on my own car?

Most organizations' customer support efforts still reflect an era when we couldn't communicate well and the inefficiencies that come with it. But it doesn't need to be this way. We'll learn how to do it better.

"Please Take a Moment to Complete Our Survey": All Take and No Give

I've been getting a bunch of surveys recently. It seems like each time I contact a company or buy something I am asked to complete a survey that "will take less than 10 minutes."

I've been interrupted by big brands that should know better, like Skype, Apple, Nike, and AT&T.

Sometimes, they send multiple emails, as if I forgot to complete the survey the first time. Sometimes they even use ALL CAPITALS, such as this one:

REMINDER: AT&T Wants To Know About Your Recent Experiences with AT&T

Dear Valued AT&T Customer,

At AT&T, we value your opinion. We strive to give you the best service possible and that can't happen without your honest feedback. Every voice matters—especially yours! By taking less than 10 minutes to complete a brief online survey, you have the opportunity to make your voice heard. We are specifically interested in talking to you about your recent experiences with AT&T.

Just click below and help us improve in order to serve you better!

How do the customer service people let this happen? It is extremely counterproductive for a company to ask for additional time from their buyers—especially when they have just expended the effort to call customer support or after they have just purchased a product. If a company is so hungry for customer survey information, create a relationship that encourages customers to want to interact and willingly provide feedback at their convenience.

Here's another one:

You recently contacted our Nike Digital Sport Customer Service team for assistance and we would like to hear from you.

It is because of feedback we receive from customers like you that we are able to continually improve our products and services. We won't rest until we've made every effort to provide you with a best-in-class consumer experience. The information you provide will be kept confidential and will not be shared with any other company.

The survey should only take 3–5 minutes to complete. We value your opinion and would appreciate it if you would answer some brief questions and tell us how we did. To access the survey, please click on the Web address below. This survey can be completed on your mobile phone or your computer's web browser.

If you require assistance for a new or existing support request, please contact Nike Digital Sport Customer Service.

Thank you for your consideration,

Nike Digital Sport Customer Service

Rather than taking, companies should be giving. Specifically, they should be delivering valuable content.

"We value your opinion" is not an accurate statement. Rather, it's "we want to take your time."

It seems to me that the problem with these surveys is that the people behind them aren't at all connected to the people who are responsible for educating consumers. (Their concern is evaluating the customer support staff using metrics that measure the satisfaction of people on a transactional basis for each telephone support call or product purchase.)

And the senior executives are so focused on spreadsheets that they can't even comprehend that the process of gathering that customer service data is actually hurting the company.

The executives in these companies pore over tiny incremental changes in customer satisfaction numbers. "Oh, look! We're up 1 percent this month!"

They must know that the metrics are based on people who have nothing better to do than fill out stupid surveys.

Don't they realize that most people, like me, are just annoyed?

"There's a Robocall on Line One. It Says It's Urgent."

Just because you have my email addresses, it doesn't mean you should email me your sales message.

Just because you have my phone numbers, it doesn't mean you should call me with your sales pitch.

Just because we're connected on LinkedIn, it doesn't mean you can add me to your distribution list.

Just because I follow you on Twitter, it doesn't mean you can try to sell me something via Direct Message.

Intrusive, interruption-based sales techniques frequently do much more harm than good. The creation of such a campaign can tick people off so badly that it can actually cause business to fall. It would have been better to do nothing.

In 2012, Democrat Elizabeth Warren defeated incumbent Republican Scott Brown to win the U.S. Senate seat in my home state of Massachusetts.

I predicted the outcome. But not based on politics.

It was Scott Brown's intrusive robocalls. I wrote a piece in the *Huffington Post* before the election in which I said the robocalls would hand the election to Elizabeth Warren. I wrote that Warren would win because voters like me are fed up with being interrupted at home by robocalls pitching Brown. At my home number, we received perhaps 10 recorded ads from Brown support groups, including the Massachusetts Republican Party. We did not receive any calls from Warren support groups.

The idea of spending money annoying people seems like a good sales idea to traditionalists. They buy a list, prepare a script, and reach out to "prospects" to ask for votes.

Are these robocall interruptions supposed to be good? They just tick me off. And I'm not the only one. Other Massachusetts residents I spoke to were also fed up.

People hate sales calls. Some three-quarters of Americans have signed up for the National Do Not Call Registry, which does not currently apply to political organizations. If three-quarters of Americans signed up to say "no" to sales calls, why the heck would a political campaign think making a sales call is a good thing?

I see examples of this behavior all the time. I am frequently added to email sales lists that I have no interest in. I got one where the person said, "Hello David Meerman. Since we're connected on LinkedIn I thought I'd let you know I added you to my email list . . ." You don't even know my name. You blew it by interrupting me with an unwanted message. Bang! We are not connected on LinkedIn anymore, pal.

If someone sends me an unwanted sales pitch via Twitter Direct Message, I immediately unfollow that person on Twitter. Gone. Bye-bye.

Just because it has passengers confined in a metal tube for a few hours on a plane doesn't mean American Airlines should wake me up from a nap to plug its damned credit cards over the loudspeaker.

I don't go to my local mall food court as much as I used to because the owner, Simon Property Group, installed a television system that loudly advertises stuff to everyone as we are seated and trying to eat.

You don't have permission.

Salespeople need to understand that ownership of an email address or phone number or being followed on Twitter is not permission to intrude with a sales message. The presence of distracting audio and video advertising while dining, waiting in line at a supermarket, sitting in an airport lounge, or at other moments when one may be trying to concentrate on personal thoughts finds few fans.

Such behavior and intrusive pitches do more harm than good. You'd be better off doing nothing.

Receiving an Email Address Is Not an Invitation to Spam

Many years ago I opted into emails from BMW because I wanted to receive a notice when the automaker released a new addition in its excellent series of original short films. For example, I liked *The Star* featuring Madonna and directed by Guy Ritchie. At the time these films were a new and exciting form of online marketing, and I wanted to know when new ones came out. I wrote about BMW's use of video on my blog back in 2007 and included a mention in one of my books.

Gradually over the years my email address seemed to be added to a number of BMW sales lists that I didn't choose to join. So I opted out of all emails from BMW.

Like most people, I am on a bunch of lists that seem to grow like weeds. Every time I buy something online, I'm added to a new list. I frequently opt out and that's the end of it, but I do not keep a tally of opt-outs. There are just too many, and most companies simply honor my request and stop sending me email.

I distinctly recalled opting out of BMW emails, so it seemed strange that I would mysteriously be placed back on the distribution list against my wishes.

When I received an email from BMW once more, I opted out again but this time I kept a screen shot as a personal record showing that I had indeed opted out from all items in BMW's list.

After that opt-out, I again got an email from BMW!

This one was from BMW of North America with a subject line "Shop BMW gifts on Cyber Monday." This email most certainly arrived after I had expressed my preference to receive no more emails and had recorded the attempt.

I posted my experience in a blog post titled "Is BMW an email spammer?" The post generated 24 comments and many tweets as people discussed what I had gone through.

Companies are frequently too eager to sell something to the poor hapless consumers who in good faith add their names to an email list. But to exploitatively abuse that trust is harmful to a brand.

Soon after I posted this story to my blog, BMW commented.

We came across your blog entry and would like to apologize for your receipt of e-mails from us after you unsubscribed from our mailing list. A now resolved software issue caused some people who opted out of e-mail to be added to two recent mailings in error.

Your entry this week was good timing as, over the last few days, we've been addressing the very issue of developing a streamlined process for managing email subscriptions and opt-outs (including "one-click" opt-out). We plan to launch it next year to resolve many of the concerns you've raised. BMW takes CAN-SPAM very seriously and we're dedicated to offering an experience that not only follows the letter and spirit of the law but is easy to use.

Thanks to everyone on the thread for your feedback; we are listening and are looking forward to offering improved experiences for managing email subscriptions in the near future.

Thank you, BMW of North America, LLC.

While the comment and explanation were appropriate, and I certainly recognize that mistakes such as the BMW "software issue" can occur, companies need to consider carefully how they use people's email addresses to sell them things.

Adding Social Media to Old School Sales and Support Is Still Old School

Many people proudly trumpet how their company has made social media a part of its sales and customer service infrastructure. While the efforts are to be commended, most of these efforts involve taking the old ways of doing things and simply adding a social component. Social media bolted onto traditional sales does not work so well.

Following the interruption-style sales model by transferring focus from telephone cold calling to interrupting people via social networks like Twitter and LinkedIn is still interruption selling. It needs to change.

The same is true with customer service. It's not enough to add a Twitter feed to your existing traditional 800 number support call center, where people must wait on hold until they finally talk to a rep who is only authorized to read off a script. It needs to change.

The Old Rules of Sales and Service

I recognize that this chapter has been a bit of a rant. I've taken you through many of the ineffective sales and service strategies and tactics that have been used in the past and either are not as effective in the world of the web or, worse, are downright counterproductive. It feels good for me to relate personal examples where companies have treated me poorly, but I am sure you have your own cases of ineptitude with the companies you deal with.

So here, in one place, are both the dynamics of *why* sales and service were so poor in the days before the web enabled real-time communications, as well as the old rules of sales and service:

In the days before real-time online communications . . .

- It was very difficult for buyers to find independent information about the products and services that interested them.
- There was no easy way for unhappy customers to voice disapproval of a company in public.
- Both buyers and existing customers couldn't communicate instantly with the companies they did business with or patronized.
- Customers had little say in the products and services they wanted to buy.

. . . therefore the old rules of sales and service applied:

- The seller had more knowledge and therefore had the upper hand in negotiations.
- Sellers had little incentive to tell the truth about their offerings.

- Companies used agencies to dream up messages rather than communicating with authenticity.
- Cold-calling solicitations were among the most common methods for salespeople to contact prospective clients.
- Customer service was conducted on the company's timetable, so it was okay to place people on hold or take weeks to respond to mail and email.
- The seller was in charge of the sales cycle, parsing out details to buyers on the seller's timetable.
- Salespeople and customer service people used scripts to push buyers and customers down a single path.
- Jargon was rampant.
- Sellers delivered only proprietary information such as their company's white papers and research reports.
- There was very little incentive to fix problems or make customers happy, because there were few outlets for complaining publicly.
- The sales process was generic, and buyers needed to fit into a one-size-fits-all culture.
- Buyers needed to ask the right questions.
- Sales were handled by the sales department, and customer service was handled by the customer service department.

Okay, end of rant.

> People hate to be sold to, but in the old days they had no choice.

None of this needs to be true in your business any longer! The world has changed, and your business needs to adapt. In the rest of the book we'll look at what you need to do to be successful in the new world.

2 The New Rules of Sales and Service

W e dislike being "sold."

We hate being treated poorly by the companies we do business with. It's time to make a change.

Okay, by now you must be saying something like: "Enough already! What exactly are the new rules of sales and service?" I won't keep you waiting any longer. Here are the ideas of this book distilled down to one set of concepts.

> The biggest communications revolution in human history means your marketplace has changed.

Setting Down the Rules

The vast majority of human beings—more than five billion of us—are connected instantly to each other via web-based and mobile communications devices.

While the communications revolution provides immense benefit, in our technology-driven life we crave humanity.

Information about products and services is available to buyers everywhere, 24/7, and for free.

Publishing valuable content has become essentially free for companies. At the same time, customers have a (loud) voice through social networks and review sites.

The New Rules of Sales and Service

Authentic storytelling sets the tone.

- People want authenticity, not spin.
- People want participation, not propaganda.
- Your organizational story cannot be dreamed up by an ad agency.
- The individual at the top of the company is the master storyteller, the conductor of the organizational orchestra.
- With social networks, every employee has a role in sales and customer service and must sing from the same hymnal.
- Buyers want information in language they understand, not gobbledygook-laden jargon.

Content is the link between companies and customers.

- You are what you publish.
- Companies must drive people into the purchasing process with great content.
- Blogs, online video, e-books, infographics, and the like let organizations communicate directly with buyers in a form they appreciate.
- Social networks like Twitter, Facebook, and LinkedIn allow people all over the world to share content and connect with the companies they want to do business with.
- Smart sellers now not only deliver proprietary information such as their company's white papers and research reports, but also curate information from other sources on the World Wide Web.
- On the web, the lines between marketing and sales and service have blurred.

Big data enables a more scientific approach to sales and service.

- The best organizations customize the buying experience for each customer.

- Because of the infinite amount of information available on the web, buyers now have more information than sellers and therefore buyers have the upper hand in negotiations.
- With a plethora of independent information available to buyers, sellers must tell the truth about their offerings.
- Online communications are infinitely measurable.

Agile selling **brings new business to your company.**

- Buyers actively use search engines and social networks to find companies to do business with.
- The buyer is now in charge of the sales process, and wants to buy on his or her own personal timetable.
- When a buyer is ready to buy, the company must respond with lightning speed.
- Instead of causing one-way interruption, making sales is now about delivering content at the precise moment each buyer needs it.
- Companies must treat people as individuals.
- When buyers have valuable information at the click of a mouse, it is sellers who need to ask the right questions.

Real-time engagement **keeps customers happy.**

- In our always-on world, buyers expect instant, 24/7 service.
- Because of independent product reviews, there is now a huge incentive to fix problems and make customers happy so they don't complain publicly.
- Customers expect employees of the companies they do business with to support them via social networks.

> Today, people like to buy because they have far more choices than in the past!

The new rules of sales and service are not theoretical. This is no academic exercise. Throughout this book, you will meet people who are implementing these rules today and enjoying high business growth as a result. But the new rules demand a new kind of leadership.

Living Up to Their Name: OPEN Communications to Customers

Now that we've taken a look at the new rules of sales and service, let's turn to a story of a company doing many great things to reach buyers and promote sales.

OPEN Cycle, an Amsterdam-based company building an extremely lightweight and strong mountain bike, was founded in 2011 as a completely open company taking advantage of the new communication tools that you are reading about in this book. Since it was a brand-new company, the founders were able to create an organization completely around their vision of the company's character and then set a goal to communicate that directly to the marketplace. OPEN's greatest assets are the fantastic engineering that goes into creating the best mountain bikes in the world, and the stories the founders convey to their customers about the bikes and the company they created. Everything they do is shared with customers, retailers, and vendors on social networks and via email in real time—it helps them build better products, keep existing customers happy, and grow their business.

"If we want to have any success, we've got to keep it simple," says Gerard Vroomen, owner of OPEN, a company he co-founded with Andy Kessler. Prior to OPEN, Vroomen co-founded Cervélo Cycles, a Canadian manufacturer of the fastest and lightest professional racing bicycle for road, triathlon, and track. He sold Cervélo Cycles in 2011 to focus on mountain bikes. He says, "Now you can really make the difference with customer service. So many businesses do such a poor job responding to their customers that even if you have the simplest company and respond effectively to emails, you're ahead of 90 percent of your competition."

When Vroomen established the company, he focused on "relentless simplicity" as the guiding principle of OPEN. This was a very strong story that his buyers could relate to. He has made a point of communicating that story to all of his constituents, including buyers, existing customers, the media, suppliers, and others who work in the bike industry. OPEN's guiding principle has established itself as a powerful differentiator, setting the company apart by the honesty and sincerity as well as the consistency with which it communicates.

In an introduction on the OPEN website signed by Vroomen and Kessler, the company story is available to all:

> Three words describe this new venture: bikes, open and simple.
>
> Bikes we live and breathe. Andy's career spans from downhill racer (back when helmets were optional!) to CEO of a mountain & road bike company. Gerard's career includes co-founding Cervélo, where he's done everything from engineering and design to sales, supply chain and marketing.
>
> OPEN means open to new ideas; from our customers, retailers, vendors and ourselves. Open to show the intricacies of our products but also our company. Open even to issue shares to some of our customers.
>
> If open is the goal, simple is the tool.
>
> "Relentless simplicity" is our guiding principle. Reduce the number of models and you simplify production, logistics, customer decision making, the website, everything. Avoid traditional advertising or sponsorships and free up precious time. Transfer logistics to third parties and you can focus on what matters most, which in our case means:
>
> 1. Designing better bikes, the first of which we introduce here.
> 2. Connecting with our customers.
>
> And when you put it that way, is there really anything else to do? Welcome to OPEN.

A great story comes directly from the passion of the top person in charge. When the founder or CEO lives his or her passion much like Vroomen does, the company itself almost becomes secondary. The key is that the passion and the story behind it intersect brilliantly with what the buyer wants. The passion results in the delivery of tangibly honest, authentic, and humane ideas, which inspire trust and confidence in the company and its products.

Once there is an honest and inspiring story built into the very heart of an organization, the first step in successful selling is to understand buyers and segment them so that marketing and sales are aligned around customer needs and integrated into a seamless selling process. (We'll look at that in detail in Chapter 4.) At OPEN, because Vroomen and Kessler are communicating with buyers on their site and through social networks like the @OpenCycle Twitter feed, Facebook, and LinkedIn, they truly understand buyers and communicate in language the buyer understands, not gobbledygook.

The OPEN concepts of simplicity and authentic engagement played out in early 2014 when the company decided to stop selling kits of bike components, an assortment of additional parts used to complete a bike after purchasing only an OPEN frame. Many OPEN mountain bikes are sold through the company's worldwide dealer network, but OPEN also sells bikes directly from its website. Prior to the change, visitors to the OPEN site could choose to purchase a frame alone or a complete bike. Since OPEN designs only bike frames, the components were taking time and attention away from the core business.

Indeed, the name OPEN was chosen, in part, to signify that the founders' approach to business was to be open to customers. So that's what informed the way they honestly communicated the decision to the market.

In a blog post titled "Simplifying parts," Vroomen wrote:

In my previous blog I wrote about how we use "relentless simplicity" as our guiding principle. With only two people running the company, it's the key to getting things done without going crazy. And therefore, we regularly look at which parts of the company take a lot of time, and what we can do about it.

Some big time sucks are unavoidable; without product engineering, we don't have a company. But one of the biggest drains the past year has been the component kits. The ordering, coordination, warehousing and shipping of these kits takes more of Andy's time than the selling of our frames. So the simple question that arose was: can we not stop offering component kits?

The direct financial impact would be negligible, since we don't really make any money on them. The only reason to offer kits in the first place is that it gives people an easy way to buy a complete bike, which obviously includes our frame on which we do make money. However, as time went on, we noticed that it really isn't so hard to sell just the frame.

Our dealers can buy the components for not much more money than we can, and sometimes even for less. . . . Most importantly, many of our customers don't just want to change a few parts, they want to customize everything. That means that a component kit doesn't bring any benefit at all.

For the past year, these component kits have merely been a nuisance (easy for me to say, with Andy doing all that work). But going forward, it will become a real hurdle. As we increase the number of frame models from one to two or three, the logistics and sales of those will take more time. This is time we will need to recoup elsewhere.

And so we have decided to stop with the unlimited kit. Not because it isn't a great spec (it is), not because it isn't a great value (it is), but because we need to spend our time where it makes a difference. And whether you build the frame up yourself or do it with your local retailer, you can find these parts all over the globe without much trouble.

What does this mean for you? Well, in the long run likely very little as we will continue to showcase specs to give you inspiration (just like your fellow customers are doing in the Owners' Showcase).

Notice how Vroomen connects with his customers by telling them the details behind the decision to stop selling components. So many companies would just announce the change and make up something to tell the market. Given the authentic nature of how OPEN is open with its customers, Vroomen chose to tell all. And within a few hours customers began commenting positively on the post, and Vroomen himself responded to each comment.

"That blog post was interesting," Vroomen reports. "Once we decided to make this change, we started to think about how to communicate it. And then after a bit of discussion we thought, 'why not provide the whole truth?' In business there is often a difference between the truth and the whole truth. You can call it spin, PR, or whatever you want, but it's so ingrained and it's easy to fall into that wordsmithing trap. It's liberating to realize we can simply tell the whole truth because no matter what it is, it fits our company philosophy to share it."

Open and honest communication means that customers feel a part of the company. They feel like owners. Heck, if you pay many thousands of dollars for a bike, you want to know who you're buying it from, right?

On the OPEN website, every page has a place for customers to leave comments or ask questions, and Vroomen and Kessler answer the questions in real time and in public for all to see. "There are a lot of good mountain bikes out there," Vroomen says. "But if we can show people that we care about them—we do that by responding to people and also being open about how we're running the company—then they will reward us. If they're going to choose between bike A and bike B, and bike A is from a big faceless company and bike B comes from a company where one of the two owners helps you decide which size to get, which wheel, and which handlebar, well, that's a very appealing proposition." At the OPEN website, visitors interact on every page, and Vroomen can observe which content has generated the most interest.

In a world in which most sales processes are generic and each potential customer is sold to in the same way, understanding the individual buyer based on the content the buyer has viewed is a revolutionary concept. It's a fundamental idea behind the new rules of sales and service. If you know how the process works, your salespeople can close more business by being less aggressive.

At OPEN, the open communications concept carries forward, informing customers how to connect directly with the two co-founders. "On every page of our website there are two buttons. One says 'Email Andy' and the other says 'Email Gerard' along with a list of the specific topics that are our responsibility," Vroomen says. "Everybody sees that on our Web pages, but maybe only 10 percent use it. So it gives a warm, fuzzy feeling with everybody aware that we are approachable, but the amount of work is small enough that we can handle it. The vast majority of the people who email us end up buying a bike. And for us a complete bike is between $5,000 and $12,000. So that's worth two emails back and forth. It's mind-bogglingly simple, right? You don't have to get the calculator out."

When an email comes in, the people from OPEN respond right away and in detail, an agile selling strategy of the first order. Vroomen offers an example: "I had an interesting case today when somebody wrote and asked, 'I'm 95 kilos. Am I too heavy for your bike?' So I responded, 'Here's our test results. Yes, the bikes are light but it surpasses the tests and etc., etc.' I gave a complete and elaborate response. And they wrote back saying, 'Oh, that's great. I really appreciate that you, one of the owners, responded to me so quickly. So yeah, I'm very confident about it, and if it does go wrong I know that you guys will react to the warranty situation promptly.' That experience really gives people confidence." Besides email, OPEN has the same level of responsiveness on Twitter, Facebook, and LinkedIn.

Instant engagement via social media is a concept that many companies are focused on today, but too often that effort is limited to merely monitoring Twitter for mentions of their brands. They aren't doing actual real-time customer service of the sort practiced at OPEN. "I think people are very aware that you cannot let a situation on Twitter spiral out of control," Vroomen says. "So they're monitoring like crazy and as soon as something happens on Twitter they jump on it. But they haven't taken the important step, which begins by offering good customer service. If you treat people well they don't end up venting on Twitter."

There are many happy riders of OPEN bikes, including me. And because of their interaction with the OPEN team during the buying process and later support, many OPEN owners feel they know Vroomen and his colleagues. Some are compelled to share the specs of the bikes they've custom-built using OPEN frames. OPEN started a public owners' showcase on the website where customers have uploaded photos and specs of their bikes.

Vroomen consciously decided to keep OPEN simple, making the personal real-time communication with buyers and customers a hallmark of the company's authentic story. OPEN is successful in a very crowded market-place because the story resonates with buyers.

After my examples of expensive consumer products and services so far in this book, you may be thinking, "This sounds fine for guys selling trips to the Antarctic or catering to the high-end sport bike enthusiast, but does any of this apply to my restaurant or my small business doing picture framing or my business-to-business company?" The answer is absolutely! The new rules can be applied to any business today, and I'll show examples from many types of businesses in the pages that follow.

The Communications Revolution That Wasn't Televised

Now that I've outlined the new rules and we've met a few people who have developed success with the ideas, I'd like to step way, way back and look at the big picture for a view of where we are today with our ongoing communications revolution and why these ideas are so important for the success of modern sales and service organizations.

This is not a view from 30,000 feet. It's the view from 1,000 years into the future.

The new rules of sales and service are a part of the much bigger and incredibly important communications revolution we're currently living through—the most important in human history.

In my thinking, there are three major periods in human communications:

Up until the mid-1400s, illiteracy was the norm and life was difficult for nearly everyone. Knowledge was the domain of specialists, often the ruling elite or the church. Information was very, very expensive, as storing it required either disciplined, time-consuming memorization or knowing how to write on clay tablets, papyrus, or parchment. Although movable-type printing (as well as paper) had been invented in China as early as the eleventh century, printing wasn't mechanized. Not until mechanical printing arose independently in Europe 400 years later did a world cultural revolution take place.

Beginning 570 years ago, knowledge became cheap because it could be reproduced mechanically. Almost anybody could own one's own books or could gain access to those owned by others nearby. However, this era of communications was essentially one-way: Information originated with a relatively small number of knowledge creators whose work was distributed to a larger population of readers around the globe.

In the past 20 years or so, information has become largely free and two-way. The long-term ramifications are huge. One thousand years from now, the two things that will be remembered in the history of the time period we are living through right now will be the first lunar landing of Apollo 11 on July 20, 1969, and the development of real-time communications instantly connecting every human on earth with every other human on earth.

Let's look at the importance of the second most transformative communications revolution in human history. Johannes Gutenberg's invention of printing with movable type (circa 1439) meant that books could be mass-produced, rather than painstakingly copied by hand. It meant ordinary people could refer to things in books, like laws. Previously much of this information had to be committed to memory. The printing press liberated people's minds from the need to memorize large quantities of information, allowing them to use that extra brainpower to be more creative. In addition, Gutenberg's communications revolution (which took many decades) hastened the spread of literacy, making vast quantities of knowledge available to average people, while raising living standards along the way. And since large numbers of people could access different ideas and philosophies, they no longer had to rely on religious leaders for the truth; now they could decide on their own whether, for instance, the earth was the center of the universe or it actually revolved around the sun.

Some 556 years later, in 1995, the most important communications revolution began. I chose 1995 because it was the year that Netscape went public on the success of Netscape Navigator, the first popular product to allow easy Internet connection and web browsing.

We're fortunate to be living at this moment in history, the time of another important communications revolution. I figure we're about halfway through it. The first 20 years or so were fast-paced, and things changed very quickly. Usage went from a few million people online to billions.

Now any person with an Internet or mobile phone connection can communicate in real time with virtually any other human on the planet. Talk about a revolution!

According to the International Telecommunications Union, there were 5.9 billion mobile phone subscriptions worldwide in 2011, and mobile networks are available to more than 90 percent of the world's population. It's not creaky old technology, either; nearly 150 countries offer high-speed 3G service.

In fact, more people have access to mobile phones than have access to toothbrushes. More people have access to mobile phones than have access to working toilets. That may sound kind of gross, but it's true. The first thing people want to buy after they've earned enough to eat and have shelter is a mobile communications device.

When people can communicate in real time with one another, it has fundamental ramifications for humanity. A handful of people in Egypt can create a Facebook group that generates support from millions of ordinary citizens and bring down a government.

Anybody can do independent research on the web and choose what to believe about the products and services they consume.

Communications technology has far-reaching influence on the world's economy. People who relied on traditional selling techniques in use for hundreds or even thousands of years suddenly have a global market at their fingertips.

I saw this firsthand when I was visiting the village of Cangandi in the Guna district of Panama on an expedition organized by my friends at Earth Train.

What's remarkable about Cangandi is that the several hundred villagers chose to move the entire village more than one kilometer to the top of a hill because that was the one place that had good mobile phone reception. In 2010, they moved the entire village, huts and all—obviously a massive undertaking.

The village of Cangandi does not have running water. It does not have electricity. But Cangandi does have cell reception (with solar power for recharging).

Having cell reception in Cangandi has already transformed the way the villagers do business. Previously, before they had mobile devices, they would load up their canoes with the cassava roots, maize, and plantains. They then paddled downriver to the Pacific Ocean islands to see who wanted to buy their goods. But it was hit or miss. If another seller had been there recently it was difficult to make a sale, so they frequently returned home after wasting several days.

Now, they have spot market intelligence via mobile phones. Islanders frequently contact them to place orders, which the villagers deliver when needed and at fair prices. This is particularly relevant for cassava and other roots because the plants can be kept alive for a long time and harvested as needed or when the offered price and desired quantity make sense.

Without the spot market opportunities via mobile devices, the villagers would frequently be stuck with a canoe full of roots out at sea skipping from island to island, only to discover that there was little need for roots at that moment, and they would have to sell their goods at a loss.

Time to Join the Revolution

Even now, more than 20 years into the revolution, many organizations still aren't communicating in real time on the web. Their sales and service organizations remain stuck in the past.

Are you one of the revolutionaries? Or do you support the old regime? Are you selling your product or service like the villagers of Cangandi, using modern tools?

The next few decades will bring a continuation of the revolution. We need to be constantly learning and updating our skills to reach buyers as they're looking for the products and services we sell.

This is an exciting time to be in sales and service. In 1,000 years, people will study this period in history to learn about the tremendous transformations in society brought about by the technological changes that have been introduced only a few years ago.

Just as we study how medieval times transitioned into the Renaissance as a result of knowledge spread by the printing press, the wide global availability of mobile technologies and web content will be viewed in the future as a decisive moment when humanity was made better.

Okay, now that I've dispensed that history lesson and my bold prediction, let's return to today, the new rules of sales and service, and what these mean for your business.

An Invaluable Sales and Service Asset: Your Employees

I really enjoy doing business with companies whose employees are friendly and who treat me with respect. It's a dramatic contrast from those companies whose people go through the motions, treat you like you're intruding on their lives, and count the hours until quitting time.

Earlier we described the power of an authentic story created by people at the top of an organization, like Hans Lagerweij of Quark Expeditions and Gerard Vroomen, co-founder of OPEN Cycle. When these stories are embedded in the very heart of an organization—with all the employees sharing a clear vision of what the company stands for and living that vision every day—then everyone is pulling together to move the company forward.

Several years ago I traveled to Lapland in northern Finland to experience life above the Arctic Circle in wintertime (fascinating!). On the first leg of the return trip, we traveled via Finnair from Ivalo to Helsinki. As we climbed the stairs to the plane, I composed an awesome photo in my mind focusing on the plane's cockpit with the terminal in the background. I thought this would be a great way to show what midday looks like in a place where the sun doesn't rise in midwinter.

I quickly got out my iPhone to take a snap. At that moment the captain turned and saw me through his window.

What could the captain have done? Well, he could have made a signal indicating "no photos." He could have pretended not to see me and turned away. Or he could have simply waved hello.

But this captain took a moment to open the cockpit window and flash a thumbs-up gesture and smile. Fortunately, I got the shot, which I tweaked with Instagram. When I tweeted it, @Finnair social media people responded in real time. Perfect.

Most pilots do what the handbook tells them to do and nothing more. They say "Your business is important to us" over the loudspeaker at the moment prescribed, and that's it.

It's not just pilots. In all businesses, many employees just don't show that they care.

A culture of caring comes from the top. It starts with how the CEO treats employees and customers. It comes from how people are hired, what skills are valued, and how people are promoted.

No matter how such a culture develops, your people are a terrific sales and service asset.

Big Data. Rich Data.

The term *big data* has gotten a lot of attention in sales discussions.

It's a concept most executives know a little about, but most don't understand big data's potential for their businesses. And very few organizations are actually taking advantage today.

I prefer the words *rich data*, a term and idea advocated by Nate Silver, a statistician and writer who analyzes in-game baseball activity and elections. Silver became well known for having successfully predicted the outcome in 49 out of 50 states during the 2008 U.S. presidential election. Today he is the editor-in-chief of *FiveThirtyEight* blog and a special correspondent for ABC News, and his best-selling book *The Signal and the Noise: Why So Many Predictions Fail—but Some Don't* dives into rich data in a big way.

No matter whether you call it rich data or big data, the concept involves using very large data sets and powerful analytics to generate real-time information that is valuable for making decisions.

Some examples: Billy Beane was the first Major League Baseball general manager to apply statistical analysis to players, quickly leading all the teams to reconsider how they evaluate players. He was profiled in Michael Lewis's 2003 book *Moneyball*, which was made into a 2011 film starring Brad Pitt as Beane. As another example, the American government monitors massive amounts of telephone and Internet traffic searching for words and phrases that might indicate nefarious activities, and routes suspicious traffic to analysts for further scrutiny.

In the context of business, big data is used in sales and marketing departments to analyze website traffic and click activity, search engine word and phrase patterns, and social media streams—all in real time.

And big data is invaluable for helping sales and service organizations understand the motivations of their existing and potential customers and anticipate their future needs. Making sense of this massive amount of data can be used develop strategies to grow revenue.

At the micro level, a company can combine someone's social profile on Twitter and other social networks with his or her customer data and market demographics to draw a detailed portrait of the person's interests and lifestyle. With this intelligence a company can deliver the right personally selected information at the right time.

To some, such massive data sifting sounds a bit creepy, but I welcome the companies I do business with to use these informed approaches. It surely beats the untargeted one-size-fits-all pitches that most companies have been sending for decades. I would be happy to have the airline I patronize realize that I take an international vacation every December with my wife so that six months in advance it might suggest options and places we might consider traveling to this year based on our past journeys. (And now, lest you think that I travel only to cold-weather places like Antarctica and northern Finland, I actually enjoy a tropical vacation, too!)

Big data is also used at the macro level to calculate sentiment analysis, the aggregate positive or negative attitudes gathered from what people are saying about companies, brands, and markets on social networks.

When sentiment analysis is calculated in real time, executives and marketers can learn whether a blog post with content negative to the company is drawing attention, and when appropriate they can respond right away. Or, in real time, salespeople could be armed with the knowledge that a competitor has just launched a new product and could know instantly what customers are saying about it.

Large companies use big data to generate revenue, either by being more efficient at what they already do or by implementing new sales and marketing strategies that would have been impossible otherwise.

For a macro example of big data at work in sales and service, consider big box home improvement stores like Home Depot and Lowe's or general merchandise stores like Walmart and how they might create specific sales strategies around the weather.

If early predictions forecast snow for a region, the store could shift inventory to outlets in the affected area during the hours preceding the storm. Things they know people purchase prior to and after snowstorms—snowblowers, shovels, generators, and the like—would be moved to locations in the affected area while keeping inventory at a manageable level.

Meanwhile, the retailer could create a dynamically updated website showcasing these weather-related products on its homepage, but only in the areas of the country affected by the storm. In other locations, the regular products would be shown.

As actual products are purchased and stock is depleted, the point-of-sale systems at each store could drive a real-time display showing how many units of the popular items are available at each store. This way, customers could expect a unit to be available (or not) and plan their visit to the appropriate store to make a purchase.

Marketers could monitor social media as well as mainstream media for keywords like "snowblowers" and comment as appropriate.

The home improvement store could also calculate (from loyalty card purchase records) which customers had not acquired shovels or snow-blowers recently and target them with a content-rich email focusing on tips to survive the storm, and could offer a video about what they need to know to buy a snowblower appropriate to their needs. In addition, the email could include incentive offers for other products likely to be needed during a storm or patterned to the buying habits of the customer.

Real-time Google AdWords and Facebook advertising could be run, targeted to the precise time and location of the impending storm. I'd imagine an online ad headline something like "Snow Blowers in Stock" and text "Popular models available right now at Home Depot in Massachusetts." The ad would point to the dynamically updating real-time product availability page.

There's a lot going on here. Big data–based sales and service strategies rely on crunching huge data sets that no human with a spreadsheet could ever manage. It's the future of real-time sales and service that's happening today in some forward-looking companies.

I'll share other examples of big data and how you can use these ideas in Chapter 6.

An Underground Business Cooks Up Innovative Sales and Service to Discover a Menu for Success

Many people I meet have a tough time using content for sales and service. This is especially true for those who have spent their entire career generating attention via paid advertising and direct sales efforts.

With that context in mind, imagine how difficult it would be to generate sales if you're running an underground business that can't use traditional sales and marketing methods because it is outside mainstream distribution channels.

That's why I'm excited to share the story of Liza Puglia, owner and chef at NOLA Buenos Aires. She relies almost exclusively on web content and social networking to fill the several tables in her fledgling restaurant.

NOLA Buenos Aires is a *puerta cerrada* restaurant. That translates to "closed door" and is a way for chefs to showcase a specialty cuisine and to bring people together through delicious food. Like NOLA Buenos Aires, many *puerta cerrada* restaurants are located in private homes. This form of underground dining is common in Buenos Aires, and the trend is growing in other cities around the world.

"*Puerta cerrada* is a great opportunity to tap into the restaurant business as an owner before making that big commitment, whether that's a financial commitment or a time commitment," Puglia says. "It's like getting our feet wet without jumping all the way in the pool."

I totally enjoyed the NOLA experience. There's the excellent food, of course. But as an added benefit I got to visit a Buenos Aires home, hardly the typical experience of a business traveler on his first trip to Argentina.

But to experience this, I had to do my homework. It's kind of like a members-only club, and I felt as if I was part of an in-the-know community once I figured out the scene.

Puglia knows this. "One of the things that really sells us is our exclusivity. We're small capacity. We're a private residence. It's somewhat difficult to get a reservation." Notice how Puglia tells the story of NOLA. It's a powerful founder's story that her buyers (like me) relate to.

When my wife and I visited NOLA, we chose the communal table and were seated with about a dozen people from all over the world who, like us, had learned about NOLA via social media. I inquired among my fellow diners and all of them—every single one—had found the restaurant via their social networks, or foodie blogs, or review sites like TripAdvisor.

"Social media is everything for us," Puglia says. "It enables us to spread the word. We know that people are coming to Buenos Aires and they're literally searching hashtag Buenos Aires on Twitter. So we'll tweet out that we have availability this Saturday night at 9:30—hashtag Buenos Aires, hashtag Palermo—so they have a little concentrated search on what it is that they're looking for. We're trying to make it as easy as possible for our future clients to find us and make a reservation."

Puglia knows that photos attract people who love good food. "Food is so much to me, esthetically," she says. "If people can see photos of the food that we're executing, they're more likely to make a reservation with us. Facebook and Twitter and blogging really allow us to share that content."

Buenos Aires has a strong community of food bloggers and many write in English, so when people are planning a trip and searching for Buenos Aires restaurant information, NOLA is there and easy to find. "Local food is one of the city's biggest tourist attractions," Puglia says. "People blog about it. And then they'll link to their blog and they'll put us on Twitter. And then we'll spread their article around so everyone is winning. They're getting more traffic to their blog, and we're getting more reservations and more exposure."

With a business that relies so strongly on social media to drive sales, Puglia has techniques to get people talking. "Twenty-four hours prior to your reservation, we send out an email to all of our clients with our exact location as well as a reminder that we'll see you tomorrow. And in the email we say we're on Instagram. We're on Foursquare. We're on Twitter. Feel free to share the word. And then after they've dined with us, we share the photos of that evening on the Facebook page, tagged with people who were there. People like that and they share those pictures and the word starts spreading."

Puglia actively encourages people to share their experiences. "When we conclude the evening at NOLA, we bring out our guestbook," she says. "We present the book to the table as a way to close the evening and to let people know that we're a small business with the hopes of getting bigger. And we're eager for feedback. Tell us what your favorite course was. Tell us anything. We want to know the good and the bad. That gives people an opportunity to speak their minds about the experience before they have a chance to write about it on review sites. In addition, we always send an email the following day, a thank you for dining with us and giving us your time. And if you'd like to spread the word, here's a direct link."

Puglia knows that reviews of NOLA Buenos Aires are important, and she generally gets very positive ones. However, as is true of all restaurants, there are occasionally people who want to express other opinions.

"It's been a mini roller coaster with the reviews," Puglia says. "We definitely don't dispute anything, because we don't want the future clients feeling uncomfortable when writing a critical review if that's the route they're taking. We know we can't please everyone; how boring would that be? However, negative reviews get me upset. It's my blood that I'm putting into this business. We're trying our hardest. And if we disappoint someone, then I'm disappointing myself. However, I believe there's a lot of feedback in the reviews, both good and bad, that can help our business and want to be aware of it. But I don't need to personally obsess about every review."

The content Puglia creates on her blog as well as on social networks like Twitter, Facebook, and Instagram is the link between the story about NOLA Buenos Aires and the potential diners she hopes to attract. "I'm extremely reliant on social media," she admits. "I don't think my business would be half as successful without it. I started my blog when I came to Buenos Aires strictly as a way to stay in touch. This forced me to use Twitter and start a Facebook page. It's really allowed me to make connections, and helped me grow as a person. And it's opened many doors for my business and helped me learn during the process."

NOLA Buenos Aires is successful today because people sharing on social media have driven interest and sales, filling the restaurant with diners who are eager to experience a terrific *puerta cerrada* restaurant. As an underground establishment, traditional methods simply cannot work for it.

No matter what industry you're in, driving sales via content creation and sharing on social networks can benefit your organization in the same way it is benefiting Puglia and NOLA Buenos Aires.

Navigating Your Sales and Service Plan

At this stage I've introduced the concepts of the new rules of sales and service. We've looked at the old ways of selling and servicing existing customers, and we've explored the basics of the new rules. I've shared a few examples of success using the methods in these pages, including those of Quark Expeditions, McGlynn, Clinton & Hall Insurance Agencies, OPEN Cycle, and NOLA Buenos Aires.

The next chapter details the concept of developing an authentic voice and communicating what your organization stands for via storytelling. This is the core of the new rules. Later, in Chapter 4 we'll focus on the idea of buyer personas and creating content for each buyer. This concept is critically important to align the marketing, sales, and service organizations of companies. Too often there is a massive disconnect in typical organizations when the marketers prattle on about products and services and waste massive amounts of money on advertising rather than focusing on the needs of their customers and creating content that directs people into and through the sales process.

Chapter 5 is a deep dive into the buying process and how your organization can build a lead generation machine. In particular, we'll be focused on how the availability of web content empowers buyers and why your existing sales process should accommodate this shifting dynamic by becoming a buying process. Chapter 6 takes an understanding of the new fundamentals of the buying process and adds the component of instant engagement. Agile selling is an incredibly powerful way to reach buyers and close more business.

Chapters 7 and 8 address how you service your existing customers. Because great customer service is one of the strongest predictors of future return business, these chapters are also part of your long-term sales strategy because they will help you grow your business.

Chapter 9 explores the need to change your personal mind-set to be engaged with your marketplace in real time. We discuss how to become active in social networks and content creation. And finally in Chapter 10, I talk about how all of the previous chapters lead toward the new paradigm of a social company that succeeds with the new rules.

You don't need to read the chapters in this order, though. Feel free to jump around as much as you like.

3

Your Story

S tories are universal. No culture has survived without them. They are widely recognized as an essential part of human cognitive development. As toddlers, when we listened to someone telling a tale, we built emotional bonds with others while developing empathy, encountering common cultural touchstones of morality and ethical behavior, and learning how to use language to express our thoughts and feelings. As social animals that crave connection with others, we find that stories—whether told orally, written on paper, or conveyed on film—are our most immediate way to enter the imaginative minds of others.

Business and commerce continue to be fundamental ways we interact outside of our family. And while we may not fully realize it, stories are an inescapable part of how we communicate professionally.

Storytelling

As you've heard me say several times, a great organizational story comes from the top. It might be the founder's story, like NOLA Buenos Aires and OPEN Cycle. Or it might be a story honed and crafted by the person who leads the organization today, like Quark Expeditions. By story, I don't mean something made up in a conference room one afternoon, nor something that an advertising agency creates on your behalf. Instead, the best stories lay the foundation for what makes an organization connect effectively with its customers.

Apple tells stories about great design. When founder Steve Jobs was alive, he was the chief storyteller and everyone else followed his lead. Jobs famously delivered eagerly anticipated speeches several times a year where he outlined the company's design vision and shared the most recent products. Today, Apple CEO Tim Cook and Jonathan Ive (the designer of many of Apple's products) are the top storytellers, following in Jobs's footsteps.

For much more on storytelling, I recommend *All Marketers ~~Are Liars~~ Tell Stories: The Underground Classic That Explains How Marketing Really Works—and Why Authenticity Is the Best Marketing of All* by Seth Godin.

"Let Me Tell You a Little Bit about Me": The Story Customers Tell Themselves

Critical to an understanding of story is how customers tell themselves the stories that define them (their worldview) and how these relate to the products and services they use. For example, I've been using Apple products for more than a decade now, and I tell myself a story like this: "I like great design and products that are easy to use, so Apple is the brand I buy." This story I tell myself intersects perfectly with the story that Apple tells about its products.

Similarly, a mother tells herself a story: "I want the best for my family, so I buy only organic food even though I know it is more expensive."

When the story that you tell customers matches the story that customers tell themselves, your business is in alignment. However, all too often, companies are completely out of alignment with their customers, which makes for difficult work. It is really tough (but not impossible) to convince someone to change their worldview and therefore the stories they tell themselves. If you sell organic food but emphasize its low cost, you're out of alignment because people accept that organic food costs more. Organic food being expensive is a deeply embedded aspect of people's worldview and it's the story they tell themselves. Since spending more on food because you care about your family doesn't square with seeking out cheaper prices, the company that sells lower-cost organic food will encounter difficulty.

As storytellers, companies need to consider customers' existing worldview as they work on the ways they communicate to the market. Going back to a few of the examples I've shared so far in this book, here are some stories that people tell themselves that align with the companies they patronize:

"I love visiting new places. I've been to all 50 U.S. states and over 100 countries and territories. I enjoy traveling to remote places I've never been to before." This, actually my very own story, framed why I was so excited to research an Antarctica expedition. Yes, I am a travel geek. Having visited six continents, I was eager to travel to the seventh. Quark Expeditions' stories fit perfectly into my worldview.

OPEN Cycle: "Mountain biking is a big part of who I am, and I don't mind paying more than $5,000 for the best bike there is."

NOLA Buenos Aires: "Small, exclusive restaurants that you can learn about only on social media are much more fun to visit."

Or consider other examples of stories that people believe:

"A $900 Louis Vuitton bag is better than cheaper bags."

"Facebook is only for young people."

"Democrats are better at running the U.S. government than Republicans." Or "Republicans are better at running the U.S. government than Democrats."

"I care about the environment so I drive an electric car."

Some companies sell to people with more than one worldview. An understanding of what I call buyer personas is essential to being able to communicate to multiple audiences. (More on this in Chapter 4.)

Call Larry: How One Entrepreneur's Story Defines a Company

Consider the worldview that many homeowners share about contractors. It's not uncommon for people to say they distrust home repair people because they suspect they are taken advantage of. There are unscrupulous contractors using a familiar manipulative sales technique plying their trade in many neighborhoods. It starts with an initial lowball bid, and after the job is well under way additional expensive charges are added on due to "unforeseen circumstances."

For the honest contractors who understand the worldview of the homeowners they serve, the market is wide open. Lawrence Janesky, founder and CEO of Basement Systems, Inc., understands this intimately, and has built a powerhouse brand and a number one leadership position in five separate industries as a result.

"We offer a marked contrast from the hard sell that everyone else uses," Janesky says. "When we go in with a consultative, educational approach, people rapidly understand they get more benefits the more they spend. In the old days the salesperson knew more than the consumer. These days the consumers are empowered and it's seller beware instead of buyer beware. Homeowners get turned off by the old high-pressure sales model."

Basement Systems is the world leader in developing and providing products that result in dry below-grade space. The company develops solutions and delivers them through its network of trained dealers.

The roots of Janesky's rise to prosperity in wet basements can be traced back to 1983, when he put an advertisement in his local Connecticut newspaper: "Carpentry. No job too small. Call Larry." He began to get calls. Eventually, he started his own homebuilding and remodeling company.

Early in his career, Janesky saw the need for basement waterproofing when one of the houses he built developed a cracked foundation wall that was leaking water into the cellar. He did some research on the problem and concluded that there had to be a better way to waterproof home basements than the technology that was available. As a result, Connecticut Basement Systems, Inc. was born in 1987, with Basement Systems, Inc. and product development following in 1990. Today, Janesky owns 27 patents on basement and crawl space products and has 345 Basement Systems dealers selling products. He is the undisputed industry leader.

This story about his company's origin is important to how Basement Systems operates. Janesky, as the entrepreneurial CEO, has set the tone for the entire enterprise, one that everyone working with him knows by heart.

While this chapter focuses on storytelling and the role of the person at the top in setting the overall tone in an organization, a company story should also drive how it interacts with the market. Therefore, I'll be sharing other aspects of Basement Systems' business in the following pages before we turn back to other examples of storytelling.

The New Model: The Salesperson as Consultant

Basement Systems makes money by selling products to professional basement waterproofing contractors. But Janesky's tremendous success isn't based on Basement Systems' product line, although the products are certainly excellent. His rise to number one in his market is directly related to his understanding of the homeowner buyer personas, how he trains his dealers to sell, the tools and services he provides to dealers, and the content he makes available that helps dealers close business with homeowners.

In short, Janesky delivers a complete system so that each salesperson in the network of 345 Basement Systems dealers is trained and has the tools to do a consultative sell with homeowners.

"I tell contractors: 'I will create a brand for you,'" Janesky says. "I tell them: 'I will train all your people. I will provide you with sales software programs. I will provide you with a database management program, which includes scheduling your sales, your service department, your production department, and GPS tracking for everyone in your company. The software we have is incredible. I will provide you with graphics. If you need an ad, just call us and we'll make it for you. I will provide you with radio and TV spots, produced in our media department. I will have annual conventions for you, where you bring all your people. I will have an owners' meeting to help them think correctly and keep growing as an individual so their business can grow. I will do all these things for you, and I'll run your Internet department, your website, and I'll get lots of leads for you. I'll do all those things for *free*, if you just keep buying product from me.' That's what we are saying, which is really, really unprecedented." And the dealers are incredibly happy with this approach—so happy that they do business with just a handshake.

For a sense of the scale of Janesky's operation, consider that he has his own in-house Internet marketing agency with 48 people, and in a recent year, the team generated 135,000 sales leads for dealers.

So that he can continue to completely understand the buyer personas that his dealers call on—the homeowners who might purchase a job that uses Basement Systems products—Janesky has continued to run his own consumer contracting business in Connecticut. "We have our own local operation and most years we are the largest dealer in the network," he says. "We do that so we can learn, and not say dumb things to our dealers. We can say we understand what your business is going through: the marketing and sales challenges. We understand people management issues like incentive programs. We understand your business completely because we run the business that you aspire to be."

Because he is still in the contracting business himself, Janesky knows his dealers' buyer persona: what homeowners need. "Basement waterproofing has changed," he says. "Before we came along in this industry, everyone thought the problem was just how to fix a leak. Fixing a leak is why most people call us, but what they really want is dry, usable space. You can simply fix a leak, but you may still have a damp, moldy basement that's not suitable for finishing or using for dry storage, one that's not safe if the power goes out, or that still has ugly, damp walls and an ugly, damp floor. We have a solution to all those things. Not everyone wants that level of service, but we invented a shopping process that caters to both the economy buyer as well as the high-value buyer who wants everything."

At the heart of the consultative sale is Basement Systems' software application. It's a proprietary visual tool that the salesperson brings to a meeting with homeowners to show, in real time, what different product options would look like in their basement, and how much each will cost.

"The sales software that we developed is incredible," Janesky says. "We take a visual image of someone's basement, and as we take them shopping for repairs and add our product, it makes changes to what the basement looks like visually. There's a shopping cart where they can see the price, and as they do more the basement gets better and the price goes up. But should you want an economy job, you can do less. The typical process when you position a company in the marketplace is to ask, 'Am I catering to the bottom of the value chain, or to the top?' Well, we figured out how we could cover the entire range, and it all flows from sales process."

At the beginning stage of the Basement Systems consultative sale is a 90-page color book, *Dry Basement Science*, which is sent to every homeowner who expresses an interest as a result of the lead generation program. The book is timed to arrive before the salesperson meets the homeowner for the first consultation. "*Dry Basement Science* educates the homeowner about the realities of wet basements, what they will need to think about, and what options are available," Janesky says. "It gets their expectations in line with reality. They aren't upset in the end if they didn't get something they thought they were getting. It really works great."

The key to the consultative approach, and the next step in the process, comes when the salesperson and homeowner meet and review Basement Systems' sales software presentation. Basement Systems' training makes certain that each contractor's salesperson knows how to use the system and is familiar with the consultative sales technique the software supports. That way, the contractors don't have to rely on hiring expensive, highly skilled salespeople who learned it elsewhere.

"We take ordinary salespeople and teach them about our products and how to use our sales system and software so that they can confidently make an extraordinary presentation," Janesky says. "When you are building systems to scale your business, you have to build systems that you can put into the hands of ordinary mere mortals that will produce above-average results. You can't count on having superstars." Note that Janesky is providing tools for the people who sell his products to tell the story that he has crafted for Basement Systems. The story itself is critical, but so is how others in the organization tell the story.

Basement Systems' consultative approach reflects the ideas I've shared in this book about the buyer being in charge. Think about the entire sales process for a moment. Homeowners have a wet basement and do a search on Google. They find a few contractors and make some calls. Some of the contractors don't even return the calls or they show up late. A few might offer a bid on the basement leak and that's all. But the Basement Systems contractor, who received the sales lead from Janesky's own Internet marketing efforts, sends out a copy of the 90-page *Dry Basement Science* book. Then the salesperson shows up with a software program allowing the homeowners to visualize their own basement with each of the available options. The salesperson relates the story of how Basement Systems was founded and talks about the benefits of dry and usable basement space.

"The homeowner is making the decisions as we go through the sales process," Janesky says. "If it yields a very large job that transforms the basement into an area with many possibilities, then that's what it yields. If it yields more of a band-aid approach and that's all they want, then okay, we can do that job too. Importantly, the customers know what they are getting. They don't have any illusions about what to expect. They don't come back to us and say 'Man, I thought my problems were over and now I realize you guys just put a band-aid on it.'"

Janesky has been so successful with his dealer network approach that he has extended the model into other services. Basement Systems, Inc., has grown to include sister companies. Janesky started a crawl space repair contractor network and in the process invented a new industry. He also started a dealer network in 2007 called Total Basement Finishing, and in 2009 he opened Foundation Support Works, focusing on structural repair to building foundations. All use the same network approach, and, not surprisingly, Janesky is number one in each of those industries, too. He now has a corporate campus in Seymour, Connecticut, with five buildings situated on

50 acres featuring hundreds of thousands of square feet of office space and training facilities.

Janesky's journey from a 1983 newspaper ad for carpentry services to the largest business in five industries was built on insight into how homeowners want to buy. This organizational story is at the heart of the company's success, and it provides the backbone to the extraordinarily effective tools and training that the company provides to sales personnel in his dealer network.

Mastering the Art of Effective Storytelling for Any Organization

Once your CEO has set the tone for your organizational story and aligned it with the worldview of your buyers, there will be an opportunity for writing (and telling) stories to your marketplace. As content takes its rightful place at the forefront of sales, I'm seeing many people fail at basic storytelling.

In the next chapter, we will look at how to align your marketing and sales around buyer personas. If you work in a smaller company, you're likely wearing many hats, and marketing may be one of them. If you're an entrepreneur, one of your jobs is marketing. If you're in sales at a larger organization, you probably have a relationship with people in a marketing department. If so, make them read this.

Salespeople and marketers alike are ineffective when they use the classic customer testimonial format and pop that onto their blog or make it into a video. "Here's our product. It is great. Here are customers who say it is great. Now buy some of our product." This just doesn't hold people's attention.

How interesting would a book or movie be were it to have this plot?

Boy meets girl.
They fall in love.
They get married.

That's what most people do with their business writing.

Unlike this boring "boy meets girl" story, the best stories drip with conflict. They have a hero and sometimes a villain. There is a story arc. As a writing teacher once told me: "Writing without conflict is propaganda."

Movies and novels have these elements—the best open with conflict in the first scene, on the first page, or even the first paragraph. Usually, it's one character in conflict with others (Batman against the bad guys). Sometimes it's a character in conflict with herself ("I really shouldn't go into this bar, but . . .").

Unlike the boring propaganda approach, here is a classic conflict-driven plotline of countless books and movies:

Boy meets girl.
They fall in love.
Boy loses girl.
Boy (and sometimes girl) is miserable for most of the action.
They finally get back together.
They get married.

The conflict involves how and why they break up and then what they do to get back together. That's where it gets interesting, where the delicious tension lies, and why people pay attention.

In her blog post "Weather Happens—Be Prepared," Kristiana Almeida writes on the American Red Cross website about her life as a kid on Cape Cod, and uses that story to educate readers about the importance of being prepared for a blizzard. Great stuff. What does the Red Cross really want? A donation. Is a donation mentioned in her post? No.

You too can be an effective storyteller. Here are a few ideas to get you thinking about telling stories that people will want to pay attention to rather than propaganda they will ignore.

- Instead of "creating copy," think about sitting in a restaurant with friends and explaining a little about your work. How would you convey your story? How would you hold your friends' interest? Write that down.
- Rather than talking about the features and benefits of your products and services, consider how you help people to solve their problems.
- Who or what is the "bad guy" in your market? Is it the big, famous company that everybody does business with but nobody really likes? Is there a silly government regulation that holds buyers back? How can you weave those into a story with conflict?
- What is the status quo? Use that as the bad guy in your story.

I've used these techniques in the book you are reading now. It's how I create many of the stories of success I share not only here, but in my blog and in my speeches. I think of the stories I tell as a movie or a novel, and I cast the people from around the world whose success I showcase as my heroes. The villain is the ancient traditional approach. Gerard Vroomen at OPEN Cycle is a hero battling the big bike companies that don't engage with customers in real time. Larry Janesky is a hero, delivering quality basement services to people in a world of unscrupulous contractors.

Your stories must be true. They must align with your buyers' worldview. And they must showcase how you are the ideal organization to do business with.

Now I'll share one of my favorite examples of how a company developed a set of stories that cast others as the bad guys and used humor in an interesting way to build a following and become the leader in its marketplace.

The Health Club That Tells Its Story by Exercising an Attitude

I've been a member of health clubs in four cities where I've lived: New York, Tokyo, Hong Kong, and now in the Boston suburbs. In each location, my decision to join a club was spontaneous. I'd think, "Oh, shoot. It's mid-December and my New Year's resolution is to get fit, so I need to join a gym." (That's exactly what happened when I lived in New York City.) Or several years ago when I decided to swim a day or two per week to keep in shape for surfing, I decided to join a club with an indoor pool. I used social media to ask my friends who live in the Boston area about the clubs they belonged to. I also hightailed it to Google to see what clubs were nearby. And inevitably, like so often when I am in the market to buy a product, I'd start to notice advertisements for health clubs in the *Boston Globe*.

I made a quick decision to join Boston Sports Clubs because I just loved the cheeky personality that came through in their online and offline strategies to reach me! They got my attention in a big way even before I walked into my local club. When I did visit for the first time, the unconventional, humorous approach of the company story continued as I saw posters in the lobby.

That's exactly the strategy the parent company has used to become the largest operator of health clubs in the northeastern United States. "When you think about joining a gym, it's because something in your life changes and causes you to come in," says Robert Giardina, CEO of Town Sports International, the owner and operator of New York Sports Clubs, Boston Sports Clubs, Washington Sports Clubs, and Philadelphia Sports Clubs. "You could come in because of a health reason. It might be a reunion or a wedding. At that point you're going to say, 'I need to join a gym—which gym do I want to belong to?' And that gym's personality has to fit who you are. You start by thinking about which gyms you know that are in your market. And that's the moment that people think of us."

Giardina has been in the fitness business for his entire career. He joined the company that was to become Town Sports International in 1981 (initially selling squash memberships) and moved up to chief operating officer in 1992. In 2002 he became CEO, expanding the business to over 150 clubs with 500,000 members and taking the company public in 2006.

The personality that Giardina has built and maintained for the branded clubs in each city—New York, Boston, Washington, and Philadelphia—is one of playfulness. "Sports clubs have always been about price and hard bodies," he says. "Clubs say, 'Let's get a price out there, let's see if we have images of a hard body or some weights, and we sell what we sell.' We did that for a while, and first, it really never set us apart, and second, it really just didn't create any conversation."

About 20 years ago, Giardina looked at the market and realized that all of the gyms looked the same. They all sold in the same way, and they all positioned themselves the same way. "We liked the product that we offered and we liked the services that we offered, but we really had to create a difference," he recalls. "People knew what a gym was. The challenge that we faced was to break through the clutter and get people talking about us."

At that time, Giardina spoke with a bunch of branding and advertising agencies, but none of the big ones showed him anything that would get him noticed. He did hear from one person who truly captured the challenge, so he began working with CJ Waldman of the tiny Octopus Creative Group, and they've been together ever since. Giardina recalls, "CJ said, 'You've got to do things that are going to make you a little bit uncomfortable because that's what will get people talking about you.'" They worked together to craft a story that resonates to this day with buyers. It's one that drips with conflict and uses humor in an interesting way.

One of the first stories that ran in the late 1990s played off a typical health club message that depicts people with good bodies presenting themselves attractively in the dating market. It was run just prior to Valentine's Day with copy that said: *"This could be the year you'll find your perfect soul mate who will love you for who you are and physical appearance will mean nothing."* And then in small type at the bottom, it said in parentheses: *"And the tooth fairy could introduce you."* "We ran the ad and all these people started talking about it," Giardina says.

When the New York Sports Clubs run such an advertisement in the local metropolitan newspapers, the narrative campaign is supported through window displays as well as on posters inside the clubs. The same promotional strategy is used in the Boston, Washington, and Philadelphia Sports Clubs, too. Sometimes, the stories appear in unlikely places like bus stop shelters. The strategy ensures that existing members like me feel good about our choice of a fun-loving health club, and believe me, it gets us to talk up the club! And that means the stories do a great job attracting people who are thinking of joining a gym at that moment.

When Reebok entered the New York market and started advertising its new large health club, Giardina had an opportunity to poke fun at the new competitor: *"Reebok's opening a gym. Maybe New York Sports Clubs should make sneakers."*

As the clubs started to develop strong personalities, Waldman and Giardina began to poke lighthearted fun at celebrities in the news, including, over the years, Bill Clinton, Anthony Weiner, and Alex Rodriguez. Some of the famous people who hit the news that Town Sports International clubs riffed off in recent years include:

Chris Christie: *"Don't worry, Chris, our members stop traffic too."*
Miley Cyrus: *"Miley, better to work out than twerk out."*
Charlie Sheen: *"Charlie, we can't offer $3 million per episode, but we can give you March for free."*
And my favorite: *"Kim Jong-un, with a great bod, you don't need a big missile."*

Giardina's approach to storytelling gets more attention because so many people talk about the latest story on social networks. In addition, the mainstream media loves to cover stories about how the clubs' talked-about marketing skewers well-known people. "The clever, a little bit edgy ones about the celebrities will end up on a local newscast," he says. "You'll also see them on *Entertainment Tonight* and CNN and lots of other places. We could never pay for that kind of coverage."

Unlike most CEOs who delegate storytelling to the marketing staff, Giardina himself is involved in all aspects of the way in which the clubs communicate. He personally chooses and approves the stories focused on celebrity, and that personal attention from the leader of the company over 20 years has been instrumental in making Town Sports International the success that it is today, growing from a handful of locations to more than 150.

When Waldman and Giardina work, they get as edgy as possible—it's an important aspect of the company brand. "CJ pushes me as far as he can, right to the line of acceptability," Giardina says. "A few times we might have gone too far, like years ago when Bill Clinton was president and we were opening up clubs everywhere. We said: *'New York Sports Clubs have more openings than Clinton's zipper.'* We're always thinking about breaking through the clutter."

Over time, the clubs have established a great reputation for their communications approach, and that has carried through to how people think of the clubs. In the same way that I did when I was choosing a club, people remember the fun-loving chain of health clubs, and many want to be a part of that. Giardina says, "If you talk to people who know us, and you ask, 'What comes to mind when you think of Boston Sports Clubs or New York Sports Clubs?,' the first thing that usually comes out of their mouths is, 'Oh yeah, I love their advertising.' People know us but we don't spend that much. We spend less than almost anyone in the industry. But our personality makes people say, 'Let me go see who they are. They're in my neighborhood. I want to see what kind of club they have.'"

Just like the sports clubs that Giardina runs, your organization needs compelling stories about what you deliver, and those stories need to be cleverly told. When this is done well, people will talk about you in social networks, and the mainstream media will want to write about you in newspapers and magazines, and broadcast about you on radio and television. A great story builds business.

"What Happens Next?": How a Compelling Narrative Builds a Following

Presidential campaigns in the United States are a fascinating case study in how marketing, sales, and customer service work together to achieve results (or not). The product (the candidate) is also the CEO of the organization. In the best campaigns, the candidate sets the tone either by having a compelling life story that people already know or by introducing a backstory that resonates with voters. This approach means that at all of the touch points of the campaign—marketing (website and other online information, the content of television ads, direct mail, signs, etc.); sales (email pitches for donations and in-person fundraising events); and customer service (ongoing campaign communications, frequently sent in the candidate's name)—must work together to support the core message: the candidate's story.

In the 2004 election cycle, Vermont Governor Howard Dean competed in the primaries to seek the Democratic Party's nomination for president. Dean, a former medical doctor, called for comprehensive universal healthcare for Americans. The Dean campaign was largely ignored by mainstream media, so the campaign built a strong underdog story with its supporters, positioning Dean as an unknown upstart who had to rely on being scrappy to win.

Nicco Mele was the Dean campaign's first technical hire and served as its webmaster. He's currently a senior fellow at the USC Annenberg Center on Communication Leadership & Policy and is the author of *The End of Big: How the Internet Makes David the New Goliath*. In 2004, Mele built and maintained the Dean campaign's online presence by launching the first presidential campaign blog, and worked on email acquisition and email fundraisers.

"When I was on the Dean campaign, there were nine candidates in the Democratic primary," Mele remembers. "And the *New York Times* wrote a story every day about the campaign and never once mentioned Howard Dean. They would say, 'candidates John Kerry, Joe Lieberman, Richard Gephardt, and five other presidential candidates.' Meanwhile we noticed that the bloggers were writing about Dean like crazy. These bloggers would go see Howard Dean give a speech and then they would come home and write a blog post saying, 'Wow, I just saw him and he was amazing.'"

Mele and others on the campaign team realized that they needed to use the story of Howard Dean being the most scrappy competitor in their narrative, and target supporters via the campaign's "customer service" outreach program.

Mele knew that to communicate effectively, the campaign had to have something compelling to say to supporters. "You have to make some kind of promise," he says. "And so the promise is 'I'm going to give you inside information about this campaign. I'll tell you things like who my vice presidential candidate is before I tell the press. The bargain is that in exchange for that inside access, I'm also going to ask you for money. You are going to get fundraising emails.' But it has to be worthwhile and compelling. You have to talk to them in a way that when you ask them to give money they believe in the mission."

This played out when the campaign went to supporters to get their help to raise Dean's profile with the reporters at the *New York Times*. At that point in the campaign, *Times* reporters were not paying attention to Dean, so campaign staffers realized that if they were to raise a large amount of money, that total would get reported. And if Dean won the money race, the *Times* would have no choice but to cover his campaign. This was a perfect story for Dean supporters—the upstart campaign being ignored by the mainstream media in New York. But with a lot of donations, those reporters would be forced to pay attention.

Campaign manager Joe Trippi wrote a guest opinion piece about Howard Dean titled "The Perfect Storm" that appeared on one of the popular blogs. In his post, Trippi explained how the *New York Times* never mentioned Howard Dean, and laid out his audacious challenge to Dean supporters. If they could band together to raise enough money to win the so-called money primary, it would prove that Dean was a financially viable candidate, and would put him on the front page of the *New York Times*. And that's almost exactly what happened. To put that in context, at the time all the other campaign managers were spending their time trying to get their candidate on CNN, MSNBC, and Fox and in the newspapers. But it was Joe Trippi's blog entry that altered the dynamics of the campaign.

The elements of this strategy can be used by any organization, not just a U.S. presidential campaign. When you have a compelling story like Howard Dean the upstart, and you craft a compelling "us versus them" narrative dripping with conflict, you have the essential raw materials. You then arm your loyal customers with content that makes them feel like insiders. This drives people to want to support the organization in other ways, too. But it has to be something that resonates emotionally and not merely marketing copy.

"The art is telling a really compelling narrative," Mele says, "a story that excites people, that engages them, a story that also is true. It resonates with what they are seeing in the press and what they are feeling on the ground. It makes them think, 'Yes, this is something I want to be a part of, something I want to succeed.'"

A Story That Sells

I was paging though my favorite newsweekly *The Week* (yes, I read it in print) and found a small review of the brand-new FluidStance Level, a sort of teeter-totter board that you stand on to elicit subtle, constant movement underneath your feet to increase your range of motion and heart rate.

I thought, Wow! That's cool. I have a stand-up desk and I am a surfer, so this looked like a great thing for my lifestyle. So I went to the FluidStance site, found they were launching via the Indiegogo crowdfunding platform, and watched the video about how Joel Heath, the founder and CEO, started FluidStance and designed the Level.

Much of the video was shot in Heath's garage, and he spoke about how the idea of the Level came to him. Illustrating the power of an authentic story, before the video was even finished I knew I wanted to buy my own Level. Heath's FluidStance story got me from curious to whipping out my credit card for the $300 product in less than three minutes. Clearly the FluidStance Indiegogo campaign was a success, because it enjoyed an 805 percent funding success rate and raised over $500,000—all because of a great story.

Here's what Heath said in the video:

I lived in Vail for 16 years skiing and riding my bike 60 to 80 days a year. I got a corporate gig, and all of a sudden I was sitting on my butt 60 to 80 hours a week. The body starts changing; you just start feeling your body caving into itself. It just didn't feel right.

So, like so many, I moved to a stand-up desk, which was great; it helped me, and I just felt more energetic like so many other people that are doing it. But I started standing on my hips really hard and locking my knees out, and all of a sudden just started feeling pain. I started to think about how I could create motion in life. It's not just about standing; standing's been great, but I really want to move.

Our product is called the Level. It's designed to work with you. You don't have to think about it; you just step on. It's enough motion to get your heart rate up a bit, and simple enough that you can multitask while onboard.

We designed the Level to create subtle instability underneath your feet so when you're working, you get out of your joints when you're standing hard like we stand. . . . But when you get onto a board like this, it allows you just to flow through; it gets you into your muscles. So step on, and see how it feels.

There's a time to sit, there's a time to stand, and there's a time to flow. Whether you're in a cube, in a common meeting space, or in your living room, it's time we all get moving. We hope to provide you the shift where you need it most: physically, emotionally, or intellectually, and, hopefully, change the way you move, through work.

We've spent the last 18 months getting the design, engineering, testing, and now the tooling in place. Help us get a little bit of motion in your day, and everyone's day around us.

As I write this, I've had my Level for about six months and I love it. And in a karma-infused coincidence, as I was walking the show floor at the Employer Healthcare & Benefits Congress where I was to deliver a keynote speech, I noticed a FluidStance display, and there was Joel Heath. So I introduced myself, told him I was an early customer, and conducted a real-time impromptu interview with him.

"We wanted to build a sense of community, and we felt that building from a community is the best place to build anything, including a brand," Heath told me. "Having people be a part of the vision, rather than telling them what the vision is has always been part of our overall core principles."

The Indiegogo campaign for the FluidStance Level was very successful, so I asked Heath what other organizations could learn from his approach using the power of story. "I think what people love about start-ups is that humanization of the brand," he says. "It's where you're buying from somebody's personal passion—how you can humanize that story and make it feel like you're buying from Ma and Pa again. I think that what we crave as individuals is to have that human connection. And that's one of the things that we've tried to do from the start. That video was filmed in my garage, with my kids, with footage of my tools. It wasn't produced to try to be something bigger than we are."

In January 2016, FluidStance celebrated its first anniversary, and early customers like me received a heartfelt thank-you email from Heath, extending the company story.

A year ago today, I had the opportunity to cast my dream out into the world. The purpose was simple: to help set the world in motion.

While I may have lost a little sleep along the way, I am grateful to have turned an idea into a shared vision. Your help throughout and after the crowdfunding process has led to amazing stories and recognition, including being named one of "The 7 Biggest Workplace Game-Changers of 2015" by *Inc.* Magazine. Beyond the recognition and a strong first year of sales, I am most proud of the stories that keep coming back to us about how people's lives and desks have become filled with movement. Couple this with the fact that we have donated 1% of all top line sales, 1% of our company's equity, and 1% of our employees' time to First Descents, an adventure camp for young adults beating cancer, and it has been a fun-filled and rewarding year. Thank you for your early support.

We could not have done it without you.

A powerful story is an essential component of the new rules of selling. As I've learned more about Heath and FluidStance, there's no doubt in my mind that the interesting story he tells, the authenticity of the way he tells it, and the way he brings the community along for the ride drove his initial success and will continue to grow his business.

Now that we've looked at how to craft a compelling story, let's turn to ways to integrate marketing and sales, and the importance of buyer personas in your sales and service plan.

4

Integrating Marketing and Sales with Buyer Personas

I spent most of my career in marketing, although for four years I was in sales. So I've seen both sides.

Back in the mid-1990s there was a great divide between what marketing did and what sales did and often people in the two departments were at odds. Much of the tension stemmed from the handoff of leads generated by marketing to the sales staff, who owned them until close.

However, in the new digital era, the great divide between sales and marketing is rapidly disappearing. Skills and responsibilities that were once clearly defined are now making a transition to allow for more agile and creative interaction.

Creating Magic by Adding Context to Content

I had an excellent conversation with my friend Greg Alexander, CEO of Sales Benchmark Index, about how marketing and sales can work together more effectively. We discussed the new buying process and what this means for salespeople, marketers, and their management teams.

In my simplistic first stab at this, I offered that marketing must create the content that salespeople need to be successful in the selling process. It could be found in a repository somewhere, or it could certainly be available freely on the web, but the important thing would be that the salesperson knows where it's located and how to access it. This means that what the marketing team creates is important throughout the entire sales process, not just for initiating the process at the top of the funnel, as was true just a few years ago.

It is, I said, the salesperson's job to understand each individual buyer or existing customer so well that the salesperson knows precisely which bit of content is pertinent to the customer's situation and sees that it is delivered to that customer.

"What the salesperson has to do is implement context," Alexander added. "This is where contextual content marketing actually happens. The marketing department is doing everything you just said, which is of huge importance, because salespeople don't have the time to go do all that. And sometimes they don't have the skills."

In Alexander's view, the salesperson, as the expert on the customer, takes what the marketing department creates and then personalizes it for each buyer or existing customer and passes it on in whatever method is best: LinkedIn, Twitter, email, or even the good old telephone. It is a reason to make contact.

"Sales reps take the information and say to themselves, 'How does this idea, this theme, this concept apply to my account and the decision makers inside my account?'" Alexander says. "'How do I make this real to them? How do I provide context for it?' That's where the magic happens."

With that magic in mind, in this chapter I will focus on the concept of buyer personas. While the ideas here are essential for the smooth running of all aspects of an organization—including sales and marketing and customer service—many ideas will also likely fall into the purview of your organization's marketing department. If you run a smaller company, it's your job to make sure this integration happens. If you're part of a larger organization, you need to make sure the marketing executives are in sync with your new sales and service plan. You might suggest to the marketers in your organization that they check out my book *The New Rules of Marketing & PR*. In it, I provide the same concepts you'll read here but with much more detail specifically written for those in the marketing and public relations departments.

I include this chapter because for sales and service to be successful, it is essential that marketing be aligned and work smoothly in conjunction with sales and service activities. The days of the great divide are over.

The Power of Content That Provides Exactly What You Need

Think about the websites you've visited recently. Have you noticed that sometimes you can glance at a site (or product page) for the first time and instantly know that it will *not* be helpful? I experience that feeling nearly every day. I might be shopping for something—say, a bike helmet. So I go to Google or to Amazon and just search for "bike helmet." At this point, I'm looking for a site that will educate and inform me, not one that is chock-full of jargon and hype. I'm expecting that the people behind the site have anticipated my need for a little education. Yes, I am interested in buying a helmet at some point, but not until I know exactly what I want. What should I look for in a helmet? What's the trade-off between less weight and more strength? What's the price range?

Usually I sample a few sites or product pages that are just terrible. When that happens, I'm gone in a split second, clicking away, never to return. You know what I'm talking about, right? You make a decision immediately. It's a gut feeling you make in real time, isn't it? In contrast, many sites have valuable and useful information. In fact, sometimes I feel that a site has been developed especially for me! It's as if someone read my mind and built a site based on my needs alone. And the site was *right there when I needed it.*

You know something? It's not a coincidence when a site feels like it was created especially for you, because that means a marketer somewhere did his or her job well! When I end up somewhere that educates me about bike helmets through a video, a few blog posts, or maybe a Q&A with some instructive photos, I'm ready to make a buying decision in just a few minutes. And guess where I am inclined to buy? Yes, the place that educated me.

If you've read my previous books, you know I talk a lot about what I call "buyer personas." Buyer personas are the representative groups of people who buy your products and services. In fact, the concept of buyer personas is so essential to good marketing and sales that I'm compelled to reintroduce the idea here. It's essential to realize that only when your marketing and salespeople work together and are united does an organization truly thrive in today's always-on world of the web, a place where people do their own research.

The Nobis Hotel Sells to David Meerman Scott

In Chapter 3, we explored the idea of story in two broad contexts. We looked at how consumers tell a story to themselves based on their worldview. These stories frequently involve products and services and inform individuals about the sorts of things they want to buy. And we also looked at how companies tell stories, with the best being a founders' story or one crafted by the top people, which everyone in the organization uses to define their mission. It is when those stories mesh that a company is perfectly aligned within its marketplace. A hotel I visited in Stockholm illustrates this example brilliantly. As you're reading, consider how you can do the same thing for your products and services.

Have you noticed that nearly all hotel websites are exactly the same?

There's the photo of the property on the front, the "reserve a room" widget usually in the top left, and a bunch of boring, superlative language. Basically the sites are interchangeable. I recently booked a hotel in California, and the three hotels I considered had websites that looked like they had all been designed by the same agency.

But it doesn't have to be that way! When my wife Yukari and I decided to spend a few days in Stockholm, I did my research and ended up booking a room at the Nobis Hotel. I made the choice myself based on—you guessed it—the content on the hotel's site. This hotel website immediately seemed different. It felt like it was speaking personally to me.

That difference continued as Yukari and I checked in and explored the property. It seemed perfect for us. We had to find out why, so we met with Oliver Geldner, an executive at the Nobis.

Geldner told us that the buyer persona of the people attracted to the Nobis are frequent travelers who are sick of sterile chain hotels and want something different. They are people who make their own decisions about where to stay using the web and social media. Their buyers want upscale luxury but in a modern style, not the old-world traditional style.

As Geldner was going through this with us, I stole a glance at my wife. "That's us!" I almost shouted. How cool that we were actually attracted to the hotel based on the buyer persona created by Geldner and his colleagues! Our worldview intersected with the hotel's story.

The most fascinating detail that Geldner shared about the Nobis Hotel was the internal description of the Nobis that is used when communicating about the hotel on social networks like Facebook:

The Nobis Hotel is a grand old lady who lives in a vast apartment in Stockholm. She's a dame of means. She has a cocktail party starting every day at 11:00 am and is slightly tipsy by 5:00 pm and that is when she is communicating to you via social networks as a friend.

The Nobis is a Swedish hotel, but she insists on communicating in English even though the majority of guests are Swedish.

She has a sense of humor and has interesting things to say. She wants to be relevant, have a sense of humor and not take herself too seriously.

Wow! How cool is this description? (Well, at least it's cool for me, which is why I was attracted to the Nobis via its site.)

Here are a few short stories I pulled from the Nobis Hotel Facebook page. I can picture the slightly tipsy grand old dame writing them:

Animal question of the week: "I am traveling with a duck, and would need a room with a tub." I can't wait to see the cleaning lady's face when she comes in to make up the room! Well, at least today we got nice weather, for ducks. . . .

And this:

Note to all parents of three-year-old boys: there is a subtle but very distinct difference between peeing in the steam room and peeing into the steam room. The first can be the sign of an emergency; the latter is a signal you might have a hooligan on your hands. . . .

Isn't this fantastic? Can you imagine a big chain hotel communicating like this on social networks? Not a chance!

Geldner told me that he does a semantic analysis of the Nobis Hotel listings on travel review sites such as TripAdvisor to find out what words and phrases visitors use in their reviews. These are then used in the Nobis marketing.

So rather than make up their search engine terms like most marketers, they actually use the terms like "beautiful modern hotel in Stockholm" that people use in social networks as their search engine optimization (SEO) phrases.

All of this communication to buyer personas drives people into the Nobis Hotel's sales and marketing process, making the actual point of sale—the moment when someone enters their credit card number to make a reservation—happen more often.

Before we dig deeper into the concept of buyer personas, let's look at how most people communicate about products and services, essentially focused on their own egos rather than on their buyers.

Making Stuff Up

I see it again and again. The way most entrepreneurs, salespeople, marketers, and product managers operate is by *making stuff up*. I spend a lot of my time talking to organizations about their sales and marketing plans and strategies, and it is amazing to me that so many of them spend their time like this: holed up in comfortable company conference rooms, sitting on nice cozy Aeron chairs, eating free sandwiches brought in from a catering company, and trading ideas about how to sell and market their products. You know, just off the top of their heads. The worst part? In these making-stuff-up sessions, everyone in the room works for the company, and therefore there is no representation of the voices of people who will actually buy the products and services. People go back and forth, saying, "Oh, I *think* we should do this" or "I *think* we should do that."

I call this "MSU behavior." The polite way to describe MSU is "making stuff up," but feel free to substitute a less polite word beginning with *S*. Many people I work with, organizations large and small, prefer the other *S* word because it emphasizes the behavior's dramatic ineffectiveness. What people who make stuff up are *not* doing is getting out of their comfortable offices and talking to people who represent their buyer personas. People practicing MSU behavior are simply guessing at what buyers need.

Annoying Three out of Four Customers

I have exercised in more than 100 hotel gyms. Some are great, fully outfitted with the latest gear. Some are tired and broken down. Recently, as I was doing my morning workout in a hotel gym, I was thinking about how these rooms get put together. Does any hotel developer actually interview potential guests before planning and constructing the gym? It certainly doesn't appear so.

Some have interesting views, like the gym at the Stella Di Mare Hotel in Sharm El Sheikh, Egypt—where I happened to be staying when I wrote this portion of the book. But most gyms are relegated to the hotel basement.

How do they decide what equipment to buy and in what quantities? They appear to just study existing gyms and copy what every other hotel does.

> "Because everyone does it this way" isn't the right way.

The accepted ratio seems to be two treadmills for every elliptical. Why?

The stationary bikes are nearly always empty of riders. Who decided to waste money on those things? (My theory is they were popular in the 1970s, but nobody has bothered to tell the hotel gym people that preferences have changed in the decades since.)

And for something really weird, consider that no matter how large or how small the hotel gym is, there is precisely one set of dumbbells! In the tiny Courtyard Marriott gym in Bangor, Maine, there was just one treadmill, one bike, and one elliptical. Yet it had a beautiful set of dumbbells. But at the Intercontinental in Cairo, which boasts a huge gym with some three dozen pieces of equipment that were mostly unused while I was there, I witnessed four people sharing one set of dumbbells.

Don't even get me started on the music. Nearly all hotel gyms play music. Loud music. But at the same time, my informal analysis reveals that about 75 percent of people in the gyms wear headsets (usually in Apple white).

So while the majority of customers listen to their personal music selection or perhaps enjoy an audiobook, or they plug into the exercise equipment's integrated television screen sound, the gym still pumps in the loud music. What results is an annoying musical clash. So unsurprisingly, people play their music at a higher volume to overpower the gym music in the background. Do hotel operators realize they are contributing to their customers' hearing loss?

As we all know, one's taste in music is about as personal as one can get. Nevertheless, many establishments believe that imposing their playlists on their customers is good for business. Why would someone decide to annoy 75 percent of customers with a practice that can be fixed in one second?

Understanding your buyers.

Why not observe and learn from what people actually do in the gym, and turn the damned music off? Why not get a second set of dumbbells?

Most people tend to be polite and avoid conflict, so rather than tell hotel staff that the music is annoying (or your product doesn't seem to be addressing needs), they simply turn away and go elsewhere.

Of course, this isn't a story about hotel gyms. It is all about understanding your buyers.

Egocentric Nonsense

The problem with making stuff up is that, unless you get incredibly lucky, you're not likely to stumble upon exactly the problems your buyers face. Even more importantly, you'll miss the specific ways they describe these problems.

According to the Princeton University WordNet database, ego is defined as "an inflated feeling of pride in your superiority to others." When companies make stuff up, they tend to create sales and marketing materials with egotistical language, usually featuring obscure jargon from their industry. I call this nonsense "gobbledygook."

> Your customers aren't looking to satisfy your ego, and they don't really care what you think about the stuff you sell. Your buyers want to solve their problems.

You know what I mean: the technology company that hypes a "world-class, mission-critical, cutting-edge solution to improve business processes." Huh?

Or how about the automobile manufacturer that prattles on and on about the obscure technology behind its award-winning antilock braking system? This is just egotistical nonsense. I couldn't care less about the subtle nuances of the technology behind any antilock braking system. However, I do want to know if my car will stop properly.

Buyer Personas

Buyer personas, the distinct demographic groupings of your potential customers, are critically important for successful marketing that leads to sales success. Creating marketing and sales initiatives that target specific buyer personas is a strategy that easily outperforms the results you get from sitting on your butt in your comfortable office making stuff up about your products.

> Organizations filled with people who take the time to understand the needs of buyers they wish to reach, and then develop information to educate and inform those buyers, are more successful than organizations that just make stuff up.

For those of you who don't work for a company that sells products or services, my use of the word *buyer* applies to any organization's target demographic. A politician's buyer personas include voters, supporters, and contributors; universities' buyer personas include prospective students who might apply, their parents who will foot the bill, and alumni who might donate; a golf club's buyer personas are potential members; and a nonprofit's buyer personas include corporate and individual donors. So go ahead and substitute the way you refer to your potential customers in place of the phrase *buyer persona* if you wish. But do keep your focus on this fundamental and powerful concept.

By working to understand the market problems that your products and services solve for members of your buyer personas, you'll gain the insight you need to quickly develop a product or service that will resonate with buyers. And once the product is ready to ship, an understanding of buyer personas transforms your marketing from mere product-specific, egocentric gobbledygook (that only you and the other employees in your organization understand) into the sort of valuable information people are thrilled to consume and eager to share. When people are educated and informed by your organization, they frequently make the choice to do business with you in return. Let's take a look at an example of how real-time buyer persona research yielded a surprising insight for a company that took the time to learn.

Consider the rental car industry. Now, I'm no industry expert, but I do rent cars from time to time. It would seem to me that rental car companies serve quite a few distinct buyer personas. Here are a few that come to mind:

- Independent business travelers who make rental decisions themselves
- Corporate travel department employees who make an approved vendor deal on behalf of hundreds or even thousands of company travelers
- City dwellers who don't own a car but who need wheels for the weekend
- Somebody choosing a car for a family vacation
- A commuter whose own car is in the repair shop for a few days but who still needs to get to work

The incredible value of creating multiple buyer personas and learning about each is that the needs they express and the problems your organization solves may be very different. In the rental car buyer persona example, a corporate travel manager who cuts a deal for 5,000 employees has very different needs (for example, to save the company money) than somebody whose car is in the shop for a week and needs a temporary vehicle because, above all, she cannot miss work. Smart organizations build sales strategies that will appeal to each of these buyers, with a focus on their unique problems. It is precisely those organizations that build sites based on buyer personas that cause you and me to go, "Wow! They *really* understand me!"

And then, because the marketing is so well targeted, the potential customer is nearly sold by the time she gets to the point where the sale happens, either in an e-commerce transaction or by contacting a salesperson.

No Red Alfa Romeo?

One way to research buyer personas in real time is to monitor the blogs, forums, chat rooms, and social networking sites that buyers frequent. A huge benefit of this form of research is that people are communicating right now, and you can see what's being discussed—for free! How cool is that? It's exactly what Avis Europe did, in order to learn what cruise passengers need from a rental car company. The company has been actively using the web to reach buyer personas since launching the rental car industry's first blog in 2006.

Okay, quick: What comes to mind when you imagine a large cruise ship berthing at a resort island? What do you think passengers would want in a rental car for touring the island for a few hours? Well, people at Avis Europe assumed that cruise passengers would primarily be couples and would prefer a sporty two-seater to tool around in. They were exhibiting classic MSU behavior. Once they began the research, however, they realized they were very, very wrong.

"By monitoring Twitter, blogs, and forums to listen in on conversations, and by following trends, we were able to gain insight into what was important to cruise passengers, like our location's proximity to the port, and the kinds of cars that they actually wanted to rent," says Paul Burani, a partner at Web Liquid Group, a digital marketing agency working with Avis Europe.

A startling insight emerged from the research. Not only had Avis Europe underestimated the size of the cruise market, but it had chosen a default car that was completely wrong for many travelers. It turned out that people tend to make fast friends on cruises, and many choose to tour islands with another couple or in groups. So Avis Europe quickly gained the insight that larger cars and vans were needed immediately at cruise ports. With this buyer persona insight, Avis Europe could adjust the makeup of the rental fleet in real time. This product reconfiguration resulted in more sales right away. This kind of valuable information cannot be made up in a conference room. The only way to learn it is to hear it directly from representatives of your buyer persona groups.

"That was an example of consumers articulating needs which were different from our expectation, and it surprised us," Burani says. "It just goes to show sometimes common sense does not work."

Because Avis Europe marketers understood how customers make rental car decisions at cruise destinations, and they adjusted the car selection and communicated appropriately, the salespeople at Avis Europe were prepared to make more sales.

Multiple Personality Order

Most organizations, like Avis Europe, serve more than one buyer persona. Your job is to identify the different buyer personas and then research each one. Of course, many people are a little stumped when confronted with a blank whiteboard and asked to identify the different buyer personas their organization sells to. What you should be asking yourself is this: What problems do we solve for our buyers? When a problem you solve is fundamentally different from one group of customers to another, then you have more than one buyer persona. The rental car market is a perfect example. For the cruise passengers, a rental car on a resort island solves the problem of how to spend a few hours with a group of new friends from the ship. For the person whose car is in the shop and who needs to get to work, the rental car solves a very different problem.

I like to talk about universities as another example of a type of organization with multiple buyer personas. An effective university marketing and PR effort would include research on the buyer persona for the high school student who is considering college. But since the parents of the prospective student have very different information needs (How much does it cost? Will my daughter be safe?), buyer persona research should also be conducted with the goal of understanding parents. A college also has to keep its existing customers (current students) happy. Of course, alumni are an important audience as well, because many graduates donate money to their alma mater on a regular basis. And maybe the university also targets funding agencies, so the people who run the foundations that dole out money to worthy causes are another buyer persona for a university's marketing efforts. By truly understanding the needs and the mind-sets of the different buyer personas, the university will be able to create appropriate marketing and PR initiatives to reach each of them.

This understanding means that instead of making up jargon-filled, hype-based, product-centric advertising, you can create the kind of information that your buyers find compelling. Taking the time to segment buyers and then listen to them discuss their problems can transform the effectiveness of your efforts. The other thing that happens is that your marketing materials will use the words and phrases of your buyers, not your own.

> Buyer persona research ensures that you market using the voice of your buyer, not of your founder, CEO, product manager, or PR agency staffer. This drives people into the buying process, making salespeople's work easier and quicker.

This concept of buyer personas can seem a bit daunting for some, especially those who have previously relied on their personal intuition or have called on assistance from an agency. Some people are wary of the concept because they don't immediately see the value of buyer personas for their specific market. I find that observing actual examples from a variety of markets helps. We will next look at the importance of interviewing your potential buyers, and how the process of segmenting potential customers into buyer personas has helped drive business.

The Buyer Persona Interview

The best way to learn about buyers and develop buyer persona profiles is to interview people one-on-one and in their own environment. The goal of the interview is to define the problems people are facing and to learn precisely how they describe those problems—the actual words and phrases that they use. For example, if your company creates products that are used by people who play golf, then get yourself out to a public golf course or country club and speak to people there! You'll need to segment the buyers you speak to, in order to develop individual profiles for each. Perhaps you might segment golfers into buyer personas like this:

- People who play golf for fun
- People who play golf for exercise
- People who play golf mainly for the social or business aspects
- People who play golf to drink beer and bond with their buddies
- High school and college students who play on their school's team
- Professional golfers

Start with open-ended questions of a general nature. A question like "Why do you play golf?" will often yield surprising answers. Ask about how golf fits into their life and work. You can then begin to ask more specific questions, but don't drive the discussion toward the products and services that you currently sell—buyer persona research is not a sales pitch! In fact, when you approach people to speak with them, emphasize that you're not trying to sell anything but, rather, you are trying to learn about how to create better products and market them effectively.

Another line of questioning should center on problems your company's services are designed to address. You should inquire about how your buyers gather information when they need to solve such a problem. Again, using the golf example, you might ask, "Do you read golf magazines? How about visiting golf websites, blogs, and social networking sites? Do you ask the club professional for advice?" You should also ask, "If you were to go to Google or another search engine to research equipment to improve your golf game, what words might you enter as search terms?" This information becomes valuable as you create and market products to golfers. And it is essential to make sure that your marketing aligns with your sales process.

I would also encourage you to ask questions related to speed. You never know how a line of questioning focusing on the real-time aspects of a business can spark ideas. If you learn that your buyer personas are frustrated with the cumbersome system for reserving tee times, perhaps your company can perfect a real-time, web-based self-registration system that works on mobile devices.

> Meet members of your buyer personas on their own turf (their office, home, school, or where they go to relax) and listen carefully to how they describe their problems. Then develop products and services especially valuable to them, and create marketing using their language, not yours.

In order to gather enough information, you will probably need to interview 10 to 20 representatives of each buyer persona. I know some organizations that have interviewed many more. By triangulating the information you gather from a dozen or more interviews, you can then easily build a descriptive buyer persona profile.

Here are a few ways to personally connect with your buyers.

Visit People in Their Offices

Perhaps you can mine your lead database for people to contact in your area. (Don't approach people while the sales cycle is in progress, though—you don't want to tick off the salespeople.) You also don't want to meet with existing customers, because they already know you and won't give good data. You want potential customers. When you contact them, say, "I am in marketing, not sales. I won't try to sell you anything. I want to learn about your business."

Go to the Conferences That Your Buyers Attend

Go as a delegate, not as a vendor. Sit in on the sessions. Meet people at the breaks. Ask other attendees open-ended questions like: "What have you learned here that surprised you?"

Watch the Webinars That Your Buyers Watch

Learn what webinars are interesting to your buyers, and sign up as a participant. The Q&A session that typically occurs at the end of a webinar is an excellent place to learn what's on the minds of your buyers.

Monitor the Social Networks Your Buyers Participate In

Monitor the social networks that are important to your buyers such as the Twitter hashtags of important events and the feeds of interesting people and organizations. Joining the LinkedIn groups that your buyers do is another excellent strategy. You can use these forums to find some interesting people, and reach out to them via the social network.

Read the Books That Your Buyers Read

As much as I hate to say this, you'll learn more about how to market to your buyers by reading the books that they read than by reading a sales and marketing book. Yep, that may sound silly from someone who has written a bunch of sales and marketing books. You might look for people who have reviewed the book on a blog and reach out to them. (Once you understand your buyers' problems and how you can solve them, *then* you can read my books!)

Uncover New and Valuable Information with Buyer Persona Research

Get Out There! (Your Competitors Probably Aren't Doing So)

Recall that the way Avis Europe learned about cruise passengers and their need for larger cars at island ports was by monitoring blogs, forums, and chat rooms frequented by cruise passengers. Just like in your interviews, pay attention to the *exact* words and phrases that are used. Again, this language will become important for your marketing materials and for understanding how salespeople should speak with buyers. But don't forget that there is no substitution for the specificity and depth of actual interviews; other strategies should be purely supplemental. Gathering information about your buyer personas helps you identify initiatives you might implement to reach people in real time, and outsmart your competition as a result. For example, the enterprise software company that takes the time to meet with, say, 10 or 20 information technology (IT) executives working in government agencies will learn a great deal that helps to eliminate MSU behavior.

Taking the time to learn what their issues are, what their problems are, and what challenges they face will reveal nuggets of information that will lead to real-time sales and marketing success. I've heard many people say, "Oh my gosh, I cannot believe that most of these people are on this one particular online forum!" Or, "Wow! Everyone said that what they are really looking for is a company that has fantastic after-sale support; maybe we can do that through a social networking site!" Many people I speak with get excited when buyer persona research reveals an insight that is so valuable that an entire product offering, marketing program, or sales initiative can be built as a result.

In other words, buyer persona research helps you uncover new information. You learn something (probably many things) that was impossible to make up, because it's actual data about the things that people need. All of a sudden you will *know* (not just assume or make up) something about customer needs (say, a Twitter feed for real-time customer support). Your competitors will ask, "Where in the world did they come up with *that*?" You'll be reaching buyers much more effectively than they are. And do you know why? Because your competitors are still in their conference rooms making stuff up.

GoPro Keeps Its Buyer Personas in Focus and Sells Millions of Cameras

Back in 2007, I enthusiastically gushed on my blog about the GoPro digital camera, which I had purchased to take photos and videos while surfing. I was a very early adopter (the digital version had been out only a month or so).

In my post, I said: "GoPro should focus on user-contributed photos and videos, but the product was only introduced a few weeks ago, so I'm sure that with a product like this, more will come very soon."

Wow, have they ever tapped the crowd! The GoPro Facebook page has more than seven million "likes," and many people post photos and videos to the page.

GoPro excels because it is focused on coming up with solutions that address the specific problems faced by its customers. And its customers are willing to spend money on a product that will solve these problems. (In my own case, as mentioned, I wanted to shoot photos and videos while surfing.)

Not long after my original post, I interviewed Nicholas Woodman, founder and CEO of GoPro, for a story in the book *Tuned In* that I co-authored.

"The larger camera companies are building product on such a massive scale that it is not interesting to sell to a small niche market," Woodman told me then. "GoPro's cameras are more specialized and complement your regular camera. You still take your Canon to a wedding, but out in the surf or on the mountain you need something else."

What's so fascinating about this example is how different buyer personas articulate problems. Photographers asked, "How can I protect my camera in the water?" But surfers asked, "How can I take photos while surfing?"

Buyer persona research yields surprising information, and when you are tuned in to a problem that people will spend money to solve and you build a product that solves it, you are on the road to success.

Since my original post, GoPro has expanded way beyond surfing. Soon, Woodman concentrated on buyer personas representing other extreme sports.

"Because surfing is so demanding from a usability and environmental standpoint, our product also worked very well for other adventure sports," he told me. For other sports, the core camera remains the same, but the associated accessories and mount are different. For example, GoPro has adaptable mounts for bicycle handlebars or to attach onto helmets and other body parts for sports like rock climbing and kayaking.

When adapting the camera to a new sport, Woodman says he has several prototypes built and then goes into the field to ask people to use the product, beat it up, and give feedback. "One of the great things about the markets we sell to is that they are passionate people," he said. "Our solutions could never evolve from a boardroom discussion; our ideas come to us when we are out playing. We go straight to the source. We don't ask our grandmother what she thinks about our motorsport mounts apparatus; we ask race car drivers."

So how is GoPro doing now, nine years after I first wrote about the company? According to *Forbes*, GoPro sales have more than doubled every year since the first camera's debut in 2004 through 2012, and in that year GoPro sold 2.3 million cameras. The company went public in 2014, and in 2015 grossed $1.6 billion—from zero a bit more than a decade ago. GoPro was responsible for 21.5 percent of digital camcorder shipments in the United States in the first half of 2012, according to IDC data. Among so-called pocket camcorders, that figure swells to one-third of shipments. Holy cow. And in a *60 Minutes* piece, it was reported that Woodman is now a billionaire. All based on buyer personas!

By breaking down buyers into distinct groups—such as surfers, race car drivers, skydivers, and others in the case of GoPro—and understanding what problems each group has and how they are solved, you make it far easier to create breakthrough products like the GoPro camera and its associated mounts.

Buyer personas also make it much easier to market your products. Rather than web content that is simply an egotistical reiteration of gobbledygook-laden corporate drivel, you create content that people actually want to consume and are eager to share.

This approach is utterly different from what most organizations do. Either they fail to segment the market, and instead create nonspecific marketing for everyone, or they create approaches to segments based on their own product-centric view of the world.

It is so exciting to see GoPro's extreme success.

Close the Gap between Sales and Marketing

In my days as vice president of marketing at several technology companies, I distinctly remember how difficult it was for my team of marketing professionals to command the respect of the salespeople in the company. We were finally successful in doing so, but only by becoming the company experts on the buyers. The salespeople didn't care about the brochures we produced or the websites we built. They rarely commented on the email newsletter or the trade shows we spoke at. But by effectively understanding and defining our buyer personas, we shortened the sales cycle for the reps who followed our strategies. Only then did the salespeople offer respect and kudos.

But most sales teams and marketing teams continue to operate out of alignment. The marketers and salespeople question the others' skills and their commitment to the job. They fight over the quality of the leads. I remember hearing of a sales team that snidely referred to the marketing department as the "T-shirt department" because they said all the marketers had accomplished was the production of T-shirts imprinted with the company logo. Others call the marketing department the "branding police." Marketers, in turn, complain about how the materials they produce fail to be used by the salespeople. They bitch and moan because the sales leads they generate are left untouched, claiming that sales staffers are too lazy to pick up the telephone.

Think about your own organization's last launch event. Were the salespeople hanging on every word as the marketers described the features of the latest product, service, or product marketing plans? If you're like most people I speak with (if they are honest), the salespeople were bored, probably poking at their smartphones instead of paying attention.

I ran these issues by my friend Adele Revella, founder and CEO of Buyer Persona Institute. My own understanding of buyer personas has been greatly influenced by her work over the past decade. I wanted to learn from her how sales and marketing can be more closely aligned.

"It's my experience that the best way to align sales and marketing is around real insights about how, when, and why buyers make the choices the company wants to influence," Revella says. "That's because the one mission that both sales and marketing have in common is to persuade buyers to choose the company's solution rather than a competitor's or the status quo, and it's incredibly difficult to persuade people you don't understand. When you look at the content of internal meetings, the conversation is all about us—our new products, story, and goals. It's easy to miss the fact that buyers can have very different interpretations of the story, or even conflicting attitudes and motivations. When sales and marketing have a way to fully understand their buyer's decision model, it's a lot easier to get past the finger-pointing and focus on what they can do to win the buyer's business."

Revella cites five specific buying insights that align the teams around the buyers and positively impact those buyers' decisions. Marketers should be able to tell the salespeople:

1. Which buyers want to meet with the company's reps and who will be annoyed by the request, as well as the circumstances that trigger these buyers' interest in meeting with a rep
2. Which parts of the solution or company story will have the most favorable impact on buyers, which parts are irrelevant to them, and which objections the salesperson will need to overcome
3. What the buyers are saying about the pros and cons of doing business with each of the competitors, and how the competition is persuading buyers that theirs is the best approach
4. How and when different roles within the buyer's organization will become involved in the decision, and what to watch out for with each of the respective influencers
5. How the marketing team is providing backup for all of the aforementioned, plus which sales tools they've built to help the reps succeed with these buyers

> Marketing needs to be the buyer expert, not just the product expert.

"One of the most important things we learn from interviewing buyers is that the company's marketing messages and campaigns need to address the perceptions that prevent buyers from choosing them," Revella says. "We need to interview real people to understand the attitudes and beliefs that cause them to walk away from the product, service, or solution we hope to market to them. You can't accept an answer like 'It's too expensive' or 'It's too hard to use' or 'It's missing X capability.' These are the answers that salespeople are likely to pass along about why they lose deals, but personas need to go much deeper into, for example, why the buyer wasn't willing to spend more to purchase the company's premium solution. Did we fail to communicate the value of that additional cost? Or are we actually charging more than buyers are willing to pay?"

Becoming the Buyer Expert in Your Company

So how, exactly, do we interview buyers to develop buyer persona profiles? These interviews are best conducted by marketing because they learn much by having conversations with real buyers. Whatever you do, don't give this responsibility to the salespeople or have them listen in. You want candid feedback about what worked and what didn't when the buyers evaluated their options. Buyers won't open up when the salesperson is present.

If possible, either record the interview or have a colleague take notes. You want your undivided attention focused on the conversation, and you want to capture verbatim quotes to use in the final buyer persona document, as that's the best way to communicate exactly how buyers talk about a particular point.

"I suggest only the first interview question is scripted, and after that it's completely unscripted," Revella says. Here's an example of an open-ended first question that Buyer Persona Institute uses to get the conversation going because it focuses the buyer on the first step in the decision process: "Take me back to the day when you first decided to evaluate [category of solution], and tell me what happened."

Buyers will usually give you an obvious answer here about the pain point they wanted to solve. To get to real insight, you need to ask good follow-up questions such as: "You probably always wanted to achieve [benefit] or eliminate [problem]. What actually happened to make you decide that this was the right time to invest in a solution?"

After that, the rest of the interview is what Revella calls "structured but unscripted." The structure is based on walking the buyer through every step in the buying decision, from the first day all the way to the point when the buyer made a decision. And, as mentioned, it's critical to keep asking good follow-up questions, because that's when buyers get invested in the interview and reveal real insights.

If you want to interview buyers about a brand-new idea that isn't yet available, you need to get them talking about the problem you plan to solve. You might start with a very general question like "How's business?" Then, once they get talking, you can segue to "We're hearing that buyers are struggling to [insert problem here]. What are your thoughts?" Spend about

10 minutes or so with open-ended questions about what they tell you. After that, you can tell them about your proposed solution and ask them for feedback. But the most valuable insights come before you've biased the conversation with your own ideas.

In a consumer setting such as when people at GoPro interviewed surfers, an opening question might be: "What do you like most about [activity]?" Open-ended questions lead down surprising pathways and sometimes reveal insights that create a billion-dollar company like GoPro from scratch.

Closing the gap between marketing and sales means the marketing staff needs to be the buyer expert, not just the product expert. Marketers need to focus on buyer personas. It's not about posters or pretty slides. It's about having deep and factual clarity about how markets full of buyers think about doing business with the company. That's when marketing is ready to deliver tremendous value to the sales process.

Which brings us back to those dysfunctional discussions between sales and marketing, the name-calling and finger-pointing that go on in so many companies. "Marketers complain that salespeople don't follow up on their leads, even those that are highly qualified. This is especially difficult when salespeople have several different products to sell. Reps will generally avoid following up on leads for new or unfamiliar products," Revella says. "But who can blame salespeople for preferring to sell products where they can anticipate how the buyers are going to react? Every rep wants to feel ready to answer the buyer's questions and overcome objections. Marketing needs to step up its game, understand what the salespeople are going to encounter, and give the reps confidence that they've got a winning hand."

If you have responsibility for both sales and marketing, you need to make certain that marketing is focused on buyer personas. If the marketers work in a different part of the organization, you need to be an agent of change. Figure out how to get them the opportunity and skills they need to interview buyers and become buyer experts. Talk to the head of sales or the CEO if need be. Marketing can deliver incredible value, but only if marketers have a full understanding of their buyers' needs and perceptions.

The Buyer Persona Profile

Once you've completed some 15 to 20 buyer persona interviews and done some additional research by reading what your buyer personas read, it's time to create a buyer persona profile. This one-page document will be your guide to creating real-time marketing and public relations programs to engage that particular buyer. Your marketing and PR will be transformed from egocentric, product-based stuff that doesn't connect with buyers to information that people notice. You will connect with your buyers at a gut level.

And, importantly, your sales, marketing, and customer support efforts will be aligned.

I strongly suggest that you go so far as to name your buyer personas, as a way to make them come alive for you and the others in your organization. I also recommend that you cut out a representative photo from a magazine to represent your buyer persona and to help you visualize him or her. Via names and images, rather than nameless, faceless prospects, your buyer personas will come to life for you and the others in your company.

A great example of a buyer persona profile is the one describing "Internet Ian," one of three buyer personas that HubSpot markets to. HubSpot is an inbound marketing software platform that helps companies attract visitors, convert leads, and close customers. Marketers from HubSpot developed the Internet Ian profile based on interviews with more than 100 web marketing managers.

What you'll see with Internet Ian is a composite profile of a web marketing manager, sometimes called an Internet marketing manager. Many of the details are consistent across nearly all of the representatives HubSpot interviewed. For example, web marketers generally understand HTML and web analytics very well. However, some of the details are more specific, representing composite or average characteristics. For example, Internet Ian is 26 years old and holds a bachelor's degree from Carnegie Mellon University. Of course, not all web marketing managers are 26, male, and Carnegie Mellon alums. The point is that including a combination of both general traits common to all web marketing managers and specific details that are still in some way representative helps marketers at HubSpot to personalize Internet Ian, and make him a little more real. The point here is that knowing a great deal about Internet Ian means it's much easier to reach him.

For each buyer persona profile, your job is to know as much as possible about this group of people so you can answer questions like these: What are the problems facing this buyer persona? What media do they rely on for answers to their problems? How can we reach them? What words and phrases do the buyers use?

HubSpot's Internet Ian Buyer Persona Profile

Job Title: Internet/Web Marketing Manager

- Understands HTML and web analytics very well
- Worries about web reputation, leads, metrics
- Original website design was $20K, but he enhanced it a lot
- Uses Google Analytics and a customer relationship management system, and uses the application programming interface (API) for both of them
- Lives his business and personal life online
- Sends hundreds of text messages per month, rarely talks on the phone
- Runs an affiliate website on the side for fun
- Has been blogging since 2005, now trying "lifestreaming" platforms
- User of Twitter, Facebook, Digg, FourSquare

Personal

- Twenty-six years old, bachelor's degree from Carnegie Mellon University
- Single, online dating, met last girlfriend using Facebook
- Loves sushi, drives Toyota Prius Hybrid, watches video online and does not have a TV, hates advertising, loves Apple/Mac
- Wears designer jeans and funky glasses; has spiky hair; does not own a suit

Expectations from HubSpot

- Wants advanced/detailed functionality, with lots of controls and customizations, is willing to do some hacking, loves beta, does not need content management system (CMS) since he edits HTML directly and likes to build custom sites; also interested in an API to write custom code to move data into and out of HubSpot

The information found in the Internet Ian buyer persona profile helps that buyer persona come alive for the marketers at HubSpot. Instead of sitting around the office making stuff up, they are constantly referring to Internet Ian. "What would Ian say?" and "What would Ian want?" are frequent questions asked in HubSpot conference rooms.

Organizations that take the time to learn about their buyer personas get out of the common egotistical sales mode and instead work to educate potential buyers. When you educate and inform rather than hyping, your marketing comes alive. Your buyer personas are then eager to do business with you and excited to share your ideas with others. The sale is made more quickly, and more business results.

Focusing on buyer personas will transform your business. That's why this concept is so critically important for effective sales, marketing, and service alignment—it's also why I write about it a lot.

How Buyer Personas and Journey Mapping Integrate Marketing and Sales

Most marketers make stuff up. They sit in nice comfortable offices and imagine what interests buyers, and then create "copy" and "campaigns," typically with the help of equally clueless agencies.

But as I've said many times in these pages, the more you know about buyers, the better aligned your marketing and sales become. The strategy of buyer persona research combined with journey mapping is an incredibly powerful way to rise above the competition.

At a recent presentation I met with Paul Mlodzik, Vice President, Marketing and Communications at The Co-operators Group Limited, and learned how he has implemented buyer personas and journey mapping. Indeed, The Co-operators is among the very best examples of marketing strategy based on understanding buyers I've ever seen.

The Co-operators Group Limited is a Canadian-owned financial services and insurance cooperative with more than $40 billion in assets under administration. Through its group of companies it offers home, auto, life, group, travel, commercial, and farm insurance, as well as investment products. The company sells to people of all ages and backgrounds and is both a business-to-consumer (B2C) and business-to-business (B2B) marketer.

The Co-operators Group's first step was identifying discrete buyer personas and then interviewing representatives of each group.

"It took five or six months to get through all of this because you really do need to sit down with a lot of people," Mlodzik told me. "We would interview them on the phone to figure out what are the common characteristics of the things that they're saying. We generated a very large database of actual verbatim quotes to see how people are thinking and the type of words that they're using."

This kind of one-on-one telephone or in-person research is time-consuming but when done well yields incredibly valuable information. To help with the process, Mlodzik and his team worked with Forrester Research.

"When we came out with the group of personas, we had a whole vocabulary around each persona about the types of things that they would say," Mlodzik says. "We learned about technology use, how they live, where they live, who they ask for advice, and how they go about interacting with different types of products and services, not just in our market but in general, and then specifically in our market."

> Name each buyer persona to make them come alive.

To ensure that Mlodzik and his team are completely dialed into each persona, they named each and then built very detailed profiles used by the team to create their marketing strategies. So that others in the company are aware of personas, they created posters out of them, which are located around the company offices. They even created an interactive persona exhibit, which will be touring offices across the company.

"By actually doing the work and doing it properly from a research-based perspective, you get a tremendous sense of confidence about things," Mlodzik says. "I really like the fact that I was surprised by some of the things we learned. As a marketing veteran, you think you know about buyers. But I like being surprised because it gives me something else to work with. It gives me a hole to plug. It gives me a new need to go after."

The confidence that Mlodzik and the team developed through research means that he can focus on only the most important strategies and tactics. It gets them away from the "list marketing" that so many people do when they are unclear about the best way to reach buyers.

"We're doing fewer things but each more intensely," Mlodzik says of how he does marketing now versus before the research. "We have found we're doing less activity and getting more results."

The process also helps to align marketing staff with the right roles. "As a result of doing this work, you end up freeing up head count," Mlodzik says. "Instead of replacing people in roles that become vacant, we created different roles with different areas to focus on based on what we discovered during the persona process. It has changed the way that we do business."

Understanding buyers is essential to great marketing. When you are properly aligned, you have confidence in your marketing strategies and your tactics are more effective.

A customer journey map, which can be used as a follow-on to buyer persona research, details a representative customer's experience and includes company interactions from initial contact through the process of engagement and into a long-term relationship. It can include virtual as well as human interactions.

Once Mlodzik had identified buyer personas and had published those profiles inside the company, the team brought groups of about a dozen people from each persona together for the journey mapping research. "These people hadn't met before," Mlodzik says. "We told them that they would be grouped with people that we felt were in the same market or had some of the same preferences. But it was very funny to watch them interact with one another because it was almost like they were separated groups of friends. As soon as they got together, they just started yakking immediately. It was hard to get their attention at times because they just wanted to interact with each other so much."

The way that Mlodzik implemented journey mapping at the Co-operators yielded surprising results that highlighted the differences between what staffers thought people do and what the customers actually do.

"The process has two parts," Mlodzik told me, using the example of a Generation Y person filing an auto insurance claim. "The first thing you do is take the subject matter experts from inside the company, people from our claims department and underwriting and marketing and whoever knows about this particular journey in depth, and you put them in a room and ask: 'How does this go? Step one: They hit a car. What happens? Step two: What do they do next?' And you go through all the different steps and all the choices and how they get their car repaired and how you think they're feeling at any given time. Then you bring in about ten customers that are actually that persona, and you do exactly the same thing. The disconnects are sometimes jarring."

It was clear that parts of the expected customer journey through the claim process did not match with what the young people said they would do. "You come into it with preconceptions," Mlodzik says. "I was interested in what was not going to match up. For example, all of the young people except for one said the first thing they would do is call their parents—not call the claims number, not call their agent, but call their parents! We assumed people would call the 1-800 claims number. But that didn't happen. We learned how unprepared they were for the claim experience and how for them it is one of the biggest things that's ever happened to them. Those kinds of disconnects were the most important revelations."

Mlodzik estimates that 25 percent of what Co-operators employees thought would happen were wrong. "That 25 percent is enough to make the whole way we communicate with them go bad," he says. "A lot of the disconnects were around communication preference—tone, language, the softer things. In a highly commoditized business, financial services and insurance, one policy does look pretty much like the next one. It's not highly differentiated like smartphones or something like that. It's all about the approach. And if you get the approach wrong, you're sunk."

Mlodzik and the team used the results of the journey mapping research to storyboard each process and make them more effective. "It's interesting because you think you're going to be fixing a product problem or a claims process or something like that," he says. "Instead, a lot of what needs to be fixed is communication. You find out that what they really need is a simple email at the right time. It's a well-timed communication that helps them through this entire process. It's inexpensive but not simple to deal with."

As an example, Mlodzik cites the journey of the "David" buyer persona, someone in his mid-40s running his own business. "This is a very entre-preneurial and independent kind of person and a perfect candidate for all kinds of different lines of insurance," he says. "They can be some of our best customers. And they also tend to be do-it-yourselfers. When it comes to wealth and life insurance planning, they think they know what they're doing, but they don't. We learned that the way to approach these people is super important. When we put our subject matter experts through their journey, they came up with a 37-step process for doing a needs analysis and getting somebody into a basic set of investments. But when we brought in an actual group of 'Davids,' they knocked it down to about ten steps, which were very quick. And the process was over in less than three weeks because they showed exactly how it should be presented to them, when the choices should be presented, how everything should work. As a result, we are completely revamping our process based on that because we had totally overcomplicated it."

Because the research into buyer personas and journey mapping yielded such surprising results and the resulting changes had such an impact on how business is done at The Co-operators, Mlodzik is even more of a believer in research-based approaches. "This has been both enlightening and rewarding because you get right in front of people and talk to them. When you get in front of people, you're always amazed by the things that they tell you."

When everybody else is just making stuff up in their comfortable offices, a research-based approach to buyer personas and journey mapping delivers a decisive competitive advantage.

Midnight Oil

Want an example of buyer persona research leading to a surprising new product?

Several years ago, Bunker Hill Community College (BHCC) in Boston became the only college in the country to hold classes beginning at midnight. *Yes, midnight.* The "midnight oil" class period is from 12:00 a.m. to 2:45 a.m., and courses offered during this period in the spring 2014 semester included Principles of Psychology, College Writing II, Statistics I, and Human Growth/Development. This all may sound a bit crazy until you consider that many people who want to take college courses in the Boston area work an evening shift (for example, restaurant employees).

When people at BHCC took the time to interview representatives of a unique buyer persona—individuals who want to take college classes but who work second shift—they learned that the preferred time for class was immediately after work, which for them meant midnight. Any college in the United States could have developed midnight classes. But BHCC led with this innovation because it stopped making stuff up and actually found out what people needed.

And the college was eager to offer courses in real time—in this case, the time that is convenient for students, not the one that works best for the college. In a fun twist, students attending the midnight oil classes enjoy unlimited free coffee! The free coffee is even part of the clever sales strategy on the BHCC site. The response from students has been wildly enthusiastic. You just can't make this stuff up.

Imagine how much easier it is for admissions officers to sell the school to prospective students who work the night shift. Again, as I've said several times in this chapter, aligning your company's marketing around buyer personas makes the sales process faster!

Sales and Marketing Working Together

With all this talk about buyer personas and how web content drives sales and marketing success, it is essential that we take just a little time to look at how the two functions differ. By making certain we understand the difference, we can close the gap between marketing and sales and grow business faster.

> Marketing generates the attention of the many people who make up a buyer persona, whereas sales communicates with one potential customer at a time, putting the buying process into context.

It is the job of marketers to understand buyer personas—essentially groups of buyers—and communicate to these groups in a one-to-many approach. Marketers are experts at communicating to many people, and typically the potential customers they reach are not yet ready to have a sales discussion.

The marketing team captures the attention of a group of buyers and drives those people into and through most of the sales process. The content generated by the marketers—blogs, YouTube videos, infographics, e-books, webinars, and the like—can influence large numbers of people. Done well, with a deep understanding of buyer personas based on research, this content generates sales leads that culminate in the buying process.

The role of salespeople is completely different because they influence one buyer at a time when the buyers are much closer to making the buying decision. While marketers need to be experts in persuading an audience of many, salespeople excel in persuading the individual buyers. They add context to the company's expertise, products, and services. Through them, the marketers' content fulfills its potential at the precise moment the buyer needs it.

People Reaching People

Recall how I opened this chapter. Do you remember the two types of websites that we all visit? The ones we click away from usually hype their products and talk mostly about the organization. But the sites that we relate to, the ones that resonate, are created with us in mind. We're human, and we crave interaction with people who know us. When you deliver information to your buyer personas, you build a relationship with people before you've ever met them.

5 The Sales Cycle Is Now the Buying Cycle

I distinctly remember when my daughter Allison began her third year of secondary school. That was the point when colleges and universities started to send her information—a lot of information! In the United States, university applications are due in the early part of the fourth year of high school, so when we started receiving thick packets in the mail we were still a year away from application season.

Allison would get beautifully designed, hundred-page, full-color magazine-like documents in the mail. Each day would bring letters galore. Then the emails started coming. Because she took the PSAT standardized test administered by the College Board and she had given permission to contact her, hundreds and hundreds of colleges and universities sent her email pitches and direct mail packages. Each of these expensive sales come-ons was designed to drive my daughter into that school's selling process in the hope that she would want to learn more about the school, visit, apply for admission, and ultimately attend.

We're Buying. So Stop Selling.

Nearly all of the print material went into the recycle bin. Every email was deleted unread. Allison had already begun her own personal buying process. Yet many hundreds of schools were still selling to her, wasting her time and their money.

Without being pushed by us, her parents, Allison had gotten interested in the process of choosing and applying to schools when she entered high school, and shortly thereafter she started her research about specific colleges and universities. She had already been in college shopping mode for three years by the time this sales material arrived in our mailbox and her inbox. In fact, by her second year in high school, because of her web-based independent research, Allison had already made her choice. She had settled on Columbia College as her first-choice school long before she was being solicited by other schools. She chose Columbia based on the story the college told her.

Columbia College, a relatively small residential college in New York City, is part of the much larger Columbia University. The college teaches an unusual core curriculum, a set of common courses required of all Columbia undergraduates and considered the necessary general education for students, irrespective of their choice in major. Allison was fascinated by the core as she read about it on the Columbia site. She learned that all students encounter the same texts and issues at the same time, and the courses are taught in small seminars. Since the core was begun in the early part of the twentieth century, every Columbia student, alumnus, alumna, and professor is connected by this common bond. The story Columbia told resonated with Allison, and she was sold on applying to the college years before applications were due.

"Statistics on a college website don't tell a story like people do," Allison says. "Citing the average SAT scores, and what percentage of graduates work on Wall Street—what does that tell you? But an alumnus who says he became engrossed with prison reform because he read Michel Foucault in a Contemporary Civilization course given as part of the core during sophomore year at Columbia, now that's interesting. When I read accounts by alumni on the website, I wanted to learn if they gained a different outlook on life because they went to Columbia and took the core curriculum. And I wanted to hear from professors and their reflections about what the core means to them."

As Allison did her research and kept coming back to the Columbia site, her mind was made up. "In addition to the strong science program, Columbia appeals to me because the core unites the student body intellectually throughout the school's history. It will stimulate my curiosity to explore all the opportunities the university has to offer in areas outside my major, and feed my enthusiasm for courses in literature and the arts. For me, Columbia is the perfect balance between a liberal arts education and a top science research school in neuroscience."

When Allison finally visited the Columbia campus a year later, she was already extremely well informed. "When I visited Columbia, it was bitterly cold with bits of brown ice covering the streets," Allison remembers. "Despite my dislike of winter, I was excited to see the university where so much history had been made. Columbia had always been my first choice. The neuroscience program caught my eye long before I had started my college search. By the time I arrived to visit that frozen February, I was eager to hear about the funding going into mind, brain, and behavior research. I imagined myself side by side with the bundled-up students I saw before me, hurrying to a class where the professor is an author I'd read, or a scientist I've studied. I wondered what secrets were held behind those doors, and if I would someday be part of the pioneering research conducted there." Allison had already gone through the buying process. Columbia didn't need to sell her. She had already told herself a story about how she belonged at the school.

By the time Allison was ready to apply to schools, it had been a four-year buying process. She was in charge. All she needed to make her decision was available to her on the web.

The best schools understood this and provided valuable information at each stage of her consideration process. When she was first looking around, the college websites delivered general information about the schools and some idea of what it might be like to attend. Often there were profiles of students and professors. There would be video content and photographs. Perhaps an email newsletter subscription would be offered. The schools that really understood the buying process knew that the secondary school students looking over their institutions were early in the decision-making process, and therefore the schools avoided a hard-sell "apply now" approach. And understanding buyer personas, some schools delivered completely different content intended to speak to a prospective student's parents, too.

Allison applied "early decision" to Columbia College in the early part of her final year of high school. (Early decision is a program that allows students to apply to their first-choice college in the autumn of their high school senior year with an understanding that they will attend the following year, if accepted. It's a nice alternative to the usual process of sending off multiple applications later in the year when nearly everyone else is racing to complete their packets.) Allison was admitted, and she graduated with a neuroscience degree from Columbia College in 2015. She was absolutely thrilled with her choice of undergraduate school and is now attending medical school.

Creating appropriate content to develop a lasting relationship over a long buying cycle is possible only when an organization has a compelling story to tell, deeply understands its buyer personas, and has considered the many aspects of the buying process in detail. It's no longer a selling process. The buyer is in charge. An effective sales and marketing strategy reflects a careful and judicious examination of a website visitor's buying cycle to create well-organized and compelling content on the site.

In this chapter we will take a close look at the new realities of the buying process and what it means for an effective sales strategy. And in the next chapter we will dig into agile, social selling and how you can implement these new strategies and tactics.

The End of the High Pressure Zone

Most salespeople and many of the executives of the companies they work for increasingly realize that the hard sell is far more difficult to successfully accomplish in a world where buyers are in charge. When anyone can jump onto your site—or those of your competitors—and can review independent commentary by bloggers or access consumer reviews on a smartphone app in seconds, it's an entirely different world from the one a few years ago when the salesperson pressured someone to buy.

Evidence abounds that the hard sell doesn't work effectively anymore. For example, Herb Chambers, a leading auto dealer in Massachusetts, tells stories about how his dealership sells. For example:

How to sell used cars without using people.

So you don't trust used car dealers. Guess what? We don't either. That might sound funny, considering we sell used cars. But look closer, and you'll see that Herb Chambers isn't like those other places. We've always been committed to doing business the right way, and we believe we deserve your trust. Why?

Let's start with our Smart Pricing program. It gives you a fair, fixed price and eliminates haggling. Second, all of our used vehicles undergo a rigorous safety inspection for added peace of mind. Third, there's no pressure. Our salespeople are here to help you buy a car and nothing more. And finally, if you're not totally satisfied—for any reason at all—bring your car back within five days for a full refund, or within 30 days or 1,500 miles for full credit. Our cars may be used. But our customers? Never.

And this one:

When you don't try to sell a customer on a car, you'd be surprised how many cars you can sell.

At Herb Chambers, we don't sell cars. We help people buy them. What's the difference? A big one. When you help someone buy a car, you listen carefully to what they have to say. Then you help them find the right vehicle. Patiently. Without pressure.

It worked for us. Sales are up, and customers tell us they love our no-hassle approach. Combine it with our other customer friendly programs, like Smart Pricing, and our 5-Day 100% Money Back Guarantee for used cars, and you can understand why last year alone, more than 48,000 people decided to buy their vehicle from Herb Chambers. Sold? We thought you might be.

Herb Chambers tells a story about how his salespeople do not practice the hard sell. And that meshes perfectly with buyers who tell themselves the story that they hate high-pressure sales and dislike haggling over price.

Sure, there are still many who practice the dubious art of the hard sell. There are financial advisors who cold-call people looking for those gullible enough to buy into "guaranteed rates of return" that are too good to be true. Every few months another Ponzi scheme is reported in the press, and we learn that many of those who jumped in had fallen into high-pressure sales traps.

The cliché used car salesman stereotype still exists, chomping on a cigar, waiting for someone to walk onto the lot in a sketchy part of town. That car salesman knows that if someone walks onto the lot, by definition he's a mark, because no educated buyer would ever be there. In a world where the unscrupulous auto dealer is instantly branded with negative write-ups on local review sites, it's risky to practice deception. But some still do. You must not.

Mingling with Buyers at the Learning Party

I've shared several personal examples of how the buying process I undertake is utterly different today than what I would have endured back in the 1990s. In the opening pages of the book, I related how I went through my own buying journey to research, choose, and ultimately buy an expedition to Antarctica. In this chapter I've talked about how my daughter Allison chose Columbia College, the perfect school for her, but one for which I had some input.

I'm sure you're doing the same thing when you buy. It has never been easier for people to learn about products and services and the companies that provide them.

When people working in sales, marketing, and service (and the executives who lead them) understand this new buying process, they help bring the buyers along so their organization closes much more business than if they did nothing or continued using traditional last-century-style selling.

"Companies need to be educating salespeople about the buying process, making them understand the buyer's journey, and educating the sales force about what things work to help move the consumer through their buying process," says Jill Rowley, formerly in charge of Social Selling Evangelism and Enablement at Oracle. "Modern sales professionals aren't actually sellers. They are businesspeople who provide insight that helps influence what people buy." Of the more than 122,000 people employed by Oracle, 23,000 are in sales or presales support, and Rowley led the effort to educate Oracle's people about how to be more effective in this new world.

One of the ways she delivered the new rules was by speaking at Oracle's eight-week residential training program for new sales employees. During a typical one, Oracle provides its 400 to 500 new hires, who are all recent college graduates, with classes on the fundamentals of business, sales, and Oracle, as well as details about specific product areas. "I actually don't even believe in selling," Rowley says. "I opened the first day with the statement, 'Everyone here may think I am here to teach you how to sell. But I'm not going to do that. I'm going to teach you how to help people buy. I'm going to teach you how to serve, and how to help. I'm going to teach you how to be relevant and valuable.' Nobody wants to be sold to, and they don't have to anymore. The world has changed. Buyers don't have to put up with our old antics."

Rowley's approach to training involves educating the salespeople on content, how buyers use it, and how to share it with them. Significantly, she refers to how buyers access content as "learning parties." She places a strong focus on teaching the skills of social selling.

"Content is how you get into buyers' learning parties," Rowley says. "Buyers are out there having learning parties without sales professionals because they can. Buyers have unlimited access to real-time information across the Web and through social networks. The salesperson is becoming less relevant. But the salesperson can be relevant by being a part of that learning party. They can do so by sharing and curating quality content that helps the buyer become educated and informed about the business issue at hand, and how your company can actually help solve their concerns."

Rowley educated Oracle's salespeople (and by extension their managers and people in other departments such as marketing) that content sharing needs to be more than just Oracle-created information. She insisted that for every piece of Oracle content being sent by a salesperson via social media, four pieces of content from outside sources should be sent. "If all I ever shared across a social network was Oracle, Oracle, Oracle, Oracle, Oracle, Oracle, no one would want to engage with me!" she says. "You need to share content and move that buyer through the buying process. You need to teach salespeople that the buying process has changed completely and they need new mind-sets, new skill sets, and new toolkits."

Rowley encourages salespeople to understand social tools like LinkedIn and Twitter and to use them to share content. "Social isn't a shortcut," she says. "They are just new channels—new ways to find your buyers, listen and relay, engage and amplify. You are still building relationships, and relationships take time. If you show up at the front door for your first date naked, you're not going to get very far. Who does your buyer trust? Where does your buyer learn? To whom is your buyer connecting? You have to build that relationship over time."

Educate and Inform

Our ongoing communications revolution has profoundly affected how sales and service are done. Buyers are now in charge! (I know I've said this many times, but it is an important concept. Humor me.) Referencing blogs, Twitter, LinkedIn, YouTube, Facebook, and other web-based tools, buyers often bypass the traditional selling model altogether—learning for themselves about your products and services, your competitors, and what customers say about you (whether true or not!).

Don't struggle to adjust to this new environment—be agile and master it. You win hearts and minds by creating low-cost (and no-cost!) measurable strategies and tactics that help buyers you don't yet know discover you. The best salespeople have become information brokers—communicating by delivering the precise information that buyers need at just the right time and in just the right way.

> Educate and inform instead of interrupt and sell.

You have the power to elevate yourself on the web to a position of importance. In the e-marketplace of ideas, successful salespeople educate and inform. They highlight their expertise by sharing videos, content-rich websites, social streams, blogs, e-books, and images rather than using the old sales playbook of hoarding information and letting it drip out. Now you've got to be on the buyer's timetable, not yours.

We also have the ability to interact and participate in conversations that other people begin on social media sites, including Twitter, Facebook, LinkedIn, forums, and review sites.

The key is to focus on the buyer's needs, not your own ego.

Stop hyping your products and services. Don't rely on interruption techniques. You'll regret taking advantage of people's time and attention with unwanted communications.

Instead you need to deliver the right information to buyers, right at the point when they are most receptive.

> Although it sounds counterintuitive, you sell more when you stop selling.

Organizations gain credibility and loyalty with buyers through sharing content, and smart marketers think and act like publishers in order to create and deliver content targeted directly at their audience.

The Buyers' Journey

The most successful organizations understand buyer personas and how marketers and salespeople work together to serve their information needs. In the preceding chapter we looked in detail at how to develop buyer persona profiles and how to integrate what the marketing team is doing to reach an entire marketplace. The marketing team creates information of value—blog posts, e-books, white papers, videos, infographics, and the like—for each stage of the buying process. Now we shift to how salespeople reach one buyer at a time.

As buyers consider a purchase, they always go through a thought process prior to making a decision. In the case of something simple or low-cost, the process is likely to be very straightforward and may take only seconds. But for a major consumer item such as buying a new car or where to hold a wedding reception, the decision may take weeks or months. My daughter's choice of which college to attend took years. For many business-to-business (B2B) sales, the buying cycle may involve many steps and engage multiple buyer personas. For example, it might encompass a buyer from the legal department, several buyers from information technology (IT), and the buyer from the group who will actually use the product. Some B2B sales may take years to complete.

Effective organizations take website visitors' buying cycles into account when delivering content and organizing it on the site. People in the early stages of the sales cycle need basic information about their problems and the ways that your organization solves them. Those further along in the process want to compare products and services, and they need detailed information on the benefits of your offerings. And when buyers are ready to whip out their credit cards or request to speak to a salesperson, they need easy mechanisms linked directly from the content that enable them to immediately and easily purchase, donate, subscribe, or whatever.

Driving People into the Buying Process

People in the early stages of the buying process need basic information addressing their problems and offering basic information about the marketplace and the product category. Don't distract them with stuff about your company and your products at these early stages. When doing initial research, people don't want to hear about you and your company. They want the essential information about the product and how it relates to solving the problem that brought them to your site.

Make web content totally free with no registration in the early part of the buying process. The job of web content in these early stages of the consideration process is just to get buyers interested in your organization and how you might be able to help them. The best thing at that point is for your prospect to think: "These guys are smart. They understand my problems. I want to learn more."

> Don't push product.
> Teach people something. Share your expertise.

It is essential that your salespeople understand that buyers go through the buying process independently of the salespeople's involvement. The salespeople need to understand the strategy behind the marketing staff offering effective content directly to an entire buyer persona. This way salespeople know what to send and when to engage individuals one-to-one as they move them through the final stages of the buying process.

The Collective Intelligence of a Million Mechanical Engineers Creates a Unique Marketplace . . . and More

Consider GrabCAD as a fascinating example of how an organization uses online content to drive people into the buying process. GrabCAD is an online community of more than one million mechanical engineers. Hardi Meybaum, a young entrepreneur from Estonia, founded the venture-funded company to serve as a place where mechanical engineers much like him could share their computer-aided design (CAD) 3-D models. People from nearly every country in the world have uploaded more than 1,150,000 CAD files containing designs for all kinds of projects. As I'm writing this, I'm browsing the community and see new designs for a hospital bed, an exhaust fan, and a pneumatic spring assembly for a car's front axle.

Community members share and collaborate, making GrabCAD the center of the open engineering movement. By connecting people, content, and technology, GrabCAD also helps modern engineers get products to market faster. However, the important first step in the GrabCAD buying process is to get members to engage in the community so that they feel comfortable sharing their CAD models.

While the GrabCAD community is totally free, the site also offers business opportunities. Companies can access the international community's brain pool by offering to pay for services or by sponsoring a GrabCAD design challenge competition in the hope that it will generate a usable design that can be put into production more quickly or at a lower cost than the company's own in-house design team could do. GE used just such a design challenge to create parts for a jet engine. The engineers who are members of the community love it because their designs are seen by corporations that might hire them.

GrabCAD also sells GrabCAD Workbench, a collaboration service that makes it easy for engineers to share files, work with partners, and complete projects on time. GrabCAD Workbench lets users synchronize local CAD files to cloud projects, lock files to prevent conflicts, and work together smoothly.

By the time a buyer is ready for one of the GrabCAD paid offerings, the sale is nearly complete because the buyer has been a part of the community for months or years. Buyers already trust GrabCAD because they are an active part of the community. They understand the benefits of online collaboration and are receptive to the idea of contests and internal collaboration tools.

No selling required!

Now Raise Your Hand (Please)

After your marketers have delivered compelling information to demonstrate expertise in the market category and provided knowledge about solving buyers' problems, you want buyers to express interest. The goal of the middle stage of the buying process is to have people "raise their hand" somehow. At GrabCAD, this comes when they register to become a member of the community. They haven't yet purchased anything, but they have given their personal information. At this point, you've found a potential customer from a huge sea of buyers you didn't yet know. But this is not the time to sell. You've still got to move them through the buying process a bit more.

When creating content about your offerings, remain focused on the buyers and their problems. Don't be egotistical and create things from your own point of view, such as elaborating distinctions between your products. As people interact with your content at this middle stage in the buying process, think of ways that you can offer something of value that will motivate people to enter a subscription so that you can learn who they are.

Possible enticements range from an email newsletter, a webinar (web-based seminar), an e-book, or a research report to something like GrabCAD's membership in a community. Be flexible; offer buyers a variety of ways to interact with your company, and make contact information readily available from any page on the website. A one-click-away option is best. But remember, if you're asking for someone's email address (or other contact details), you must provide something more valuable in return. You want buyers to think, "This is an organization I trust. I can do business with them. They have happy customers, and they are responsive to me and my needs."

Got Square Footage?

Chuck Gordon is co-founder and CEO of SpareFoot, a company that makes it easy to find, compare, and book a self-storage unit. The SpareFoot service is free to people looking to rent a unit; space owners pay SpareFoot a fee when a deal is closed. "The storage business is just like any other asset or real estate: It's all about occupancy," Gordon says. "The more units you have rented, the more money you make. We market units for space owners on our network of websites, and they only pay us when we send them someone who moves in."

SpareFoot offers free information to self-storage facility owners to drive them into the buying process. At the middle stage of the buying process, the company offers the ability to sign up for the free quarterly *SpareFoot Storage Trends* report, which is based on surveys of hundreds of storage tenants as well as pricing and reservation data from the SpareFoot network of more than 6,000 storage facilities. Because the SpareFoot business is essentially acting as a storage facility broker, it has exclusive information that facility owners find incredibly valuable, such as the average price for a 10-by-10-foot storage unit in all 50 U.S. states. The information included in the *SpareFoot*

Storage Trends report is so valuable that Wall Street analysts and investors subscribe to the reports as source material for making investment decisions.

In the middle of the buying process, the *SpareFoot Storage Trends* report is ideal for salespeople to start conversations with potential customers. "The report definitely gives salespeople more to talk about," Gordon says. "They can say, 'Hey, let me shoot this thing over to you. Check it out, and we can talk about it on our next call.'"

SpareFoot salespeople also use the report when they've had an opportunity to speak to a potential customer who doesn't end up buying. The report keeps their company in the buyer's mind as the first place to return to should the buyer revisit this situation in the future. In a sense, it keeps that potential customer in the buying process even though the person already said "no" once. "When we get a 'no,' then we ask them, 'Would you be interested in signing up for our quarterly trends report? It doesn't cost you anything and we send you lots of free data and it's interesting,'" Gordon says. "Many people say 'yes,' and that keeps them in the marketing loop. They continue to get these quarterly reports, and then after a while they have seen SpareFoot enough times that either they call us back and sign up for our service, or when we call them back they have seen the value we provided, so they are more likely to sign up."

The other fascinating aspect of the report is that the actual data reported within it can help a storage facility increase its sales. Imagine you're running a storage facility with only 60 percent occupancy and an average price of $140 per month for a 10-by-10 unit. Then your copy of the *SpareFoot Storage Trends* report arrives showing that your city averages 75 percent occupancy of storage units and they garner $150 per month on average. You'd be much more likely to consider SpareFoot to help you rent your available units! It's content like this delivered at the right time that moves people through the middle stages of the sales process so they are ready to be closed by the salesperson.

The Merging of Sales and Content to Facilitate the Close

As each individual buyer approaches the end of the buying process, you must provide content and tools that facilitate the sale. This is where salespeople earn their commissions. Buyers may be unsure which of your products is appropriate for them, so you may need to provide online demonstrations or an application that allows them to enter specific details about their requirements and then suggests the appropriate product. At this stage buyers want to know what to expect if they do become a customer, so offering stories from your current customers can help.

Salespeople have a critical role now. In well-oiled sales and marketing machines, marketers have provided salespeople with details about each sales prospect based on the actual content the prospect accessed. Together with the form the prospect filled out, marketers should tell the salesperson details like, "She clicked the 'I'm a financial executive' link from the homepage and then requested our white paper." When your salesperson contacts the prospect, he will already know additional details about her besides those that appear on the lead form. At the moment that salespeople interact with individual buyers, they need to use their selling skills to discern the customers' needs and then offer them even more focused content. The salesperson can offer to add the prospect to the subscription list for an email newsletter, invite her to a webinar, alert her to the corporate blog, offer her online calculators, feature comparison charts, and make use of other tools.

"Salespeople get invited into conversations much later these days because of online content," says Neil Fletcher, product sales manager in the United Kingdom for Siemens Metals Technologies, a company that focuses exclusively on the metals production industry. Fletcher's direct responsibility is a range of measurement systems used in the flat products part of the steel industry: steel mills rolling hot strip for making things like automobiles and refrigerators, and plate steel used for pipelines and shipbuilding. "A buyer's first protocol is the Internet to find out who's saying what about the products they are interested in," he says. "But I think the modern salesperson needs to be able to weld together old-school techniques with the useful new techniques."

Fletcher got his start in sales in the era before the web. But unlike many others, he has successfully made the transition, understanding the role of real-time content to educate today's buyers. He has adapted the skills he learned in the old days to the new realities. "As a salesman, you need to bring something new to the party," he says. "Now the buyer is very well educated when you get to his doorstep. So you can't just regurgitate what he's already seen on the Internet. You have to be much more switched on. And you need the understanding of his business. I think that's always been the case, but it's more critical these days."

Fletcher says that many of the techniques that he learned in the days before the web are just as important today. Success is driven by the knowledge of sales fundamentals paired with an understanding of how buyers go through the buying journey. In particular, he emphasizes that an ability to deliver content as a way to help move potential customers toward closing a deal has always been an important sales technique.

"Content curating is a fancy new label," Fletcher says. "And I don't mean that in an insulting way. One of the things I remember learning a long time ago is if you read a story in the news that you think would be relevant and fresh to a customer, clip it out and send it to him. Now you just use Twitter to do that. It's exactly the same technique, but it's much easier. That absolutely has to be part of the modern salesman's toolkit. But large companies are often very slow to catch on to modern trends."

In an increasingly competitive marketplace with its complex sales processes, web content will unlock success, even in highly competitive industries where smaller players are often beset by larger, better-funded competitors.

> Tremendous success comes when great online content and an educated and interested buyer meet a skillful salesperson who understands the new realities of the buying process.

A Customer for Life

Once the deal is closed, there are two more steps. You must continue the online dialogue with your new customer. Add her to your customer email newsletter or customer-only community site where she can interact with experts in your organization and other like-minded customers. You should also provide ample opportunities for customers to give you feedback on how to make the products (and sales process) better.

At this point, you'll also want to measure what content is being used and how. Understand through web metrics what's working, and constantly tweak the content to make it better. Meet regularly with salespeople to gain insights into the buying cycle and how your web content is helping the process.

How the New Rules of Selling Contributed to a Math Education Program's Success

Imagine you're an educator charged with developing a brand-new graduate-level program in math. You've got to attract men and women to the program.

How about doing this within a school that has been an undergraduate-only, all-female liberal arts college since 1837?! The graduate program is brand-new. The co-educational aspect is brand-new. You're venturing into uncharted territory on multiple fronts.

What would *you* do to promote the program to the world?

That was the challenge faced by Mike Flynn as he took on the role of Director of Mathematics Leadership Programs at Mount Holyoke College in South Hadley, Massachusetts. Prior to joining Mount Holyoke in 2012, Flynn was a successful elementary school teacher and in 2008 was named Massachusetts Teacher of the Year.

"The program that I run used to exist at Mount Holyoke as a professional development organization called Summer Math for Teachers, where professionals would spend a week or two on campus to learn new ways to teach math," Flynn says. "I inherited a program that had a long, solid reputation over 30 years, but it was known as a summer program. But we were launching a new master's degree program."

While the existing program was known around the United States, its name, Summer Math for Teachers, became a misnomer. "With the new year-round master's degree program and other program offerings throughout the year, this name didn't make sense," Flynn says. "So we changed the name to Mathematics Leadership Programs, which is more descriptive of what we do: training teachers to be teacher-leaders in mathematics."

When Flynn started to generate interest in the new program, he did what most people do—traditional sales strategies.

"The first year I was doing everything wrong!" Flynn says. "I would do cold calls. I'd create Facebook posts, which were just advertisements. I was that guy who was just handing my business cards out saying, 'Come to this program,' and it just wasn't working. I also registered as a vendor at a national math conference because I thought that would be the place to go—just pay the fee to have a booth at a big conference and have all our materials there, and then stand around and hope people come to our booth. And that didn't work because we didn't get any applicants from it."

The first year he ran the program, six people expressed interest and just four applied for admission. "They were four really good teachers," Flynn says. "But the thing that was interesting is that out of those four who applied, three of them we knew really well; they were people who were already within our network who knew us. Just one person applied who was outside our circle of colleagues that first year."

Flynn clearly faced a massive challenge. He had to increase the number of applications significantly or his program would be in jeopardy.

"If we're not bringing in enough participants to cover the costs of the program, then they can't hold on to us," Flynn says. "I started to worry about the program and my position."

Flynn began to focus on content creation to generate interest in his program. He created a site separate from the Mount Holyoke site at mathleadership.org where he started a blog and offered other information of value to teachers.

"What resonated with me was that we are known for having really good classes," Flynn says. "People who experience our work come back time and time again. Because we knew we had strong educational content, I started developing free webinars to give people a taste of the math work we do for teachers. And those started getting well attended. But we don't do it from a sales perspective. I wouldn't even mention our program other than having the website and my @MikeFlynn55 Twitter handle. There was no sales part of it at all. I would just give something out that helped teachers immediately in their classrooms. And what I found was that people were very appreciative of it and they would tweet about the experience. The next time many would come back and they would bring a couple of colleagues with them."

Flynn also created content for use on other sites to attract people to his program. "I would guest blog for big names on Education Week," he says. "I didn't try to sell, but rather I was simply showing my perspective as a way of developing my expertise in the field. That started bringing traffic to both our website and my Twitter feed."

The focus on guest blogging helped Flynn to develop a following among educators. "It helped me incredibly because I now had access to all of these great thinkers who were sharing their blogs and their great ideas," he says. "I would retweet and/or comment on their work. And I started to grow myself professionally as a result of following these people. But then they also started following me and we started to develop this huge collaboration. For example, I connected with Dan Meyer, who is well known in the math world and has done a TED Talk, and he's got nearly 40,000 followers, and it's amazing. He and I connected on Twitter and collaborated on a huge event called Shadow Con at the National Council of Teachers of Mathematics annual conference. I'm connected with this guy only because of my work through Twitter and approaching it from the angle of helping other people and sharing their work and driving people to them. Then they in turn will drive people to me. What's nice about it for me is that it's genuine. I'm not engaging in this community as an effort to draw sales or to draw people to our program."

Flynn went from four applications to 40 as a result of content creation! He made the program a success and in the process assured himself a fascinating career that he loves. How fantastic is that?!

At this point, Flynn says they have firmly established the program because they are now reaching the broad demographic that they need to reach. "We're now inundated with master's degree program applications," he says. "We filled our program and are on track to do it again. More and more people are contacting us for professional work. I just got back from Abu Dhabi training teachers out there, and my presence on Twitter has doubled since applying these ideas."

Flynn says he learned that it doesn't work to be always selling. "Instead, engage the population that you want to attract in a way that's meaningful, in a way that you're seen as an authority and respected by what you offer," he says. "Once you do that, then people naturally want to know more about what you're doing. The selling happens naturally as opposed to forcing it. It's night and day how we changed our approach and the effect it had on our program."

While Flynn is an educator and is responsible for developing a program around education, his experience is not unlike others in countless other lines of work. I see examples like this all the time, so I know the ideas around creating content work for all industries, products, and services.

"As a teacher, we have a skill set of an educator," Flynn says. "We spend all our time learning how students learn. We don't learn business. I never took a marketing or sales course. It's not something that you can just take for granted. It's not something that comes easy and that the things that seem obvious as an outsider are actually all wrong. People think they should use the old ways to [sell], but that's not the way that people search for programs. They're not looking for advertisements. They're looking for content."

Lead Generation Calculus

I've shared several examples in this chapter, including those from Oracle, GrabCAD, SpareFoot, and Siemens Metals Technologies, illustrating the realities of today's buying process. Savvy marketing professionals and salespeople alike understand that sales and marketing must work together to move buyers through the pipeline. This is especially important in the complex sale, with long decision-making cycles and multiple buyers. Fortunately, web content hastens people through the process and shortens the sales cycle for any product or service—especially complex ones that involve many steps and take months or even years to complete.

For decades, the traditional demarcation point between marketing and sales was the lead handoff. This was the moment when name and contact information about a potential customer were delivered to the salesperson.

Every salesperson loves leads. And marketing people spend a lot of effort to provide them. But now that buyers learn about products and services through their own web research, and because they are already educated by the time they raise their hands, there is no reason for the artificial demarcation between sales and marketing. Too often sales leads go directly into a sales bucket, never to be marketed to again. This happens especially in B2B transactions. What a loss.

Think about the average corporate website. There are usually only two steps. A visitor goes to the site and there is a "contact us" form or some sort of offer (maybe for a white paper). At most companies, that lead is passed on to sales and all too often it is viewed as a "crappy lead" and ignored. Even worse, at most companies that site visitor receives no additional marketing. What a shame.

Or consider the business-to-business trade show. Many companies spend thousands of marketing dollars to design, transport, build, and staff exhibit space at important industry events. But after the show concludes, marketing staffers usually just tie a pretty ribbon around the business cards they collected from prospects who stopped by the booth, and then toss these leads over their shoulder to the sales manager.

In the auto industry, salespeople at the dealerships who obtain consumer email addresses hoard them as "our property" and never pass on the contact information to the automaker so that its marketers can send information to the potential buyers of its cars. That means people who want to receive information about new model rollouts cannot. Ugh.

Of course it's the salespeople's job to follow up on leads. But you might consider how you can integrate marketing with sales by, say, sending each of your trade show visitors an appropriate thank-you offer, such as a free trial of your service or a complimentary download. Or add the sales lead to your email newsletter list.

> Break down the walls between sales and marketing, and your business will improve.

We're in a world now where sales and marketing coexist throughout the entire sales process. Buyers are evaluating your offerings throughout the sales process based on what the salesperson does and says, and what they see and do on the site and in social media.

Smart marketers need to educate the salespeople so they understand that we're in this together. We are no longer in a world where marketing passes the baton to sales, and sales leads are seen as the primary measurement of marketing's success. Marketing needs to create content for each step in the process. And salespeople, if they are active in social media, can drive prospects into the top of the funnel.

Growing Business in a Shrinking Industry . . . without Leads

Before we dig into a deep discussion on sales leads, I thought it a perfect time to share the story of a company enjoying success by understanding its buyers and building a sales process that fits its market perfectly. Notably, the company doesn't rely on the traditional marketing and sales demarcation, nor follow the sales lead approach so common in business-to-business outfits. Keith Spiro serves as entrepreneur in residence at Kendall PRess, a Cambridge, Massachusetts, commercial print shop. That Kendall PRess—a 28-year-old business in a nearly 600-year-old industry—continues to grow in a shrinking field provides evidence that a reliance on the old sales lead model isn't right in today's world. Spiro was initially hired as director of sales and marketing at Kendall PRess because of his experience at a very large corporation, which had trained him to work through a sales process to achieve positive results.

As so many others have noted, Spiro reports that the biggest change that he has witnessed over the past few years is that buyers are now more educated. "They tend to come in with much greater knowledge, and they often think they know exactly what they want. There's so much information online and companies like Microsoft have created products where everyone can be a publisher. So my role evolved very quickly from how do we market the company to what do our customers need? More importantly, we also need to focus on where the future customers are coming from, and what is it that's not getting resolved for them?"

Kendall PRess does no advertising. People learn about the business primarily through word of mouth and web searches. Kendall PRess has an extensive library of content on its site numbering many hundreds of pages, because Spiro knows people are using Google and other search engines to research print shops and also to check up on the reputation of Kendall PRess. "We have an unusually large number of Web pages for a print shop," Spiro says. "There are no barriers, no walls. There are no sign-up forms. People realize we don't have an ulterior motive, because we don't make them register to receive content. And we try to prove that by giving them plenty of information about what they need at every step of the process. And we also provide additional information about things that we can't anticipate. The core to how we function as a company is to try to answer these questions: 'How can we help you? What do you need? When do you need it?'"

Spiro understands the words and phrases buyers frequently enter into search engines, and creates his content to rank as highly as possible in search results. "When a buyer has a problem and they're looking for a printing solution, they search using whatever words they know such as 'perfect binding' if they know that, or a phrase used in professional book production or printing. We've worked very hard to make sure we're as high up in those listings as possible."

The web content serves to provide the initial information, but most people want to connect with Kendall PRess to discuss their specific needs. This is where the "non-sales-lead" approach kicks in. Rather than forcing everyone to fill out a response form and let a salesperson take the next step and make a call, Kendall PRess allows buyers to contact them in whatever way they are most comfortable. And the company has no salespeople. Rather, it often is Spiro, or the CEO, or somebody else who responds to the inquiry. "When the right information hits, we want people to contact us in the way that's most convenient." Spiro says. "I learned that in Sales 101. If somebody sends you an email, you send an email back. If they call you, you phone them back. If they write a formal letter, you respond with a formal letter. So we have many ways for people to contact us, including a mobile site where there are three buttons: 'call us,' 'email us,' or 'get directions.' When we did that, our smartphone hit rate doubled."

Spiro joined the company several years ago as employee number 10. Now there are 14 employees. In today's always-on web-based world, many people talk about the demise of print. Newspapers are going out of business, and magazines are folding. Companies aren't sending as much print-based marketing material as they once did. While all that is certainly true, Kendall PRess proves that you can grow your business using the new rules of sales and service even in difficult markets. "We have created a true inbound environment," Spiro says. "And it's working."

Please Don't Squeeze the Buyers

Okay, take a deep breath. Really. Nice and deep. Because we're about to have a sensitive discussion. About sales leads. And it might get uncomfortable. Ready?

The debate about putting a gate in front of valuable content on a site rages on. The question: Should you require buyers to provide an email address and other contact information before they are permitted to download information such as e-books, white papers, research reports, and the like? Or, like Kendall PRess, should you be completely open and require no registration?

At countless organizations, barriers are erected. Sometimes called "squeeze pages," these sign-up forms are put in front of the information so that the only way for buyers to get the good stuff is to fill out the registration details and disclose their personal information. But other organizations like Kendall PRess make all of the information on the site freely available—no registration forms at all.

To squeeze, or not to squeeze? Those who advocate requiring an email address and other personal information prior to being permitted to download content contend that each person is a potential sales lead. Advocates for open unrestricted content, including yours truly, contend that far greater value results from many, many more people consuming and spreading your content than would otherwise occur if a gate was in place.

This really is a bit like debating religion or politics—each side strongly believes in their position, and many are eager to argue passionately in its behalf. It's just like there are those who believe that global warming is an acccelerating trend happening due to human activity on planet Earth, whereas others contend that what has been observed in recent years is merely a sign of our planet's natural cycles. And just like the global warming debate, once people have made up their minds about squeeze pages, it is virtually impossible for them to change. You believe one thing or the other.

Let me state clearly—I do not believe in squeeze pages under most conditions. Rather, I think that all organizations should take a page out of the Grateful Dead's playbook and allow people free access to content.

Can I Have Your Phone Number?

A guy goes up to someone he finds attractive at a bar, and the first thing out of his mouth is: "Give me your phone number."

A girl sees someone she finds interesting at the local coffee emporium and starts the conversation off with: "So . . . how much money do you make?"

If you're a famous celebrity or amazingly hot, this approach might work. However, for mere mortals, you're not likely to get very far in the dating world acting like this.

Yet this is exactly how many companies behave when they require personal information, including an email address and a phone number, before sending you a white paper.

Their inane "contact us" forms require you to reveal intimate details, such as how many employees work at your company, before you can even speak with a human.

> The next time you have to design a sales strategy, think about how you would approach it if you were trying to date the buyer instead of sell to them.

Lessons from the Grateful Dead

Starting in the 1970s, the Grateful Dead encouraged concertgoers to record their live shows, establishing "taper sections" where fans' equipment could be set up for the best sound quality. When nearly every other band adamantly said "no," the Grateful Dead created a huge network of people who traded open-reel and cassette tapes among themselves during the pre-Internet days. More than 4,000 shows from the band's 44-year history have been taped.

The band was happy to have Deadheads trade tapes and make copies for friends. The cult of the Grateful Dead concert became a viral sensation before Mark Zuckerberg was even born, driving millions of fans to the band's live shows for more than 30 years and generating nearly a billion dollars in ticket revenue. Photography was also encouraged back in the pre–mobile phone camera era when it was the norm to ban cameras at concerts and shows. The tickets for other bands' concerts came with a printed warning: "No cameras or recording equipment." Almost all the other bands of the era—The Who, the Rolling Stones, and Pink Floyd—coldly declared "no" while the Grateful Dead said "sure!"

While I hope to convert you to my religion of making your content freely available during the early part of the buying process, I recognize it will be difficult to sway the opinion of those who have long advocated the use of registration forms to generate leads. So let's begin by taking a look at the facts:

- Registration through squeeze pages is a holdover from the days of direct mail, when a business reply mail card was the way to fulfill a white paper request and collect names and addresses. When direct mail experts flocked to the web in the early days, they adapted the strategies they knew best. Is a postal direct mail technique right for today's hyperconnected web?
- Requiring registration greatly reduces the number of people who download something. Think about your own behavior. How willing are you to provide an email address to register for an e-book or white paper from a company? I've had marketers tell me they've run tests that indicate that the number of content downloads can be 50 times greater when no registration is required. Stop and let that soak in! You can get 50 people (and potential customers) downloading your report if no

registration is requested, or you can have just one reader (and potential customer) if an email address is required. You need to consider this: Do you want 100,000 people exposed to your information so they can learn about what you do? Or do you want 2,000 email addresses instead?

- Because bloggers and people who share on social networks like LinkedIn and Twitter do not like to send their followers to something that could cause them to get added onto unwanted email lists, a registration requirement is a disincentive for people to talk something up on their own blogs and social sites. So if you do use registration forms, you need to assume very few people will share your content.
- When lots of people link to your stuff because your content is freely available, your numbers will rise in the search results. For example, MailerMailer's *Email Marketing Metrics Report* is number one for its important phrase "email marketing metrics" as a result of free content. My own free e-book *The New Rules of Viral Marketing* is on the first page of Google for the phrase "viral marketing," and the e-book has been downloaded well over a million times. Many other people tell me that offering valuable free content causes them to rise to the top of the search engine results, too. With a squeeze page, you're lucky to get into Google's first 20 pages for a phrase like "email marketing metrics" or "viral marketing."

Here is the detailed calculus showing the two different approaches to delivering a typical white paper to buyers.

Content Delivered with Squeeze Page Requiring Registration

- No sharing is done on social networks.
- No inbound links are created.
- Every single download captures an email address lead.

    Ten thousand people initially exposed to the white paper content offer, × the 5 percent who register their email addresses to download the white paper.

    RESULT = 500 email addresses are captured from people who read the white paper. But there is no sharing on social networks, and no inbound links are created.

Totally Free Content

- Lots of sharing is done on social networks.
- Inbound links are created.
- Zero traditional leads are captured.

Ten thousand people initially exposed to the no-registration white paper content offer, × 50 percent who download the no-registration white paper, + 10 percent of those who read it share on social networks to create an additional 5,000 people who download the free content.

RESULT = 10,000 total people download the white paper. Lots of sharing on social networks means inbound links are created. But zero email addresses are captured, so there are zero traditional leads.

It really comes down to goals. Do you want a few email addresses? Or would you rather have a small city of people exposed to your ideas?

The Hybrid Lead Generation Model

When asked about this religious discussion in my live presentations, I also offer a third option, which is a hybrid.

I suggest the first offer be totally free, such as an e-book or white paper. Then within the offering, have a secondary incentive that requires registration that you can use to capture leads. A secondary offer might be a webinar that is related to the content in the white paper and educates people further on the topic.

Hybrid Model with Initial Free Content Followed by a Secondary Offer

- Plentiful sharing on social networks
- Lots of inbound links
- And a bonus capturing of traditional leads!

Ten thousand people initially exposed to the no-registration white paper content offer, × 50 percent who download + 10 percent of those who read it share on social networks, creating an additional 5,000 people downloading the free content.

RESULT #1 = 10,000 total people download the white paper. Inbound links are created from social networks.

Additional secondary offer within the white paper offers a registration-required webinar; 5 percent of the 10,000 who download the free white paper register for the webinar.

RESULT #2 = 500 email addresses are captured from people who attend the webinar.

Clearly, while the gated-content approach simply generates email addresses from people who want a white paper, the hybrid approach yields stronger leads of people who have not only read the white paper but now are likely to want more information about your company and its products and services. Their eagerness to take the second step and attend the webinar distinguishes them as serious core customers.

Simply put, the hybrid model leads are hot, while the white paper leads are not.

Defining Your Business in the Marketplace

There are many ways to compete in a marketplace. But are you really conscious of your place in the landscape?

How do your customers define you? How do you define yourself? What makes you special? You've got to know what you do better than the other guys and deliver even more of that.

You cannot do everything, so letting the other guy offer the cheapest price or have the slickest product is just fine if you're offering, say, the very best service.

When I traveled to Morocco a few years ago, I became fascinated with the local produce markets. I went to several daily markets in the city squares of Marrakech, and visited a country market held once a week in Asni at the foothills of the Atlas Mountains.

The produce sellers offer the same basic items—carrots, potatoes, onions, tomatoes, apples, and the like—and they sell from very similar stalls. But lingering and observing, I noticed the ways the proprietors differentiated their presentations.

Location—Some sellers got a prime position near the entrance to the Medina, the ancient walled city in Marrakech. A similar strategy was to stake out a location near the entrance to the marketplace in Asni. I'm not sure if these spots go to the first to arrive in the morning or if somebody has been paid a bribe, but there are definitely good and bad locations.

Product—It was orange season in Morocco. The oranges were at nearly every stall and were delicious and cheap. I ate so many I thought my skin would turn the same color as someone who applies low-quality instant tan lotion. If everyone basically sells the same thing, how do you differentiate product? Then I noticed that some sellers had beautiful green leaves still on the oranges they were selling. This indicated that the fruit had just been picked, because the leaves quickly wilt.

Comfort—A few stalls had coverings where people could shop away from the direct sunshine. While this might be comfortable while haggling over some fruit and veggies, sunlight enhanced the look of the products in the stalls without a covering, so . . .

Display—When artfully arranged in direct sunlight, the items simply looked tastier.

Service—Being friendly, offering a free sample, tossing in a few extras, and providing two bags instead of one to ease carrying the purchase home are all indications of good customer service, and another way to differentiate one seller from the nearby competition.

Price—When everyone sells the same thing, there's a lowest-cost provider. But with thin margins, that's a tough position to be in.

Advertising—Some of the sellers called out information about their fruit and vegetables. Most stayed silent until approached by a buyer.

Kindness—Some sellers smiled and caught your eye.

Sales—Others tried to hustle people into their stalls. But usually the hard sell didn't work.

There are probably other ways the produce sellers differentiated that I didn't notice or understand. Certainly, as I don't speak the local Berber language, there was a lot happening that I didn't catch.

We all compete for business in a crowded marketplace of ideas, services, and products. There are many different ways to compete and differentiate your offerings. Just copying the other guy is a tough way to succeed.

You've got to know how you're different from the competition. You've got to stake a claim as being the best at something.

These are all important aspects of the story you tell to the marketplace.

Are You Watching Your Direct Competition or Your Customers?

In late 2012, Apple CEO Tim Cook asked Scott Forstall to resign, reportedly because Forstall, the head of Apple's iOS Software, refused to sign the company's apology issued after the crappy Apple Maps debacle that was then part of the latest iPhone software. I was glad to read this at the time, because it signaled that Cook put greater value on his customers than merely "beating Google," which was probably the only reason Apple changed the mapping platform on the iPhone.

Many companies obsess about the other guys. Why in the world would you name your business Seattle's Best Coffee unless you were directly competing with Seattle-based Starbucks?

My sense is that the various social platforms (Facebook, Twitter, Google+, and the like) are spending far too much time worrying about each other (the competition) and not enough time worrying about their users.

For example, Google worries about Twitter. So Google eliminated the excellent real-time search feature that had delivered tweets as part of Google's search results. While tweets no longer appear, Google will happily show updates from Google+ in search results.

Most executives and nearly all salespeople have a relentless focus on the direct competition and use that as a benchmark for comparison. They look at the competition's products, price, and marketing, and try to do the same but with an incremental increase.

But the strategy of comparing your business to your close competitor means that you are likely to become a me-too enterprise that's just a little better, faster, or cheaper. That's no position to be in.

True leaders forget about the competition. The best salespeople don't focus on what the other guys are doing. Some benchmark themselves against people and companies in other industries, not their own. For example, in highly regulated industries like pharmaceuticals, healthcare, and finance, the competition is very likely to follow the pack and be fearful of engaging the market with compelling content and social media. "If none of the hospitals in our area have a YouTube channel, why should we?" Smart marketers don't worry about other healthcare providers. If they did, they would say "no" to blogs, Twitter, YouTube, and the like. Instead, they look to the best of consumer products companies as their model for success.

Learning from Outside Your Comfort Zone

It's always fun when nonprofits look to for-profit businesses for inspiration. Successful B2B outfits take a page out of business-to-consumer (B2C) playbooks. Service businesses look to product companies for inspiration, and vice versa. A lawyer markets like a novelist. And a novelist communicates like a journalist.

Try to get away from the comfort of your peer group and see what you can learn from those outside your industry.

As for me, I'm a huge live music fan and I'm interested in how musicians and bands perform as well as how they market themselves. So I compare myself to them in my speaking business. Most public speakers either stand behind the podium or, if they venture out, they just hang out near the center of the stage. Some go back and forth to the corners like a metronome. True professionals work the entire stage like a rock star.

I model my live presentations on the stage performances of the masters. As of this writing I've seen 630 live shows. (Nerd that I am, I actually keep a spreadsheet.) In my live speeches I apply lessons learned by watching live the likes of Mick Jagger, Bob Marley, Joey Ramone, Frank Zappa, Madonna, David Byrne, Michael Jackson, Pink, Perry Farrell, Matt Berninger, and Miley Cyrus. For example, in the summer of 2013 I went to two Rolling Stones shows in Boston, a field trip to observe Sir Mick working the stage. Jagger knows exactly where he is at every moment. There is not a wasted gesture, move, or step. He knows where the other Stones are, where the spotlight is, and most of all what the audience is doing. He's probably the most self-aware performer I've ever witnessed. I want that, too!

I've got no musical ability, but I've always loved watching how rock stars move and interact. How cool that I can learn from observing the savvy dynamics of the music pros but in a different business! Sometimes at my gigs I jump onto a large monitor for a moment. I've never seen another speaker in the hundreds of events I've attended jump onto a monitor. The move was inspired by someone outside my direct competition—I learned it from a rock star. I'm convinced that by observing musicians and bands, I've developed a more personal style than had I just copied other business authors and speakers.

How about you? Do you copy the direct competitors? Or do you look outside your industry for inspiration?

Do You Even Need Salespeople?

With all the pages I've devoted to the new buying process and all the reasons I've illustrated about why buyers are in charge today, companies may ask the question, "Do we need salespeople at all?"

Just a few short years ago, questioning the need for salespeople inside any expensive consumer product company or at most business-to-business companies would be absurd. Of course you need salespeople! Otherwise, who would educate buyers? But today, with the web, a completely different sales model not only is possible, but is being used successfully by many pioneering organizations.

With e-commerce on the web, everybody knows that many products and services are now self-serve online, bypassing salespeople. I buy many of my everyday products such as electronics, clothes, personal care goods, and the like on sites like Amazon. So do many others. Products and services of all kinds can be easily purchased on the web, even relatively costly ones like an intercontinental business-class air ticket at $5,000 or more.

But how about expensive consumer purchases that have always required working with a salesperson—cars, for example? Sure! Tesla Motors, the American company that designs, manufactures, and sells electric cars, encourages consumers to purchase their cars on the Tesla website. Consumers go to the online "Design Studio" to choose and customize the car based on options such as battery type, color, wheels, interior finishing, sound system, and much more. The base car plus each option has a fixed price, and the site calculates the final price, required deposit, and wait time for delivery. Buyers have a choice of paying the full price or financing the purchase, which is available right there on the site in the same transaction. All of this eliminates the need to speak to a salesperson for those who have done their research and know exactly what sort of Tesla they desire and how tricked out they want it to be.

And Tesla is making this business model work. Tesla Motors said it delivered 11,580 vehicles in the third quarter of 2015, which was 49 percent higher than the third quarter of 2015 and the sixth consecutive quarter of sales growth. And this for a car where the starting price of the Model S is about $70,000.

It seems totally radical, doesn't it? In an industry notorious for pushy sales techniques, here is an automaker that sells online, with no need to speak to a dealer at all.

Within the marketplace, business-to-business enterprise software is noted for its hardcore salespeople. They sell products used by businesses to manage complex tasks throughout the organization such as accounting, human resources management, collaboration, security, billing, and payment processing. These software products and associated services can cost tens of millions of dollars for a large-scale installation of enterprise software in a global organization, and the sales process has traditionally followed the quota-carrying sales representative whose income was based primarily on sales commissions.

The enterprise sales marketplace started undergoing radical change with the "freemium" model of marketing, which grew in popularity in the middle of the last decade. In the freemium model, a company offers a free version of its software to use that includes an upgrade option to a more powerful version of the software for a price. In most cases, people begin to use the free product without interfacing with a salesperson at all. But once they start using the free version, the company will engage them using email, telephone, and other sales techniques to attempt to persuade the free user to upgrade to a paid service.

Executives in some forward-thinking companies have thought, well, if it is possible to run a freemium product without salespeople, maybe we can run our entire business without salespeople! That's exactly what Atlassian, an Australian enterprise software company that develops products geared toward software developers and project managers, has done. The company has no salespeople, and using only a self-service model to sell its product it has passed $300 million in sales with tens of thousands of customers, including Microsoft, Facebook, Cisco, Oracle, Procter & Gamble, Exxon, BMW, and NASA. The company went public in the stock market in late 2015 and has more than a $5 billion market capitalization.

The Product That Virtually Sells Itself

"We have a very untraditional sales model," says Jay Simons, president of Atlassian. "It's true that we don't have any traditional commissioned salespeople, but we have a lot of people who still help clients. The simple philosophy behind our model is that the most important entity within our company selling our product is the product itself. If you can establish within the fabric of your company the belief that the product needs to sell itself, then you end up investing more in engineering and R&D to make sure that the product lives up to expectations and that it will be self-sufficient."

Many tend to consider enterprise software as one of the less sexy product categories. It is notorious for being cumbersome and very expensive to implement. Enterprise software also has a reputation for requiring a lot of hands-on human sales involvement, thus explaining why many companies overinvest in their sales department and often leave the installations department without sufficient support. In contrast, the Atlassian model invests its resources in the product and its implementation rather than in the sales process.

"Salespeople introduce friction into a transaction when they say something like 'I can't give you pricing for 3,000 users (or more) until I understand the magnitude of your problem,'" Simons says. "We empower the customer to self-serve. We reduce friction by printing a price list rather than bartering over each contract and we make it easy to understand the purchasing process.

"Even before they try it," says Simons, "buyers first ask us: 'How much does it cost?' If you are building a business that doesn't require human selling, then you eliminate all the things involved in taking a sales phone call. So our pricing needs to be transparent."

A starter license for Atlassian is $10 per month for a 10-user team. The company donates that money to Room to Read, a nonprofit organization for improving literacy and gender equality in the developing world. Once an organization goes above 10 users, the price goes up to $1,200 for a 25-user, small team license. For companies that have more than 10,000 users, an Atlassian product can cost $24,000.

The Atlassian sales process largely depends upon the distribution of free content that is accessible on its site. The content is designed to arm buyers with everything they might need to make an independent purchasing decision. There is no registration form on the site except during the final step in the process when the buyer is ready to download the product. Unlike most enterprise software companies that keep information under lock and key, Atlassian makes it freely available. "We don't care about qualifying people," says Simons. "Rather, we want the software to qualify the buyer."

Many buyers learn about Atlassian via word of mouth and social media. Additionally, company representatives create awareness by participating at events, speaking at conferences, and making sure their content is found in the search engines. When potential buyers learn about the company and are curious to find out more, they will encounter a wealth of free content on the Atlassian site. In a typical month, Simons reports that there are 1.5 million unique website visitors. As people interact with the content and learn more, about 15,000 will download a trial version of the product.

While Atlassian makes a very simple product available for people to try on their own without needing to ask for help or for permission, the company recognizes that some people will need help or will want questions answered. "If you try our products, we will send you an email," says Simons. "It says, 'We are thrilled that you are giving our Atlassian product a try. If you need any help, we are at the other end of this phone number or can be contacted at this email address. Write or call us anytime, and we will be delighted to help you.' The only difference is that we are empowering you to make a bunch of decisions on your own. We don't need to persuade you to make that decision. If we arm you with all the answers to questions others have asked in the past, we will make it easy for you to discover that you are smart enough to decide whether or not the product does what you need it to do, and if it's right for you, you'll buy it."

In an average month, this strategy converts around 800 new customers, representing about 3,500 licenses.

In the enterprise software world, there continue to be skeptics about this kind of sales strategy. "When we were really young, we hit a million dollars in revenue and people said: 'Great, that's cute. You've got a self-service model that got you to a million, but you'll never get to five,'" Simons remembers. "When we got to five million dollars, they said we wouldn't get to ten. When we got to ten, they said we wouldn't get to a hundred. And when we got to a hundred, they say we won't hit a billion dollars. We say, 'Bullshit, we will get to a billion.'"

Simons says there are many doubts that still arise about doing business using this model. Often someone at Atlassian begins to suspect that the company may need to add salespeople. But maintaining faith in this model as the right one for the company has so far proven the wisdom of that decision.

Good for You, but What about the Rest of Us?

While doing business without salespeople like Tesla and Atlassian are doing might seem tempting, for many organizations that's just not possible. After all, both of these companies were founded using a model that doesn't rely on salespeople. When you establish a new start-up, you can build the entire infrastructure around a business model that does not have a sales team. That's very different from taking an existing company with an army of salespeople and making the change.

But running an existing sales team doesn't mean you must continue to follow the same old paradigm. After all, buyers are in charge. In the next chapter, we'll look at agile sales with examples of companies implementing quick, flexible, real-time sales, and suggest ways that you can implement this ideal in your organization.

6 Agile, Real-Time Social Sales

Recently, I moved the little hideaway office I maintain as a quiet writing space. It was a very simple move from the first floor of the office building to the second floor of the same building.

I researched moving companies in my area by doing a Google search, leading me to visit their websites. I also checked out review sites like Yelp. Within five minutes, after quickly looking at a dozen firms, I narrowed my search to three companies. To each of these three, and at about the same time, I sent an email through each company's "contact us" page that included: the simple requirements for my move, the dates and times I'd like to do it, and a few photos of my current office so they could see what I needed hauled upstairs.

One company salesperson got back to me within two hours, providing detailed information and a price quote based on my email to that firm. Another company representative phoned me about six hours after I sent my email; he left a voicemail asking me to call him back. The third company got back to me by email the next day and quoted a price that was lower than the one I had received the day before.

Guess which company I went with?

The Quickest Wins My Business

It wasn't the cheapest. It wasn't the one whose rep had left me a voicemail. I chose to go with Big Foot Moving & Storage because they got back to me quickly and they were prepared with detailed information based on my initial email. They didn't waste my time with back-and-forth negotiation nonsense. I chose Big Foot because the story I told myself went something like this: "I don't like waiting for service people to arrive. I want to have people do what they promise, and I don't mind paying a little extra to get better service."

Big Foot was the quickest to get back to me and was prepared with an answer based on the information I had given. So it won my business because, in my mind, Big Foot was the company most likely to show up to my office at the appointed time and do the work as agreed.

This chapter is about agile selling. It is about how the concept of instant engagement with buyers is an important way to close more sales. I'll show you how you can win more business by being agile in many more ways besides responding quickly to inquiries.

The Ideal: Agile Sales

Today buyers are in charge. The idea of mystery in the sales process is over. We research someone online before agreeing to a first date—is he a creep? We fire up LinkedIn an hour before an initial business meeting—does she have anyone I know in her network? We watch on-demand movie trailers before deciding which film to see that night at the theater. We check out restaurant reviews and browse menus before booking a reservation.

We're in a new world. But you know that—not because I say it a lot in these pages, but because you're living in this new world every day.

Even though sales managers understand the role of web content in the buying process, many still run their teams the same way they did 20 years ago. Intellectually, we all know what's happening, because we all use the web to research products and services. I find it fascinating that many sales directors I've met go online regularly to purchase expensive products without talking to a salesperson—a set of golf clubs, for instance—but then tell me their market is different and insist the salespeople they manage use the cold-calling, hard-sell approach to sales that they learned in the 1980s. It's amazing that vice presidents of sales will go to the mailroom and systematically throw all of what they call "junk mail" into the recycle bin without reading it and a moment later march down the hall and insist that the marketing department create a "direct mail campaign." I don't understand why these sales leaders don't recognize the hypocrisy at work here—they themselves don't respond to traditional sales techniques, yet they insist that the salespeople who work for them practice the same outdated strategies. There's a huge disconnect between the sales strategies and tactics that worked last century and what works today. And today, as buyers operate in real time, sales strategies must include being agile as well.

Fortunately, just because you rely on salespeople to interface with buyers, this doesn't mean you need to stick to the same old strategies and tactics. Rather than a one-size-fits-all sales strategy, evidence suggests that an agile sales approach works best today. *Agile* refers to both the individual as well as an entire sales team focused on being hyperresponsive to buyers. Instead of forcing buyers into the company's sales process, an agile company responds to individual buyers based on what they are doing and how they are interacting.

"When somebody had to buy something 10 or 15 years ago, the only way to truly conduct a transaction with due diligence was to talk to a salesperson," says Mark Roberge, Chief Revenue Officer, HubSpot Inbound Sales. Prior to his current role, Roberge served as HubSpot's senior vice president of worldwide sales and services from 2007 to 2013. During this time he increased revenue at this inbound marketing software platform company over 6,000 percent, expanded the team from one to 450 employees, and was instrumental in HubSpot reaching number 33 on the 2011 *Inc.* 500 Fastest Growing Companies list.

"Previously, a major aspect of the sales process required everyone in sales to memorize the price book and be intimately familiar with the competitive landscape. Salespeople had to be ready with quick responses about how their company was different from the competition," Roberge says. "You had the power and control. And you could use that to your advantage to win over the prospect. Now, buyers conduct their research at any moment of the day or night—perhaps even midnight on a Saturday night."

As an example, the buyer locates the top six vendors. She researches what their products do. She looks at their price books. Sometimes she can try their product for free. And oftentimes, she can even buy it right on the website. However, in this case, the salespeople need to bring more value to the buying process than just basic information found on a website. And that value is being able to transform the website's generic messaging into specific information tailored to the needs of a particular buyer. "Today successful salespeople play a role much like a consultant," Roberge suggests.

Roberge describes the best salespeople as participating in a kind of doctor–patient relationship. In the same way that a doctor knows that every patient is unique and that a judicious medical response can come only after first carefully listening to and observing the patient, an effective salesperson in today's world must use analytic skills not dissimilar to those of a doctor—skills that can be mastered only with practice.

"A consultant comes into your business to learn about everything that's going on, and learn about what you're trying to achieve," Roberge says. "And then they can tell you if their product is a fit or not—because it's possible it might not be. And if it's not, they need to tell you so, honestly and up front. And if the fit is good, they need to explain it within your context, using your vocabulary, using your business strategy, using your business goals, just as a consultant would. That's where sales is going today. The best salespeople out there have the business acumen to be able to have that conversation with a buyer at a company, and have the required intelligence to be able to tell a slightly different story on every single sales call—a story that's precisely attuned to that buyer."

Gerhard Gschwandtner agrees with Roberge's assessment of the consultative sale. Gschwandtner is CEO of Selling Power, Inc., a media company that includes *Selling Power*, the world's leading sales management magazine, the sales management portal at sellingpower.com, and Sales 2.0 conferences held around the world. "A salesperson has a unique advantage," he says. "They are speaking to maybe 200 or 300 customers on a regular basis, and listening to challenges, problems, and situations that are all similar in some ways. Through conversations, a good salesperson learns her customer's typical concerns and applies that knowledge to other situations that her customers encounter."

When a particular buyer has done as much self-education as possible and is now ready to have a conversation about his or her particular needs, the agile sales component comes into play. The buyer has read content on the company's site, followed its blog and Twitter feeds, and perhaps has participated on a webinar. The buyer is ready to discuss details.

"We live in a society where software is getting more and more intelligent," Gschwandtner says. "Companies have an almost infinite choice of the kind of software they can patch together to create a customer-focused company. And yet there's a paradox. There are always holes in that equation. I've never seen a company where they have a sales and marketing ecosystem that's seamless without any gaps. It's the salesperson's role to identify the gaps—gaps in information, gaps in understanding, gaps in insight—and ask the questions: 'How can I be the catalyst between the company and this particular customer? How do I fill those gaps?'"

The Decisive Advantage: Speed

With buyers having access to much more information, salespeople now enter the buying process later, at a moment of enormous opportunity. When a buyer raises her hand, it's very likely she has already educated herself based on the content on your site and elsewhere. She knows the basics and wants more. She's indicating that she wants to speak with you about something specific. But this also poses a challenge. Not only do buyers need a salesperson with more knowledge than what appears on your company's site and blog, but they also expect a much quicker interaction.

> When buyers express interest, they expect contact right away. Now. Not tomorrow. Not this afternoon. Now!

It's easy to tell people to respond in real time. But it's not easy to actually implement this strategy. The best organizations use a combination of humans and technology, much like an air traffic control system. Technology can take you only so far, but eventually you'll need someone to make a decision about each inquiry that comes in. And just like that air traffic controller, it must be done instantly or there might be a crash.

"There's a lot of evidence indicating that if you respond to leads in a minute, rather than in a day, there is an enormous difference in success rates," HubSpot's Roberge says. "So as you build to a higher volume of leads, you will need to systematize the response. But in the beginning, you shouldn't overcomplicate it. You can assign leads to someone—perhaps a junior salesperson—who can eyeball the inbound leads and assign them to salespeople for real-time follow-up. But it's important to set realistic expectations and realize that only a fraction of the inquiries received are going be a good leads. And you need to clearly define what you're looking for, because you'll get leads ranging from a VP at a Fortune 5000 company to a PhD student in Japan. The first is obviously a great lead; the second will likely never be a buyer. And unless you do that legwork up front and pass on only the qualified companies to sales, they'll get really frustrated. That happens in almost every implementation that I see. As long as you establish that expectation up front, you'll be in better shape."

If your marketing team does an excellent job creating content for your buyer personas, it's also likely that the number of inquiries will grow quickly. Over time, you can start to use technology to do a first pass on lead qualification in real time; however, it's important to monitor the filters carefully when they are first instituted to make sure the parameters are properly defined. It is best to use an algorithm when dealing with high-volume responses because the clock is ticking, but implement this only with constant human monitoring, and quickly adjust and make changes as required.

Context: The Key to Unlock Every Buyer

Once you've got a system in place to manage your inbound leads and respond to them in real time, you'll need to define the buyer's needs within its context. Returning to Roberge's analogy of the doctor–patient relationship, think of the ideal salesperson as someone who treats each buyer as a unique individual, with focused attention on the buyer's specific concerns. "The buyer context needs to be leveraged right from the beginning," he says. "I still get cold-called 25 times a day, and I'm amazed that every single call is the same. 'Hey, Mark, it's John from so-and-so. This is what we do. Give me a call back.' No context. Same thing two days later, the same call. I get it six times."

Roberge cites a particular example of dysfunctional salespeople in his own life. HubSpot, a venture capital–funded company during its start-up phase, issued press releases when it had a new round of funding. And because Roberge is listed on the company's management page, people knew he was a HubSpot executive. "When we raised venture capital, I got phone calls from every single wealth manager," he says. "And yet, when I visit J.P. Morgan's website, I don't get a phone call. If I were to mention J.P. Morgan in social media, I don't get a phone call. When I open the prospecting email they sent me, I don't get a phone call. That's a great example of a company that has access to my interest and the context of my actions, but J.P. Morgan's salespeople are failing to leverage my initiative. In this inbound sales environment, that needs to change."

The cold-calling approach doesn't work with a buyer who has done his research. Roberge has built the HubSpot sales and support team around the idea of context, and that's a huge reason for the remarkable growth the company has enjoyed. "When you get called from HubSpot, it's contextual," he says. "It's a dialogue. It's 'Mary, this is Mark from HubSpot. I noticed you downloaded our e-book on generating leads through Facebook. I reviewed your Facebook company page and have a few quick tips. I'll email them to you now. Give me a call if you'd like to discuss.' And two days later, I'll contact again and say, 'Hi, Mary, as it turns out I found a case study of a customer of ours who's been quite successful in your business. I'm going send you their story and what they actually did to trigger some ideas.' Each message we send relates to the context of their situation, and the impact it makes is very powerful."

Whenever a HubSpot salesperson makes a call or sends an email or contacts a buyer through a social network, it is to be helpful and provide something in context to that particular buyer's educational journey.

Newsjacking to Find Buyers

Agile sales means engaging the marketplace at precisely the right time. It means understanding what buyers are doing and what they will likely react to at that moment. There are a number of real-time techniques discussed in this chapter, starting with one of the most powerful, and one of the most fun to implement—newsjacking.

The idea of newsjacking is quite simple: It is the art and science of injecting your ideas into breaking news, in real time, in order to generate social attention and media coverage for yourself or your business. It's the subject of a 2011 book I wrote titled *Newsjacking: How to Inject Your Ideas into a Breaking News Story and Generate Tons of Media Coverage.*

Thousands of people have used the technique to get their names into news stories, such as when marketers at Oreo tweeted an image with the line "You can still dunk in the dark" during the 2013 Super Bowl blackout. That one tweet was seen by millions of people.

Today's online tools can notify you instantly when something is said about your industry or marketplace. By monitoring keywords and phrases on the web and Twitter, you will instantly see the stories that you might be able to contribute to.

Frequently people push back and say that newsjacking is frivolous. "So what if you get into the news?" they say. "We're interested in making sales." Well, there is no question: Newsjacking drives new business!

While my *Newsjacking* book is about generating attention with the media, the same techniques can be used to generate real-time sales leads.

Many companies now use newsjacking not just as a PR technique but also as a tool to generate B2B sales leads and drive new business for consumer brands. It works for nonprofits and other organizations, too. Newsjacking works even in highly regulated industries like healthcare and finance.

For example, MultiCare Health System, an integrated health organization made up of hospitals, primary care and urgent care clinics, multispecialty centers, and hospice, home health, and other services, located in Washington state, newsjacked the name of a disease that marketers there knew was on the minds of millions of people.

The MultiCare Health marketing team sprang into action, publishing real-time content to become a part of a conversation happening online after an emotional episode of the popular TV drama *Downton Abbey* dealing with eclampsia, an acute and life-threatening complication during pregnancy.

The MultiCare Health team wrote a blog post right away and shared it on Facebook and Twitter. The post "Doctor Q&A: *Downton Abbey* Highlights Dangers of Eclampsia" was available the day after the episode aired right when people were discussing eclampsia. Within the blog post were links where interested people could learn more or book an appointment with a physician.

The team also shared on Facebook and on their @MultiCareHealth Twitter feed with this tweet: "Wondering about #eclampsia after last night's *Downton Abbey*? We've got answers here," and included a link.

The MultiCare Health digital content team includes four former journalists who bring a real-time newsroom mind-set to content creation.

The blog post quickly generated well over 1,000 page views, with people spending an average of five minutes on the page.

Marketers at MultiCare Health can directly trace about 30 click-throughs to the MultiCare Find a Physician page in their Women & Children care line, the place where new patients can book appointments.

Newsjacking helped drive people into MultiCare Health's buying process. And it all happened because of agile, instant engagement.

It's this same real-time mind-set that many salespeople and entire sales teams are using to drive success.

Ronnie Dunn's Real-Time Disruption

Most music artists use the usual route to launch a record—try to get radio airplay and attempt to get the media to write a review. Then they hope that people will buy it.

That's not what Ronnie Dunn did to launch three new songs. Instead, he performed a guerrilla gig from the roof of a restaurant, playing as Country Music Television's CMT Music Awards audience was filing out of the venue next door. Dunn newsjacked the CMT Music Awards!

Dunn is well known to the country music world—his duo Brooks and Dunn won more Country Music Association (CMA) awards and Academy of Country Music awards than any act in history and sold 30 million records—so thousands of people gathered to watch the gig. He created quite the scene!

Live video of Dunn's performance was projected onto the walls of Rippy's Bar & Grill (where he was playing) and two other nearby music venues, Tootsie's Orchid Lounge and Honky Tonk Central. At the same time his @RonnieDunn Twitter handle and hashtags were projected onto the roof of the nearby Ryman Auditorium.

At his home in Nashville, I interviewed Dunn about pulling off the disruptive sales strategy. "We didn't ask for permission," he says. "We had done a deal with the owner of the restaurant so we had our lights and production all set up. As everyone came out of the arena, 15,000 people all funneled through this little spot."

The hoopla generated tons of real-time attention for Dunn's new music as people shared on social media. Soon mainstream media and the music press wrote about the surprise appearance, too. For example, *USA Today* wrote a story, "Ronnie Dunn Debuts New Single on Nashville Rooftop," while the *Country Weekly* headline was "Ronnie Dunn Ambushes CMA Music Fest."

Dunn played by the unwritten rules of the music world for two decades. While he enjoyed tremendous success, now he was testing the limits. "Mainstream is the road to mediocrity," he says. "It took me 20 years to realize that. It got to the point where we'd get cut off at the pass every time we wanted to do something that was fairly innovative. It's time to be different."

Agile sales and marketing strategies like those from Ronnie Dunn and MultiCare Health drive people into the buying process in real time.

The Art and Science of Newsjacking to Reach Buyers and Create Real-Time Sales Opportunities

The original concepts in my book *Newsjacking* were aimed at marketing and public relations professionals, and I talked about how the technique generates awareness for organizations. However, in the several years since the book was released, I've studied the phenomenon of newsjacking carefully and realized that the ideas are just as applicable to sales. There is no doubt that the technique should be in your sales arsenal, because I've witnessed dozens of examples where newsjacking produces real-time sales successes.

You may find newsjacking opportunities on two levels: (1) within your immediate sphere of business activities and local or personal interests, and (2) in the wider sphere of national or global news. The trick is to devise news-monitoring strategies that keep you instantly informed on both levels.

To cover the immediate sphere, you will want to monitor media you may already know, including influential blogs and trade publications that cover your marketplace. If you run a local business—a restaurant perhaps—then your hometown paper is a perfect place to start. We'll take a look at how to monitor this news first, then turn our attention to news you don't yet see coming from outlets you may not know.

The first priority is to follow bloggers, analysts, journalists, and others who cover your business. Start by identifying as many voices as you can. To find these voices, start by checking the search engines (Google, Yahoo!, Bing, etc.) for relevant keywords and phrases: your company, customers, competitors, prospects, product categories, buzzwords, and whatever else you can think of.

The next step is to begin monitoring what these outlets say in real time. As its name suggests, the really simple way to do this is to use RSS (sometimes referred to as really simple syndication), a tool that allows you to harvest content from hundreds of blogs and news feeds without having to visit each one. RSS feeds update each time a site changes, alerting you to relevant information on topics that you specify. I use NewsFire for this, but there are many RSS readers to choose from.

The goal here is to know what people say immediately, so you can comment in real time when appropriate. And that becomes much easier once you have identified people likely to talk about the subjects that you can comment on with authority. For example, if you are a real estate agent and your local newspaper does a story on the market for homes in your area, you can comment on the story, blog about it, or tweet your thoughts on it, all in real time.

Once you're keeping an eye out for the important voices in your marketplace, it's time to monitor those you don't know yet.

Create a comprehensive list of search terms relevant to your business or interests. Include anything that you might want to see become the second paragraph of a story related to your interests. Again, search for anything relevant: industry terms, competitors, customers, prospects, and products, plus any relevant buzzwords or phrases—every term you can think of.

Set up news alerts on Google News or another platform using those search terms. This will automatically inform you in real time when any of your search terms crop up. Set up alerts on blog search engines, too. Note that if you choose Google Alerts, you can set the alert to let you know when a phrase appears in multiple content types, so one set of alerts can help you monitor blogs, news feeds, websites, and more.

For serious newsjackers, there is no tool more essential than Twitter. It is both a primary source of newsjacking feedstock and a powerful channel to get your message out in real time.

Twitter is a great way to stay on top of breaking news, as many media outlets now use the service to drive traffic to fresh content as it appears. Monitor your search terms on Twitter, too. Use a Twitter monitoring tool like TweetDeck or HootSuite to catch your key phrases. You can also use Twitter's own search function for one-off searches.

A word of caution: Be very careful when newsjacking a story that carries a negative connotation. For example, on September 11, 2013, AT&T tweeted an image of a smartphone taking a photo of the site of the World Trade Center in an attempt to generate interest in the AT&T brand. The image, sent from the @ATT Twitter ID, said, "Never Forget." The negative reaction on Twitter was swift. For example, @ryanbroderic, with nearly 10,000 followers, replied, "@ATT your cool photoshop makes the memories of watching my parents cry in front of the television a lot easier to deal with today." AT&T responded quickly, but the damage was done. Its tweet, "We apologize to anyone who felt our post was in poor taste. The image was solely meant to pay respect to those affected by the 9/11 tragedy," wasn't enough to prevent more than 50 mainstream media outlets, including ABC News, *USA Today*, the *Washington Post*, and the *Huffington Post*, from writing about the error in judgment. If a story like the anniversary of the events of 9/11 has negative connotations, it is best to stay away from commenting in public.

When news breaks, we know that many people immediately turn to Twitter in search of news on the topic. If the big news of the day is somehow related to your business and you tweet your take to the world, you just might influence those buyers who are evaluating your products and your existing customers who follow you on Twitter. And you could grab attention from many others who are not yet in the buying process. Just like MultiCare Health, your tweet just might make a sale you otherwise wouldn't have made.

Newsjacking: One Lawyer Considers the Legal Implications

For a terrific example of newsjacking as a technique to drive sales, consider how Mitch Jackson, a senior partner in the California law firm Jackson & Wilson (with the fantastic pointer URL mylawyerrocks.com), uses his blog to newsjack stories in the news that have a legal twist. Jackson & Wilson are an established firm, with local lawyers and past clients frequently referring cases to them.

Even though the firm has plenty of business, Jackson writes a blog where he comments on the legal aspects of stories in the news and shares via social networks. And he gets a plethora of attention as a result. His popularity has resulted in more than 26,000 followers of his @MitchJackson Twitter feed.

For example, his post "Michael Sam Is Gay and the NFL Team That Drafts Him Will Face Major Litigation Exposure" resulted a few hours later in being invited to appear on a Fox Sports show to talk about the NFL and Michael Sam.

Did I mention Jackson is a lawyer? Many people tell me that the ideas I discuss like real-time marketing and newsjacking aren't for them. They say their business is different.

Jackson's blog post "Who Is Responsible for the Death of Philip Seymour Hoffman?" was written soon after the actor's death was reported, and gave people a different way of looking at the story. "Several of my recent posts have increased views by 500 to 1,000 percent," he says. "The Philip Seymour Hoffman post generated a nice level of dialogue and comments on Facebook, Twitter, and the blog. All links with modified teaser captions were shared on my social platforms such as Twitter, Facebook, LinkedIn, Instagram, Vine, Pinterest, and Google Plus."

A few other real-time stories that caught my eye include: "Oscar Pistorius and Reeva Steenkamp South African Murder Trial," "What Will Happen Next in the Amanda Knox Murder Case?," "Unregulated E-Cigarettes Mask

Hidden Dangers," "Bill Cosby Gives His Deposition Today in California," and "Justin Bieber Shows You the WRONG Way to Give a Deposition."

"My goal is to continue enjoying an expanded sphere of influence through sharing my expertise on social media as opposed to needing to get the phone to ring," Jackson says. "Although the phone does ring with these efforts, that's not really the focus."

Jackson's personal favorite was writing his take on the Rebecca Sedwick bullying case, which gave him a chance to share tips and tools with families experiencing bullying and to offer legal solutions. "Readers from across the country have reached out to thank us for sharing ideas and resources found in the post about the tragic Rebecca Sedwick bullying case," he says. "Bullying is a huge problem right now, especially on social media, and many people and families experiencing bullying have no idea how to go about protecting their children. Several years ago, one of our jury trial verdicts involved protecting a family who was bullied for years by their neighbors. I'm proud to say that on appeal, we helped enact a new California law because of the case. Established professionals have expertise and opinions that can help bring solutions to so many people."

Live Stream Your Take on the News with Periscope

To quickly get his take into the marketplace of ideas, Jackson frequently live streams on Periscope, a service that turns your smartphone into a virtual TV news station. Periscope (and similar services from Meerkat and Snapchat) are used to share with the world what you're seeing right at this moment, so others can experience it with you in real time. The basic idea is to extend the functionality of photo- and video-sharing applications such as Instagram. Unlike YouTube, which generally requires you to upload your video, Periscope allows you to broadcast live from your smartphone.

For example, Jackson live streamed "11 Insurance Claim Tips for Snow and Earthquake Property Damage Victims" after news stories started appearing about people's damaged homes from natural disasters. The use of Periscope is even faster than writing a blog post, and, because new Periscope feeds automatically appear on Twitter, the use of a hashtag allows nearly instantaneous commentary about any breaking news story.

Periscope turns anyone into a citizen journalist—you're the TV reporter, live at the scene of breaking news (or live from your "studio" at your home or office). Periscope feeds are also available as a reply but only for 24 hours, which gives people an incentive to watch before the stream disappears.

For salespeople, live streaming opens up the possibility of sharing all kinds of information that can serve as a way to reach potential customers. A live operation at a hospital, a tour of a home for sale, a peek backstage at a rock concert, a manager's pep talk before the big game, or a product design meeting at a company all become shareable in an exciting and intimate way.

I use Periscope to broadcast sections of some of my live presentations. For example, when I delivered a two-hour session on real-time marketing at the Tony Robbins Business Mastery event in early 2016, I had somebody hold my smartphone to live stream about 20 minutes of the talk via my @dmscott Periscope account.

I'm amazed that more than 1,000 people tuned in to watch the live Periscope broadcast or viewed the replay while it was available for the next 24 hours. There were nearly as many people watching the feed as were in the room where I presented!

We're in a new world where you can share interesting events with everyone on the planet, and this has important ramifications for businesses of all kinds. Live streaming is a new way to share content, and many people love watching streams.

If you're interested in learning much more about newsjacking, I've created an online course called Master Newsjacking. For the past five years I've taught the newsjacking technique to hundreds of live audiences in more than 20 countries, and I've taken what I've learned to create Master News-jacking. The content of the course includes eight lessons with a total of more than 40 videos and eight downloadable infographics. Best of all, there is a step-by-step action plan for how you can learn the art and science of newsjacking to generate sales leads, add new customers, get media attention, and grow your business—all at no cost and with little effort.

Newsjacking can work for all sorts of outfits and people—it doesn't matter if you are large and well known or tiny and obscure. This technique is already being used by nonprofits, political campaigns, business-to-business marketers, and even individuals like Mitch Jackson.

People you will meet in the course have generated thousands of new sales leads by newsjacking. A few have made millions of dollars by using the ideas taught in my course. Some of generated thousands of news stories about their company. It can work for you, too. To learn more about my course, please visit www.newsjacking.com.

Newsjacking is about putting your ideas out there at the precise moment when people are thinking about your area of expertise. If you do so in a clever way, you will find people lining up to do business with you. Let's move on from the concept of newsjacking to look at other aspects of agile selling.

Automation Runs Amok

With all this talk of big data, real-time engagement, newsjacking, and using social tools like Twitter to communicate instantly, some people have taken the ideas too far, moving beyond welcome interaction into annoying interruption. This frequently occurs when people try to automate the entire process of communicating with the market or individual buyers.

Crunching massive amounts of data to target specific people certainly has benefits. However, there are distinct drawbacks to relying too much on technology alone to reach people by using targeted data. My research indicates that being completely automated, while a noble goal, is very difficult to implement in practice. It is much better to automate when you can, but have smart people as part of the work flow.

My friend @luckyrenee tweeted me from the New Orleans Jazz & Heritage Festival because she knows I am a big live music fan. "I wonder if @dmscott is rocking out at #JazzFest2012." I tweeted back right away: "@luckyrenee No, I'm not at #JazzFest2012 but it sounds like fun. If you are there—enjoy."

I was surprised when, soon after, a tweet from @Acura_Insider mentioned me. I checked who @Acura_Insider was from the Twitter bio: "Acura's official Twitter account. Get the inside scoop & other Acura news. On duty: Alison w/Acura PR."

The tweet read: "@dmscott You're a click away from access 2 the Acura VIP Area at JazzFest2012. Visit the Acura Tent or click [link]." The link pointed to a PURL (personal URL) that offered me a VIP experience at Jazz Fest. The text of the linked page read: "Stop by the Acura tent and check in with one of our representatives for access to the Acura VIP area. There's music, delicious food, refreshing drinks, a special viewing area and a shady spot to relax in."

I then checked the @Acura_Insider Twitter ID, and found hundreds of other people who had received such a spam message directed at them. In fact, at that time the account was in broadcast-only mode. There was no interaction at all, no humans involved. For the previous two days of Jazz Fest, the account had been generating hundreds of examples of this nonsense.

While I'm all for an automobile manufacturer getting creative and implementing real-time sales and marketing strategies, this was spam, plain and simple.

Just to be sure, I tweeted back to @Acura_Insider and got nothing. It would appear that nobody was monitoring the feed. Heck, it was a weekend. In my experience most companies are active on Twitter only during regular business hours, so would they be checking Twitter?

Obviously, I wasn't at #JazzFest2012, and anyone who bothered to look at my tweet back to Renee would have seen that. This is a perfect example of where a clever automated strategy of offering VIP access via Twitter could have been a great sales tactic had actual humans been monitoring what the automated system was generating. Real people should have had control of a button that sent each tweet after a quick review to make sure the person was actually at the music festival. And then, should someone bother to reply, they could respond instantly. It was a giant missed opportunity. I frequently go to music festivals, and it can get hot and I can get tired. If I tweeted that I was tired at #JazzFest2012 and then I got a tweet back inviting me to the VIP area, I would be psyched. I would have taken them up on the offer. Then if I enjoyed it I would have talked it up on Twitter. That would have worked.

I'm sure Acura spent a boatload of money sponsoring Jazz Fest. And it probably paid an agency a bunch of money for this stupid campaign. But this machine-generated stuff is not a good way for Acura to generate attention. The negative feelings of those who are spammed far outweigh the good vibes of Acura being on-site.

When I blogged about this soon after, more than 20 people commented on my post and dozens tweeted about it.

Soon, Alison from @Acura_Insider commented.

Thank you to everyone for your feedback regarding this situation. As I have communicated to David, we are also disappointed about the tweets that were sent out under the @Acura_Insider handle, offering VIP access to people who were not attending Jazz Fest. The intention of this program was to provide an exclusive VIP experience during the festival to those checking in and tweeting from Jazz Fest. The program worked well during the first weekend of the festival, but it appears that the company we were working with changed something for the second weekend and messaged people that they were not supposed to; essentially anyone using the hashtag regardless of whether or not they were there. For those in attendance, they were grateful for the opportunity and pleased with the VIP treatment.

I manage the @Acura_Insider account and take pride in how the account is run. I personally send out nearly every tweet and try to engage with as many people as possible. It is our goal to truly provide an insider's perspective into Acura and it is extremely rare for us to work with an outside company or send an automated tweet. We have learned from the negative effect of this campaign and will be sure to prevent such occurrences in the future.

Real-time sales and marketing present amazing opportunities. The technology available to us today for free would have been unthinkable just a few years ago or, if one could have imagined it, it would have cost thousands of dollars per month. But just like bond trading, real-time, agile sales require a combination of both people and technology to be successful.

When Real-Time Sales Put You at the Front of the Line

I was feeling smug in the back of a Lincoln Town Car, grinning like an idiot while nobody could see me through the tinted windows. I had just arrived at San Francisco International Airport on a flight from Boston for a speaking engagement at Dreamforce, the biggest cloud computing event of the year. With something like 100,000 people attending, there was a crush of people arriving at the airport and I was confronted with a massive line for taxicabs, perhaps 100 meters long. The wait was more than one hour (I asked people at the head of the line).

So why was I so happy? Because as soon as I saw that ridiculous line for taxicabs, I pulled out my iPhone and fired up Uber to reserve a car. In just five minutes I was being whisked away in style to my hotel. Brilliant. The Uber iPhone app (it is also available on Android) is a real-time way to book private driver service, typically in a black limousine, in major cities in 26 countries around the world.

For a passenger, you use the app to see if available cars are nearby. Then you tap a button to request a ride and immediately see how long it will take for your driver to reach you, all done in real time with geolocation. You get a message with your driver's name, mobile number, and car license plate number. And in just a few minutes your ride appears. Uber pricing is between a regular taxi fare and the fare for a typical telephone booking of a private car service. I paid $65 for my ride from the San Francisco airport into the city, and the Uber app took care of billing and a tip for the driver.

Uber is terrific for passengers, but for limousine drivers, this agile, real-time application is a fantastic sales tool, transforming the way they do business. I had lengthy discussions with about a dozen Uber drivers to listen to their side of the story. The drivers told me they are independent owner-operators who sometimes use old-style telephone broker services to book business as well. The drivers are incredibly enthusiastic. I heard the following: "I love Uber!" And: "I target $300 a day from Uber and almost always hit my goal." And: "I average 15 rides a day through Uber." For these drivers, this is additional business above what they would normally get in an average day. And because the app is real-time, the drivers can choose to offer rides and close the sales based on the other jobs they are working that day. When they have downtime, perhaps while waiting for the theater to let out, they can accept a ride, make some extra money, and still be back to the theater to meet the client who booked ahead using traditional telephone services.

The iPhone and Android Uber app used by drivers is just as slick as the passenger one. If they are free, they get a beep on their phone and can instantly see that a passenger is waiting for a ride. They can choose to accept or decline the ride. If they accept, the passenger's name and mobile number are made available and the passenger's exact location displayed. When the ride starts, the driver hits the start button, and then again at the destination, the driver terminates the ride on the app. The geolocation and clock functions on the mobile device calculate the cost of the ride based on miles driven and time waiting. Because the passenger's credit card number is charged and the credit made to the driver's Uber account, no cash changes hands and it is very quick. Both passenger and driver can rate one another on a five-star scale much like eBay. Easy!

Like many businesses before it, the market for private car services is being transformed by real-time mobile sales technology. Just as the publishing of books has changed with the advent of instant e-book downloads, real-time sales from services like Uber are disintermediating traditional businesses. So the question, of course, is this: Is your industry already being disintermediated? Or is it the next marketplace to be a part of the revolution? Because real-time, agile sales are growing everywhere.

Who Is Selling Whom?

At the many hundreds of live music venues I've visited, getting a drink is the worst experience.

The venue is loud, of course, making it tough to communicate. It's dark. But the biggest problem is that there never seems to be enough bar staff. That usually means that thirsty patrons must jockey for position and try to make eye contact with bartenders. Some people wave tens or twenties in their hands. Some make their way to one end of the bar or the other, hoping that when the staffer moves, they will catch his or her eye.

It is one of the few places where the buyer–seller relationship is reversed. At a crowded bar, the buyers need to work the angles to get the seller to serve them. Thirsty music fans need to work hard to spend money.

Obviously, an understaffed bar also means that people don't order as many rounds as they might if there were no hassles.

If I'm enjoying the show, I might take a few minutes to grab a drink. But I won't bother if it looks like I'll be there for more than five minutes waiting. Multiplied by lots of people, that could be thousands of dollars lost per night in a crowded venue if people forgo drinks.

One fine evening when hitting some of the live music spots in Nashville, I was surprised to see at Tootsies World Famous Orchid Lounge the bartenders raising their hands and making eye contact with customers. Wow. What a difference! Bartenders looking for us! Gotta love it.

In your market, who is selling whom? Is there a way you can turn the equation around?

Agile Sales Require a Real-Time Mind-Set

The real-time mind-set recognizes the importance of speed. It is an attitude to business—and to life—that emphasizes moving quickly when the time is right.

For decades the typical Wall Street bond trader has worked in a high-pressure atmosphere ready to make split-second decisions based on information scanned from real-time data and news feeds. The traders peer intently at bond prices displayed on the Bloomberg and Reuters screens, poised and ready to commit huge sums of money when the moment is right. Data from futures markets and stock exchanges update the instant a trade is made.

Fortunes are made in seconds; reputations are lost in a minute.

Now, the same real-time news and data that financial firms used to pay tens of thousands of dollars for each month are available to everyone for free on the web. All of us now have a new currency of success: the ability to gather, interpret, and react to new information in fractions of a second—in real time.

But success requires a new way of thinking. With such a real-time sales strategy, you need to develop an agile mind-set, an attitude that recognizes the importance of speed. It's an approach to business—and to life—that emphasizes moving quickly when the time is right. To implement this, your organization must support real-time sales with the technological infrastructure to monitor and react quickly.

Developing a real-time mind-set is not an either/or proposition. I'm not recommending that you abandon your current business-planning process. The smartest answer is to adopt a both/and approach, covering the spectrum from thorough to nimble. Recognize when you need to throw the playbook aside, and develop the capacity to react quickly.

Larger organizations will want to develop guidelines that permit speedy communications. Try to design and implement an effective code of real-time communications and proactively embed it throughout your organization. Train it, demonstrate it, discuss it, and review it until this becomes second nature to everyone. Have your people internalize it as deeply as the instincts that tell them when it's safe to turn left at a traffic light (or turn right if they're Brits). This is fully possible. IBM's code is called Social Computing Guidelines. The IBM guidelines include all manner of helpful instructions: *Be who you are. Be thoughtful about how you present yourself in online social networks. Respect copyright and fair use laws. Protect confidential and proprietary information. Add value. Don't pick fights. Don't forget your day job.* But the single most important guideline in the IBM document is this: *Speak in the first person.* In fact, I believe that speaking in the first person is essential to understanding what we're really talking about here. When you speak in the first person, you are representing both your company and yourself, and it should be understood that the reputations of both are intertwined.

> An immensely powerful competitive advantage flows to organizations whose people understand the power of real-time information. And when it's provided with authenticity and sincerity, the difference can be palpable.

Developing an agile capacity requires sustained effort: encouraging people to take the initiative, celebrating their success when they go out on a real-time limb, and cutting them slack when they try and fail. None of this is easy.

Agile Sales Mean Going Off Script

In most markets, there is a "best practices" playbook that people know is the right way to do marketing. There is an accepted script that people know and follow, and most treat that script as if it were law and there is no other way to work.

For example, venture capitalists have long insisted that the companies they fund must invest a monthly retainer to a traditional public relations agency.

Rock bands have long focused on the major-label record deal as the ultimate goal.

However, I've discovered as I travel the world that the greatest successes frequently occur when a company goes off script. Those salespeople and marketers who improvise—coming up with something new and interesting that the competitors aren't doing—get noticed and build business.

Yet, the business world traditionally rewards the safe approach. Salespeople are encouraged to stay on script. People and companies are afraid of veering from the "best practices" script.

Amanda Palmer fired her record label. Rather than following the traditional rock star script, she self-funded her album via Kickstarter, and the buzz she generated put the album on the top 10 *Billboard* album list when it was released.

Here are a few beliefs people repeatedly cite as part of their playbooks that are worth reconsidering. I'm sure you can think of others:

- "Facebook is for personal connections, and LinkedIn is for business."
- "Older people are not on the web, and seniors don't use social media."

- "You can't reach physicians with online sales."
- "Because of strict regulations, the pharmaceutical, healthcare, and financial services industries cannot use social media."
- "Newspapers are a dying medium."

What conventional wisdom that "everybody knows" can you challenge? How can you go off script?

Big Data Plus Real-Time Technology Drives Sales

It's impossible to overstate the impact of the innovations in computing and telecommunications on the financial markets of the 1980s, the time when I worked on a bond trading desk at a Wall Street investment bank. Within a decade finance was transformed from a clubby old boys' network to a 24-hour global trading system. A new currency of success emerged: the ability to gather, interpret, and react to new information in fractions of a second—in real time.

Those exact same dynamics are playing out today in your business. You can instantly see what people are doing and saying on social networks like Twitter, Facebook, and LinkedIn. Free, web-based services like Google News display real-time news feeds in the same way that bond traders see them.

In the emerging real-time business environment, where public discourse is no longer dictated by the mass media, size is no longer a decisive advantage. Speed and agility win.

Today, sales can be made by watching real-time data feeds in the same way that bond traders do. Take the example of Avaya Inc., a specialist in telecommunications technology used in call centers. People at Avaya carefully watch social networking sites and monitor what's being said to achieve sales they otherwise wouldn't realize.

The strategy delivered a quick payoff when somebody tweeted, "[The name of a competitor] or Avaya? Time for a new phone system very soon." The tweet was spotted in real time, and just minutes later Avaya tweeted back using the @Avaya_Support Twitter ID: "Let me know if we can help you—we have some Strategic Consultants that can help you assess your needs." The individual who tweeted was indeed evaluating telephone systems right then and engaged with Avaya, resulting in a quick $250,000 sale. Less than two weeks later, the customer sent a tweet in which the company was identified: "We have selected AVAYA as our new phone system. Excited by the technology and benefits for our company." The customer was so happy with Avaya's services and the people he interacted with that he tweeted again a few months later: "Getting ready to install our new Avaya phone system—our customers will love it."

A 57-character tweet became a sales lead that resulted in a $250,000 sale just weeks later.

> The Internet has fundamentally changed the pace of business, compressing time and rewarding speed.

To support real-time business, you need a technological infrastructure every bit as sophisticated as what's found on a financial trading floor. The good news is that smaller organizations can rely on free services like Google News and TweetDeck. This is the combination I currently use every day. Larger organizations will want to invest in backbone technology and a real-time data environment that feeds the dashboard used every day by your marketers, PR professionals, salespeople, and executives.

Predictive Analytics

Every move you make on the web can be measured and tracked and used to help move you through the sales process. This played out for me when I was poking around the True Religion brand jeans website. True Religion jeans fit me really well, so I have a few pair. But they are expensive, so I tend to wait for a sale to pull the trigger on a new pair.

I noticed a particular model called Men's Ricky on the Road Jean, but the retail price of $395 was way more than I would spend. So I popped over to eBay and searched on "Men's Ricky on the Road Jean" to see if there were any on offer there at a lower price. There were, but I didn't buy on eBay.

The next morning on Facebook there was a personalized ad from eBay sitting on my homepage as a "Suggested Post." The text: "Still Interested? Don't miss out on this item!" And there was a photo of the jeans I had been interested in the day before! Wow. Talk about real-time personalized targeting. I'm on eBay and look at a very specific item. The next day an ad for that exact item pops up within a social network I'm in.

In the past, I've noticed examples of ads that appeared on my browser that had been triggered either by a site I had recently visited or by my recent

Google searches. But those ads tended to be much more generic. This was a first: One of my specific searches was redeployed as an in-context ad that appeared within a completely different site. And it was targeted right down to an image of the thing I was looking for.

Our world has been heading to this level of targeting for a long time. Salespeople might use such tools to target a specific buyer in interesting ways. Imagine a B2B salesperson inserting an ad into someone's Facebook stream shortly after the person downloaded a specific white paper.

The idea of predictive analytics is a very powerful one. Let's look at a few more examples.

I buy stuff from Amazon.com nearly every week. I don't buy just books. I use the service to shop for electronics, personal care products, even clothing. Sure, I love the selection and Amazon Prime's two-day free shipping. But what I really love is how quickly the Amazon.com search engine shows me exactly what I'm looking for. And when I find an item, I can see information about other products that people who did a similar search also shopped for. I can see reviews of the product and quickly browse other products in the category. And Amazon.com will suggest other things I might be interested in based on my buying patterns. This way of selling couldn't have existed just a few short years ago, because it relies on massive computing power to analyze the purchase behavior of tens of millions of customers. Amazon.com bases predictions on the purchasing habits of millions of people by focusing on those individuals who are similar to you. Perhaps they live in the same location and bought the same kind of sporting gear and books. What did they buy next? Amazon.com has a remarkable recommendation engine at work, which has helped lead to Amazon.com becoming the world's largest online retailer, with $107 billion in sales in 2015.

Other well-known companies using recommendation engines to sell in a new way include Pandora Internet Radio, a music streaming and automated music recommendation service, and Netflix, the on-demand Internet streaming movie and TV media company. Pandora will recommend new music to me based on my previous choices, and Netflix will serve up a list of movies I might enjoy. The massive databases and computing power behind the scenes drive sales.

Those same predictive analytics engines are now being deployed at much smaller organizations as well, providing salespeople with critical information that will help them sell more. In a simple incarnation, real-time website data can help a salesperson with what to say to individual buyers based on what they are doing on the site. For example, as a buyer visits your website and registers for a webinar, an alert is triggered on the salesperson's real-time dashboard, providing details about the buyer based on the page that person is visiting. The alert notes that the person downloaded a white paper a few days ago. In fact, the alert is flagged as high priority because that combination of actions—white paper download plus webinar registration—is highly indicative of a propensity to buy.

The alert, a trigger event, instantly pulls up information on the buyer's company. Is it already a client? Have others from this company visited the site before? Even the buyer's LinkedIn and Twitter profiles appear. And all this happens in real time. It is this kind of technology that informs an agile sales strategy, transforming the one-size-fits-all sales efforts of the previous decade with just-in-time intelligence.

> Trigger events predict that a sales prospect is moving toward a decision to buy.

This is just a simple example of a trigger event that might happen in real time based on somebody visiting a website. Predictive analytics can be so much more when combined with external data. In the nonprofit world, trigger events are being used to gather information about active and potential donors. Intelligence gleaned from publicly available resources such as recent real estate transactions, reported executive compensation, and political contributions can be harvested by a nonprofit organization to estimate the level of an individual's ability to donate. Until very recently it was extremely difficult for a small nonprofit organization to access such valuable information in detail, as it was unlikely to have the staff, time, or resources to conduct background research on active members, past supporters, and potential donors.

For a nonprofit, cultivating financial support usually requires a deft combination of diplomacy and nuanced verbal choreography. Louisa Stephens, executive director of the Associates of the Boston Public Library, a small nonprofit with only two full-time employees, describes the challenge. "If you enter a delicate conversation about possible gifts, it's always helpful to have some idea where you stand," Stephens says. "When you lack sufficient background information, you could either leave a lot of money on the table or worse. If the donor was considering a gift of around $20,000 and you ask for only $5,000, they will say, 'Sure, I can give you $5,000.' But if you were to ask for $200,000, they are likely to laugh at you."

Stephens's development efforts for the Associates of the Boston Public Library further its mission to ensure continued public access to the Library's irreplaceable treasures by underwriting its cataloging, repair, restoration, digitization, and exhibition expenses. The fruit of many of these efforts is now available online for everyone and includes items from John Adams's personal library; letters, documents, and papers documenting the antislavery movement in the United States; medieval manuscripts; and even photographs documenting the history of the Red Sox.

Stephens now uses the Raiser's Edge, a fundraising and donor management software package to research active members, potential donors, and others she communicates with during her workday. "With a click of a button I can see who purchased tickets to our annual black-tie benefit dinner, Literary Lights, or view a list of past donors to reveal who failed to respond this year," she says. "That allows us to swiftly target and follow up our most important lapsed donors, something that would have taken a lot of manual work in the past."

More significantly, when the internal data held by a small nonprofit in its management software is combined with external data and trigger events, systems like the Raiser's Edge become powerful tools. "When development officers research someone, they pull information from a number of sources and areas of interest," Stephens says. "What real estate do they own? What's that worth? Is there any information about other charitable gifts that they recently made elsewhere? If they have a family foundation, you can pull down the IRS 990 form to see the grants they made. This information helps inform us when the board chairperson and I sit down to make that ask, so we are not requesting something that's completely unrealistic, a figure that's either too low or too high."

To learn more about trigger events and predictive analytics, I spoke with Brian Kardon, chief marketing officer at Lattice Engines, a technology company providing data-driven predictive applications that help companies market and sell more intelligently.

"Formerly, when salespeople made a call they would know little more than the buyer's initial interest, their company's profile, their revenues, and where they lived," Kardon says. "Then about five years ago people started going on LinkedIn to learn about the buyer. 'Oh, this guy likes to play tennis and he's from my hometown.' So you could begin to personalize things. And then maybe three to four years ago you knew from marketing automation that they went to your website and they looked at the product page or the pricing page. But now there are thousands of bits of information about each individual. We all leave digital footprints everywhere. It's about you personally, but it's also about your company."

Kardon says the companies doing the best work with predictive sales analysis understand it requires both technology and human interaction. "Sales reps alone can't get all the information they need," he says. "It's just too hard to find. You can use bots to find and deliver the information to the salesperson, but it's more than any human can process. People often ask me if a computer is smarter than a person. The answer is no. They're just faster. So a computer can process all this information and rationally organize it to aid a very personalized selling experience."

Recall my earlier example about Acura mining tweets for the New Orleans Jazz & Heritage Festival hashtag and then sending an automated tweet with an offer. That was technology with no human intervention and it failed, harming the Acura brand in the process. At its base level, the sales process is still about one human connecting with another human. The personal touch is best achieved when technology informs the salespeople, thus enabling them to deliver a unique experience to every buyer based on the buyer's individual background.

To be effective, salespeople need more than their gut instinct and sales skills, and that's where predictive analytics comes in. "We have a client who sells foreign exchange services. We've learned that if someone opens an office in a new country they're 18 times more likely to need this company's foreign exchange services," Kardon says. "In the past they treated everyone the same. Everyone had the same close rate, 3 percent. Now they differentiate and personalize every customer's experience. A customized, contextual conversation is provided based on the individual challenges faced by the unique customer in combination with knowledge gleaned from working with thousands of other clients."

Some of the data types that can be used for predictive analysis include online shopping carts, changes in executives, new hires, patent filings, opening up offices, and new funding. There are many others as well, depending on the type of business. Most companies make use of both proprietary data as well as a wealth of information available on the web from news feeds and social media.

According to Kardon, Staples, an office supply store with more than 2,000 locations in 26 countries, has a thousand salespeople and they personalize every sales call. "Five years ago they would call a little company and they would say, 'Do you need more office supplies?' Now they call and say, 'I understand you're hiring 20 new people. You probably need more desks. And you probably need more ink cartridges because you've been buying them every six weeks and eight weeks have gone by.' So you now have much more information to personalize the experience based on very specific parameters."

Interestingly, this kind of analysis also allows sales teams to operate in a leaner fashion because there is no longer a need to contact every single lead that comes in. "If a company used to have 20 job postings and now they have none, and their credit score just went from A to C and they just shut down two offices, that's valuable to know," Kardon says. "If you knew that, would you call them even if they came via an inbound lead? No, don't call them. There are all these things that are largely invisible to most salespeople. Now we can know a lot more, so the first step is not to treat them all equally and expend resources; instead you can discriminate."

Kardon says, "We used to celebrate the sales rep who called 10, 20, 50, a hundred times and finally got the meeting. What we've learned is that there's folly in doing that because if you haven't reached them initially, your chances of converting them go down dramatically. You're wasting all your time trying to reach someone who's never going to buy."

Social Selling and Your Customer Relationship Management

As you consider real-time technology to help you with agile, social selling, you'll need to be very careful about the role of your customer relationship management (CRM) software. Many medium-size and large organizations have an enterprise CRM system in place that the entire sales force uses. Frequently the marketing and customer support staff use the system as well. CRM software is used by organizations to manage a company's interactions with current and future customers. It is used to manage the process of how people inside a company interact with existing and potential customers, and typically it includes an automated component that tracks a particular buyer's history of contacts by a salesperson. There are many specialized CRM systems for industry-specific applications such as the insurance industry, healthcare, and nonprofits, as well as general systems for B2B and consumer businesses.

The large providers of CRM software designed their products in the 1990s, and the category of enterprise CRM grew quickly with the widespread availability of networked computing during the 1990s, and then the shift to software as a service (SaaS) computing in the first decade of the 2000s. And that's the fundamental problem—these software systems were developed in the era of traditional selling, when salespeople made cold calls and followed up on sales leads. CRM as it exists today wasn't designed and built for a world in which the buyer is in charge. Contemporary CRM software still reflects the old paradigm in which the salesperson initiates the action, and therefore it is flawed.

Today, the buyers decide when they want to engage a salesperson. When the salesperson was in charge, the old CRM work flow model—charting a path from initial lead, to the first call, to a face-to-face meeting, to the negotiation phase, and ending with the close—made sense. No longer. Today, if I'm interested in buying something, I go to a dozen websites and do the research. And then at some point when I've built up my body of knowledge, I reach out, typically electronically, and tell the company that I'm ready to take the next step. The old CRM systems don't manage this process well.

> Customer relationship management (CRM) platforms were built in an era when sellers controlled both information dissemination and the selling process. The problem with CRM systems is they don't work well when buyers are in charge.

The word *relationship* in customer relationship management isn't even that accurate, because the software isn't really about relationships at all. Instead, CRM systems are a transactional database for management reports. They're optimized for sales management reporting based on a hierarchical, top-down, command-and-control process where sales management doesn't trust salespeople. While there is certainly benefit for salespeople to use today's CRM platforms, most people in sales don't like them because the platforms require them to log in and record their every action with a potential customer. This takes valuable time away from their primary task—selling—and diverts it toward updating and maintaining the activity log so that sales management can see what they are doing. Salespeople are required to estimate the likelihood that the deal will close primarily so that sales management can run a forecast report for senior executives.

"Sales force automation is in trouble," says Greg Alexander, CEO of Sales Benchmark Index, a sales force effectiveness consulting firm. "This software was originally sold with the promise that it would increase the productivity of the individual sales representative. Vendors insisted that if you are a sales rep and use it, you would sell better. But in fact, that didn't happen. Why? People installed the technology prematurely. An automation tool is meant to automate a process, but if you don't have a process, you make chaos. And you end up performing chaotic activities more frequently. It actually hurts. It doesn't help."

CRM systems should do a better job of helping sales representatives understand buyer context, but CRM wasn't built to do that. Instead the systems were created to help sales reps organize how they're going to take a prospect through the sales process, and bubble it up to the sales VP. And now, in a world where there are so many signals coming in from potential or hungry buyers when they visit your website, interact with your email campaigns, or enter discussions on social media, modern and effective CRM technology should be aggregating all this data. For example, if someone posts a comment or a question to your company blog, there should be a mechanism that analyzes the context of the post against all potential customers and alerts salespeople to exactly which buyer would be interested. Yet existing CRM systems don't do this. CRM should be much more focused on helping salespeople to deliver a better buying process.

CRM pioneer Jon Ferrara agrees that CRM systems as deployed today aren't up to the task. Ferrara founded GoldMine CRM in 1989 with a college friend and built a business that achieved two million customers. GoldMine ranked number 154 on the 1997 *Inc.* 500 and was sold to FrontRange in 1999. A decade later, Ferrara founded Nimble, a service for small businesses that unifies email, calendar activities, and popular social channels—including LinkedIn, Facebook, and Twitter—and links to business contacts. "The whole idea of CRM goes back to the command-and-control mentality of the old-school company," he says. "I believe enterprise CRM was invented because management was concerned that the salespeople had their contacts, but management didn't have access or control of the information, and they couldn't report on their sales activities properly. Management wanted to lock up the contacts and own them; they wanted to keep track of what the salespeople were doing and chart the process. They forced salespeople to put their contacts into the CRM. But most don't fill in their real contacts; they keep the keys to their golden contacts in places like LinkedIn, and they only put enough into the CRM to get paid their commission."

> Buyers control the buying process, not you.

The problem here is huge. Modern social selling just doesn't work on the CRM platforms that were built during an obsolete era when sellers controlled both information dissemination and the selling process. And it certainly doesn't work on burdensome systems that were designed as reporting tools for senior management.

"We now have an opportunity to break free of the traditional CRM approach to selling," says Greg Alexander. "For example, LinkedIn is getting into social selling with an app called LinkedIn Context that salespeople populate with simple things like telephone numbers, email addresses, Twitter handles, notes about how you met this person, and how you are connected. I can tag somebody as an influencer in my connection taxonomy, for example. A client would be tagged as a client, and a prospect would be tagged as a prospect. The best part about it is that the data entry administration is offloaded. The salesperson has been freed from managing this information because their social profiles are kept up-to-date by their contacts. It's no longer necessary to constantly scrub the database to see if an email address is correct or a telephone number is current. The big burden associated with sales force automation—data entry—is gone."

Jon Ferrara believes that sales software should be about how a salesperson can participate in a buyer's journey by telling buyers things they don't know. He says aligning salespeople to the buyer's journey will benefit all. "We need to connect and build relationships with our customers, and CRM doesn't do that. It's no longer a sales funnel, or even a circle. It's a pretzel in which you have no idea where the journey starts and stops. But buyers will view you as a trusted advisor if you join them during the journey and share with them a nugget of information or an article you discovered. You're building relationships, and that's how you build your brand and your network. A salesperson's personal brand plus their network equals their professional net worth."

Obsessing over Sales Forecasts Does Nothing for Your Buyers

Just one manifestation of the disconnect between how people buy today and the ways that most companies use CRM systems is around sales forecasting.

Many companies spend huge amounts of sales managers' time micromanaging each salesperson's pipeline so they can come up with forecasts of how many deals might close in a given month or quarter.

The data they generate gets filtered up to top managers, who ask questions or themselves nitpick, all of which then gets pushed back down the line to the individual reps. It's an unproductive and never-ending cycle.

Indeed, many CRM and salesforce automation software products are primarily used by managers to forecast sales rather than being used by salespeople to work with buyers. Obsessing over sales forecasts and having sales leadership focus on "managing" salespeople to forecasts is a growing problem. It a big reason why salespeople are less effective today.

The sales cycle is no longer. Now it is a buying cycle because potential customers have near-perfect information on the web. But you know that already. Buyers can see what your company is up to, how your products work, what the competition is doing, how much others paid for your services, what your CEO is saying on social media (or not), and much more.

A micromanagement of salespeople via CRM and salesforce automation systems leads to failure because those systems were built and the algorithms developed in the old days of selling. As soon as you obsess over forecasts, you've lost.

Instead, focus on the buyers and their problems, and let salespeople do their jobs without interfering and forcing them to enter ridiculous amounts of data into your systems.

Brawn or Brains?

Over a few beers, on several sun-soaked days during the summer of 2013, I had an opportunity to explore the ideas of social selling, real-time engagement, and how technology can help salespeople to be more effective with HubSpot co-founder and CEO Brian Halligan. Like me, Halligan was also a sales representative early in his career, and he rose to run very large international sales teams. Halligan has evangelized about new marketing with his writing and speaking, and we co-wrote the book *Marketing Lessons from the Grateful Dead.*

"I started my sales career in 1990 at Parametric Technology Corporation as the secretary to the vice president of sales," Halligan says. "At the time, the company had $3 million in revenue. Ten years later, I was a senior vice president of sales and the company had achieved $1 billion in revenue. I had a very nice run and learned a ton about selling and the sales process. But it's remarkable how radically different that sales process needs to be today. The way people shop has really changed." While marketers have adapted to the new realities of the web by delivering information that helps them get found, Halligan agrees that salespeople and sales management are reluctant to change.

"Back in the 1990s, I as the salesperson had the leverage in a relationship because I controlled all the information," Halligan says. "In business school we used the term asymmetric information, which means I had unfair power against the buyer because I had better information. Today, when the conversation finally takes place between the buyer and the seller, the information is symmetric, or the buyer might even have more information than the sales rep. The power has completely shifted."

Yet Halligan observes that sales teams are resisting the inevitable change. "Sales needs to lean into change and embrace it," he says. "For instance, many companies today still don't publish their pricing on their website, which is kind of ridiculous."

Halligan believes today's successful salespeople need entirely new skills. "Rather than your cold-calling abilities, now it's all about how smart you are, and how you can solve your buyers' problems," he says. "Companies need to get their act together and embrace change to really delight customers. The element of friction between sales and customers has been dramatically lowered. Rather than worrying about unhappy customers and the implications of negative word of mouth, salespeople should concentrate on delighting customers. Helping their business and making them feel positive can have a far bigger impact today. It's so easy now for people to spread the word that they are happy. At Parametric, I had five criteria for hiring reps, but at the top of the list was being aggressive. In a world where cold-calling isn't the name of the game any longer and the prospect has an information advantage, the number one criterion today should be brains."

Halligan reiterates the same problems with CRM as Jon Ferrara and Greg Alexander. "I've spent millions of dollars on sales software and I've used a lot of it," Halligan says, "and I've got two big issues with it. First, they haven't adjusted and transformed it to match the way people actually buy today. It forces sales reps to be stuck in the 1990s. Second, it was built to monitor progress and help the VP of sales produce forecasts, while providing the salesperson with little more than irritating busywork."

Buying Signals!

Halligan says useful technology for today's marketplace must adjust to the new reality, and build that into the systems that salespeople use on a daily basis. In particular, Halligan says buying signals are essential for salespeople to know about, yet they aren't part of a typical CRM implementation today. "When a marketer sends an email to a list, the marketer gets incredibly valuable intelligence about who opened that email, what they clicked on, and other analytics," he says. "But this is 500 times more valuable to the sales rep! So why not build these signals into the salesperson's Outlook and Gmail? Every email that a prospect opens will create a signal that will report to the rep, 'Oh, they just opened their email.' When that potential customer clicks on a link, there's another signal, 'Here's the link they clicked on.' Or it signals, 'That potential customer's on your site right now.' It pops up and tells them in real time. Another signal might be sent with the message, 'That potential customer just changed their job title on LinkedIn,' or 'They just tweeted using your keyword in the message.' These signals can pop up within your browser and within your email."

In mid-2013, Halligan created a start-up company within HubSpot to build and launch a new notification app called Signals that would do exactly what he envisioned. It's designed to show real-time notifications based on signals coming from emails you've sent, your website, your CRM system, and social media. The Signals app integrates with many of the tools that salespeople are already using daily, including popular email programs and CRM systems from Salesforce.com.

"The Signals product is designed for the sales rep, not for the VP of sales," Halligan points out. "It's not designed to manage salespeople. It's built to enable the sales rep dealing with a potential customer who already has a lot more knowledge than he has. It provides the means for the salesperson to have more relevant, context-driven conversations with prospects and move them through the buying process in a more efficient way."

In this new landscape, successful selling requires new thinking as well as new technology. Today's successful salesperson is active on social networks, focused on the signals that buyers are sending, and fully aware that the buyers are leading the process.

Now we will shift our focus to customer support. There are equally radical shifts happening there as well.

7 The New Service Imperative

Our dishwasher abruptly stopped working. Oh, crap.

It was eight years old, so my wife Yukari and I decided against repair.

We discussed how to choose a new dishwasher and the best way to have it installed. To be honest, we weren't looking forward to the process at all. Based on our experience with appliance purchases in the past, we assumed it would be an unpleasant ordeal. It wasn't about money—we would gladly pay for a quality product and good service. No, it was the reality of losing a day waiting around for plumbers and electricians. We dread dealing with painters and plumbers and delivery companies and snowplow people, because we have come to assume that poor customer service is part of the package.

We considered various options for replacing our dishwasher, including buying it at a big home improvement chain or online at Amazon.com. However, if we decided on either of these two retailers, which were the least expensive options, we'd have to hire our own plumber and electrician to do the installation as well as figure out how to dispose of the old unit. Too much hassle.

Busted Dishwasher. Great Service

So we chose to work with Yale Appliance + Lighting, a company that we had used in the past. And it worked out great. We spent a bit more, but the fantastic service was worth every penny we paid above the DIY options.

The excellent customer service actually began with the sales department. Unlike our experience with the salespeople at other appliance outlets who seemed to be interested primarily in a commission, Yale Appliance + Lighting didn't pitch particular models or push to close a sale. Customers have a choice of how to interact—you can phone them, use chat, or communicate via email. Yukari chose to speak with the representative on the telephone, and after quickly learning about the various models and their availability she made her choice.

While this experience might appear to be very similar to services offered by other companies, it was the postsale customer support that was amazing. We instantly received the receipt and extended warranty via email and were assured that this information is always stored in the company's systems, so we needn't worry about saving the paperwork.

We were offered several delivery dates to choose from. Unlike many other service people who force customers into a rigid schedule, Yale Appliance + Lighting let us be in charge. Once the date and time were agreed, we received a helpful email that included this:

> Thank you for your recent purchase from Yale Appliance + Lighting. We wanted to send you some important information about your upcoming delivery. The information in the video below is vital to ensure a safe, successful delivery without any complications.
>
> Yale Appliance + Lighting has been family owned for over 80 years thanks to our loyal customers. Thank you for taking the time to watch this, and please contact me by email or by phone if you have any questions.

The video provided information about how to prepare our home for the delivery, including measuring to make sure the new unit would fit in the door. It detailed things that can go wrong and provided advice on what to watch out for.

Then, the day before the delivery, we received a phone call reminding us of the agreed time the next morning.

It was the morning of the delivery when the real-time customer service aspects of Yale Appliance + Lighting caused us to say, "Wow!" Yukari received a telephone call about 7:30 a.m. from the delivery/installation person, who was phoning from his truck to say that he might be late due to an unexpected traffic delay. He gave Yukari the highway exit number where he was at that moment, and they chatted about the traffic situation. A quick look at the traffic display on Google Maps showed that indeed there was a problem at the location the driver was calling from. He confirmed that ours was the first delivery of the day and that he would call again when he was nearing our home, which he did when he was five minutes away.

Once the crew arrived a short time later, Yukari knew what to expect. They were almost like old friends. Rather than frustration at being late, the vibe was relaxed and open. Soon our new dishwasher was installed, and in the months since we've been very happy with the model we chose.

> Great service means more repeat sales and happy customers sharing their experience, which results in faster growth for your company.

What's so remarkable about this customer service experience is that it is so simple, yet so unexpected. Many companies give you a time window in which the service call will take place, but frequently they don't keep to their schedule, making customers wait hours. Certainly it's rare that a company lets you know the exact status of what's happening on the road. It's a wonder that so few organizations practice excellent customer support like Yale Appliance + Lighting. A quick peek at the Yelp consumer review site shows that many dozens of other customers are just as happy with its service as we have been. That's why people keep coming back.

What Is Customer Service Anyway?

Sadly, unlike Yale Appliance + Lighting, most organizations have reactive customer service. They set up a toll-free telephone number, and when customers call they inevitably hear a recording saying, "Your call is important to us," and must wait a few minutes (or more) until a poorly trained representative reads off a script. Within an organization, customer service is usually an afterthought. Worse, it's not uncommon that customer service is considered a cost center, and executives are rewarded for reducing expenses instead of keeping customers happy. When executives are rewarded for controlling the costs of this one department, they miss seeing the larger picture by failing to understand that great service drives sales.

It certainly doesn't have to be this way. Great customer service actually helps increase sales because people will return again and again and spend more money. There is no doubt that when we next need an appliance, we will once again be contacting Yale Appliance + Lighting. And happy customers talk about their experience to their friends and share on social networks and review sites. In fact, studies show that an investment in customer service generates more revenue than an investment in sales because happier customers spend more money. It's far easier to keep your existing customers than it is to search for new ones.

The Elements of Customer Service

Let's take a quick look at the basics before we dive into specific examples later in this chapter.

> Customer service is how an organization helps customers before, during, and after a purchase and can range from customer support and handling complaints to professional services that enhance a product experience.

Customer support is the art and science of keeping customers happy by communicating with them about the company's products and services. Good customer support is often proactive, such as Yale Appliance + Lighting's decision to send a video outlining what we should expect when our dishwasher was delivered and installed. And customer support also has reactive elements, including handling customer inquiries by telephone, email, social media, or in person.

Handling complaints is an essential part of customer service. When customers aren't happy, fixing the problem should be seen as an opportunity to turn people from being unhappy to being delighted.

Professional services are those additional elements provided by a company (or its partners) that help customers to install, learn about, or use a product. Frequently associated with large enterprise software installations, professional services ensure that a customer has the product up and running quickly. In the example of our experience with Yale Appliance + Lighting, the dishwasher itself was the base sale, and the delivery and installation were the professional services element of our purchase.

Customer Service and Corporate Culture

The best organizations infuse great customer service into their corporate culture. Customer service isn't a department; it's a state of mind. It's a corporate culture founded on doing the right thing.

It comes from all employees understanding the corporate story, the defining characteristic of the company, which is developed at the top of the organization. That's what we looked at in Chapter 3 of the book.

Organizations that hire good people and treat those employees well have the raw materials to build a culture. Without employees who care, great service won't happen.

When Yukari spoke with the representative at Yale Appliance + Lighting, she felt the person cared about serving us. The rep wasn't just hustling a commission, but trying to solve our problems. Customer service is an embodiment of corporate culture.

Do you care? Or not? The obvious difference here is the human touch. While automation can certainly help to make a customer service team more efficient, automation should be implemented only when it serves the human element. Technology shouldn't be used to completely replace people who are empowered to help customers.

Content Creation

In the new world of web and mobile content delivery, the best organizations communicate with customers in any way they prefer—by email, telephone, text message, face-to-face, or via social networks like Twitter and LinkedIn.

Because the new tools of the web allow the easy provision of content, creating information—videos, images, text-based documents, graphics, and the like—and sending it to customers as they are learning about your product or service, these tools provide a highly effective new form of service. When Yale Appliance + Lighting sent us the video, we could watch it on our own time.

The accessibility of just the right content at the right time will delight customers and set the tone of the relationship. Costa Rica Expeditions, a Central American ecotourism company, sends customers who have booked a trip a link to 27 *Things to Do before Leaving Home*, which provides very specific items that will make customers' impending trip more enjoyable. The list, which includes things like "photocopy your passport; put the phone number of your airline in your cell phone's speed dial; and pay all bills that will be due while you're away," covers things many people don't consider. And it's simple for Costa Rica Expeditions' customer services staff to email the link to the information a few weeks before each customer's journey begins.

Great Customer Service Drives Sales

Throughout the year that I had been researching and writing the first edition of this book, I had the pleasure of interviewing hundreds of people who are involved in serving customers. I was stunned by the number of them who revealed to me that they had turned their customer service function into a "secret weapon" of revenue growth. People shared the secret that when customers are happy, they keep their product longer, they spend more over time, and they share their happiness with others either in person or on social networks. It seems so simple! Yet few companies actually use this secret weapon of business growth.

Several people shared actual metrics, and I learned that investing money in customer service efforts resulted in more revenue and profit than investing the same amount of money in sales efforts. Yet the vast majority of companies, when looking to increase revenue, invest in hiring more salespeople.

Getting Sales and Service into Alignment

Here's something curious: Many companies have completely different cultures and procedures for their customers depending upon which department is interacting with them. The manner in which salespeople engage potential new customers when trying to win new business is often light-years removed from how these same customers are serviced by the same company only months later. It's no surprise that in the course of my research

I learned that this strategy doesn't produce good results. Focusing a great deal of attention on buyers during the buying process and then relegating those same buyers to poor postsale service means customers are far more likely to leave. This can lead to a churn cycle in which companies add more sales resources to replace the customers who abandoned them, and around and around it goes.

You keep customers happy by doing exactly the same things that won them in the first place. You win customers by focusing on their needs. You keep them the same way.

In this chapter we'll look at all these aspects of customer service. In the following chapter we'll focus on the concept of agile, real-time social service.

Poor Customer Service Is the Norm

Unlike my first-rate experience with Yale Appliance + Lighting, good customer service is difficult to find. And poor customer service inevitably means that the salespeople end up working even harder. In contrast, great customer service not only results in more repeat customers, but those delighted customers talking about you become your unpaid covert sales force.

> When a company delivers a fantastic experience to the market, it serves as the best sales strategy there is.

I'll be sharing other great examples of customer service like the one I experienced at Yale Appliance + Lighting. But first, a few examples of what, sadly, seems to be more typical of how companies treat me. I'm sure you can produce your own examples of poor service.

I travel a great deal, nearly 100 hotel room nights per year. Like most people who travel this often, I've got a deck of airline frequent-flier and hotel frequent-guest cards that I whip out whenever I check in for a flight or hotel stay.

Imagine my surprise when I got an email pitch from Hilton Hotels for an American Express Platinum card that basically threatened to cancel my

Hilton HHonors membership if I didn't sign up for the offer. While this happened several years ago, it still makes me wonder how an organization can be so clueless.

Sure, the email signed by Mary E. Parks, Vice President, Marketing, Hilton HHonors Worldwide, said: "You are very important to us." But the tone and content of the email screamed the opposite.

This "offer" was so outrageous, I checked to see if it was a phishing attempt. No, it turned out it was a legitimate email from Hilton.

Subject line: Don't let your HHonors membership lapse.

As a member of Hilton HHonors, you are very important to us. That's why we want to give you an opportunity to reactivate your HHonors account before it is closed and the HHonors points you've already earned are forfeited. Plus, you can earn an additional 10,000 HHonors bonus points—enough for a free night.

Apply for the no annual fee Hilton HHonors Platinum Credit Card from American Express® and earn 10,000 HHonors bonus points on your first purchase after you're approved. By using the Card, you will reactivate your HHonors account and build upon your current point balance.

The email goes on to tout the Hilton HHonors Platinum Credit Card from American Express. While the email details other ways to keep my HHonors account open beyond the cutoff, such as staying at a participating Hilton Hotel property, I read the email as basically a threat: Open a credit card account or your frequent traveler account will be terminated. The email concluded with:

If you do not take one of the actions above by [date], your HHonors account will be closed and all accumulated points will be forfeited. Prior to your account closing, you may redeem your HHonors points for any eligible reward. After the points are redeemed, your account will be closed by the date above and all remaining points will be forfeited.

This is simply not a good way to treat a customer who has stayed scores of nights in Hiltons over the years. So what could the people at Hilton have done instead?

Using rich data, they could have mined their database and learned that the last time I stayed at a Hilton property I paid with an American Express Platinum card. They could have then concluded that I don't need another one!

If I am very important to them, they could have sent me an email saying, "You didn't stay in a Hilton property for the past nine months, so we're extending your qualification period because we want you to come back." Why threaten a customer? Do they think I'm going to stay at a Hilton now because I'm so eager to keep my status?

But most importantly, why allow their loyalty card to expire at all? What's the point of revoking it?

Teaching Customers to Wait for a Sale

Indulge me just one more example of poor customer service related to travel. When I needed to travel to Toronto to speak at the Microsoft Worldwide Partner Conference, I chose to fly Porter Airlines from Boston. The Porter Airlines flight and service were excellent. I particularly loved flying into Toronto City Airport, which is located on an island situated in downtown. The travel time from the airport into the city is significantly less than from the main international airport located outside Toronto. The travel experience itself was top-notch. In contrast, Porter Airlines' email communications were poor.

After I booked my flights, I signed up for the Porter Airlines email list. I expected to be educated about Porter and the destinations the airline services. I was not. Instead, on a regular basis, all they've sent me are fare sales. I've gotten dozens of email offers since I've been on the email list, including "Summer Splash Sale; Crisp fall air and big Porter savings; Save big on your holiday travel!" and "Biggest sale ever—with our lowest fares on select flights!"

Here's the important point: I received my first email offer shortly after booking my flights, and I realized that had I waited, I could have gotten a much cheaper fare. It annoyed me that I paid a lot more for my flights than I should have. But I couldn't switch, because the fare sale emails said new bookings only.

I get what they are doing. They want to fill seats, and it's a lazy person's drug to run sales on a regular basis.

But offering frequent fare sales also trains customers to wait for a better price on Porter Airlines. It also annoys customers like me who (stupidly) paid too much.

Porter Airlines is providing good *flight* service. In fact, it was named Best Small Airline in the World in the 2013 Condé Nast Readers' Choice Awards. But imagine how much better it would be if its email customer service communications were equally good.

I keep waiting to see emails from Porter Airlines talking about the other destinations it serves. Why not tell me about, say, Halifax? Maybe I'd like to go there, but I don't know much about it. Or maybe Porter could provide ideas about why I should return to Toronto with my family. Or it could introduce its people: "This is Captain Smith." But the airline doesn't do anything like this. It's all about the fare sale.

Your email program should be used to build a long-term relationship with your customers. You should educate and entertain them. I'll fly Porter Airlines again. But next time I'll only book a fare that is on sale. In what seems to be a boneheaded move, Porter Airlines doesn't use its customer email list to educate and inform; rather, it is simply a tool to pitch the latest sale prices.

A Clear Picture of How Great Service Generates Additional Leads

When you provide superior service, people talk about you online, and that drives new business. Doug Weil runs Clearly Resolved, a company that provides video calibration services throughout the Midwest. Video calibration is the art and science of adjusting high-end video displays—such as those used in home theaters, media rooms, and professional production suites—so that the on-screen image matches original source content when the director signed off on the film-to-video transfer or as it appeared on the director's monitor during a live broadcast. When properly calibrated, the video image looks just like one in a movie theater or ballpark or concert stage. When the calibration is off, the colors can be out of whack, sometimes dramatically, because factory settings are optimized for showroom floors and are typically much too harsh. A proper professional calibration requires expertise, equipment, and several hours. Since starting his business in 2002, Weil has calibrated nearly 2,000 systems.

"Diehard film buffs are probably the most enthusiastic consumers of video calibration services, because they often have invested considerable time, money, and effort into putting together a system that will match (or exceed) the downtown movie house experience," Weil says. "Most of my customers initially become aware of video calibration either through a Best Buy shopping experience or via one of the dozens of online home theater or consumer electronics websites and discussion boards, such as Engadget, Gizmodo, CNET, or the biggest of its type, the AVSForum."

Many people who are introduced to the concept of video calibration from a retailer or other home theater site eventually use a web search engine to learn more. And when doing such a search, they frequently find AVSForum. "AVS is where 90 percent of the customer reviews about my service appear," Weil says. "Due to the volume and density of the AVS site, it's impossible for me to know about every review written about my service, but I routinely hear from new prospects and customers that they found me through reading positive customer reviews. I think about 25 percent of all my new business comes via either a review or a customer referral."

After Weil finishes a job, he sends each client a Calibration Report a day or two later. "I don't aggressively seek reviews from customers and I never suggest it before or during the calibration process," he says. "I do mention that I appreciate reviews in the cover note of the Calibration Report. And in that note I provide links and suggestions about where they might post them. But I make it clear I have no expectation that they will take the time to write one."

Providing excellent service also prompts favorable word of mouth from happy customers. "The only thing better than an online review for generating new business is a client referral," Weil says. "Referrals are typically the friends, work colleagues, or family members of happy customers, and they're superior to online reviews primarily because it typically indicates that the new customer has actually seen a calibrated display and knows what to expect. That reduces the selling process and also means it's not necessary to spend a lot of time framing expectations."

Happy customers. Positive reviews. Good word of mouth. New business. It seems so simple. Provide excellent service and people will talk you up. And when they do, you make more sales.

A Nonprofit Changes the Rules of Charitable Reporting While Also Changing the World

All organizations must start with an authentic and compelling story and communicate that to customers. This strategy is essential for companies, educational institutions, individuals, and, yes, nonprofits too.

"We fundamentally believe that helping people see their impact is the most important thing that we do," says Paull Young, director of digital at charity: water, a start-up nonprofit whose mission is to provide clean and safe drinking water to every person on the planet. The company is reinventing how charity works, focusing on a 100 percent model in which every penny donated is sent to local partner organizations to directly fund water projects. And the 100 percent model is communicated to donors with actual proof. Every water project that charity: water builds is reported online with a GPS location and photos. As of early 2016, charity: water had raised well over $100 million and had funded 16,000 water projects. And every one of them is photographed and marked with GPS so people can see the results of the funds they've donated.

Like any very successful organization, charity: water has a compelling story: serving more than 5.2 million people by providing clean drinking water to remote villages in 24 different countries, and promising donors that 100 percent of their contribution will go directly toward funding water projects. Charity: water has around 100 super-supporters primarily from the technology start-up world, including Jack Dorsey, co-founder and co-creator of Twitter, and Sean Parker, co-founder of Napster and the first president of Facebook. The backing from charity: water's super-supporters funds the organization's administrative expenses such as employee salaries and office costs, allowing every contribution raised to go toward serving the mission to providing clean water. "If you go to our website and donate $20, every cent of your $20 goes to a local partner," Young says. "We even pay back the credit card fee. We think about how our business can compress time and compress distance by bringing our donors and fundraisers close to our local partner organizations and the recipients of the work in the field."

From its origin in 2006, charity: water has engaged in interesting ways to serve its contributors by delivering content about how their money is being utilized to bring people water. Even with a small donation, customers can go to the charity: water site to see precisely where that money was spent. For example, a recent campaign brought 100 villages in India clean water. Each community was given a village water tower, and in every household three individual water taps were installed—one in the kitchen, one in the bathroom, and one to the shower—which provide water piped from the community supply.

Such customer service is unusual in the nonprofit world. Most charities do little reporting indicating of how specific donations are used, or they send a few generic photos. Charity: water is different because every dollar is earmarked for a particular project, and information about that project is reported back to those who funded it. While charity: water is a nonprofit, similar customer service strategies can work for all sorts of organizations.

"From day one it's been about photos, GPS, and Google Maps to see all of the water points," Young says. "You can search for someone's name and see the project they funded, right down to the very village that will be served. Donors get as close as possible to really feeling like they're giving directly to individual people. And the more that we can do that, and the more that donors feel as if they are part of our projects, we believe people will stick with us and the more they'll care about our issue."

As an example, thousands of donors in the September 2011 campaign funded Yellow Thunder, the first charity: water drilling rig located in Tigray, Ethiopia. Yellow Thunder was funded so the organization's local partners in Ethiopia could drill more wells. A Twitter feed at @cwyellowthunder and a project page on the charity: water site allow people who supported the project to follow its progress and track it on a map to see evidence of the project in action. As I write this, Yellow Thunder is over 1,500 days in the field, helping to bring clean drinking water to more than 40,000 people a year in northern Ethiopia.

In a world where it is not unusual for charities to take people's money and plow a significant portion of these contributions into funding salaries, office space, and advertising, charity: water uses a customer service model that shows donors exactly where and how their money was utilized to help people. "Our belief in showing people how their money is spent provides an amazing customer experience," Young says. "By giving this detailed reporting, not only do we prove the impact people have made, but we can build a deeper relationship with donors, which in turn will not only bond them more closely to charity: water, but will make them care about the water issue. If they choose to give their hard-earned money, or even more so, to give their time and energy to fundraising, we owe them not only proof of where their money goes, but also to give them a great experience with the brand."

This same approach to customer service works for any organization. When you have a compelling story to tell and you tell it well, your customers will be eager to do business with you.

Charity: water's focused delivery of meaningful content to its donors strengthens customer support for the organization while additionally stimulating further donations.

Now let's turn to how an organization can handle complaints and transform an unhappy customer into one who publicly sings its praises.

"I Hope Everyone Who Works for Your Company Burns in Hell"

Imagine seeing this on Twitter referencing your company:

> @aimee_ogara: @Epson_Store The printer I'm trying to set up is the most retarded process ever I hope everyone who works for your company burns in hell

Whoa. Now that is an unhappy customer! And the fury is being displayed via Twitter for anyone to see. It is this kind of customer complaint that Ron Ploof, manager of social media at Epson America, Inc., searches out and helps to solve. Epson America is the local sales, service, and support company of Seiko Epson Corporation in Japan. It's a large company with businesses that include printers and projectors, augmented reality glasses, robotics, and chips. Ploof works throughout the organization to make sure that social channels are used effectively.

When somebody is so frustrated that they want to vent in social media, they are surprised when someone from the company actually responds. Most people expect that no one will bother to read their tweets, posts, and updates in social networks like Facebook.

> @Epson_Store: @aimee_ogara Before I put on my fire resistant clothing, is there anything I can do to help?
> @aimee_ogara: @Epson_Store Haha I guess I'll forgive you just because this tweet made me laugh . . . and I got it set up so I'm good now #thanksanyway

@Epson_Store: @aimee_ogara That's good to hear. If you have any Epson questions in the future, feel free to ask.

"There is a human touch that can diffuse a situation," Ploof says. "It's a voice. I can understand when someone is frustrated; they want to do something. They want their printer to work. We see these things all the time. In the past, we just kind of let that go. But now I want people to know that we are listening, that there are real people here. We're not just Epson Store; there's a real person at the other end, we heard you, and we're here to help. That's the voice that I'm trying to help develop here at Epson."

Ploof has developed a process for finding and reacting to people on social networks. If people mention Epson in any way, Ploof and his colleagues know what's going on. The Epson Social Media Support Process flowchart is primarily designed to bring customer service calls found on social networks into the Epson America formal customer support process.

The Social Media Support Process flowchart ensures that those people such as the frustrated printer customer who tweeted that she hoped everyone who works for Epson America burns in hell are brought into the same customer support and complaint infrastructure as somebody who telephones the toll-free number.

"When I first came to Epson in October 2012, I started noticing something which I thought was really bizarre," Ploof says. "I'd see someone reaching out to us on Twitter or Facebook, and the response process at the time would be a note like, 'We'll have someone from customer support call you.' And then they'd send an email to our director of customer support, who, in turn, would send it on to a manager. And the manager would then send it on to somebody else. I realized this was not a very sustainable way of doing support. So we took telephone support out of the loop because there was no reason why they should have to take every single one of those calls. And that's how the flowchart came about. Now if someone reaches out to us with a problem, and if we can find out what the model number is, we can immediately point them to a URL for a product web page with all kinds of support information, such as drivers and frequently asked questions. And there's also a phone number they can call if they need more help. Most of the time people say: 'Oh, thank you. That solved my problem.'"

Most organizations force customers into an existing support structure, much in the way that Epson America used to. If you complained on Facebook, they'd respond by giving you a telephone number to call.

However, truly excellent customer support and complaint resolution is best handled in the medium the customer prefers, be it Twitter, Facebook, email, or the good old telephone.

Because many of the issues that arise at Epson America are fairly common, Ploof has been working with his team of bloggers to create content around products and services that can be used to answer questions on social networks. "I ask bloggers, 'Rather than answering a question 86 different times, what if we actually wrote a great blog post about that particular feature that's in your product or service? How can you come up with useful content that people are searching for?'" That content serves as the information that people are directed to when they need help.

This proactive approach to solving customer problems is working at Epson America. "I have seen us save customers," Ploof says. "Some say they're never going to buy an Epson again. But we turn them around and they later write, 'You guys are all right.' You can't put your head in the sand. These conversations are happening with or without you. So you have to decide: Are you going to participate or not? I would rather participate and know what's going on than just ignore the whole thing."

Great Customer Service Starts in Person

With all the discussion of terrific online customer service—such as the examples set by Epson America and charity: water—it's possible to lose sight of the fact that excellent service does not depend on how it is delivered. It can occur face-to-face, by telephone, or even by postcard. And it's important always to listen to your customers.

For example, Metro Bank is building success through its own brand of great customer service. Founded in 2010, Metro Bank is the first new High Street bank in the United Kingdom in 140 years. The market prior to Metro Bank's arrival was an oligopoly controlled by a handful of big banks including Barclays, Royal Bank of Scotland, Lloyds TSB, and HSBC Bank. Anthony Thomson, co-founder and chairman of Metro Bank, knew there was an opportunity for a new entrant in the market because customer satisfaction among the established High Street banks was dire.

Interestingly, Thomson and his colleagues didn't look to other banks for market research. Instead they considered and studied how retailers like John Lewis and Apple deliver outstanding customer service. This led to Metro

Bank's decision to open its retail bank branches seven days a week, 12 hours a day.

Metro Bank is also pet friendly, a feature that has prompted media attention. "It says to people, if they can bring their dog into our bank and we don't mind if he pees on the floor—or worse—which is what dogs do, then maybe we care more about you as a customer than we do about constantly maintaining our pristine decor," Thomson says.

Metro Bank even ran a contest where dogs were given samples of three tasty treats and asked to vote for their favorites. The biscuit that garnered the greatest number of votes across Metro Bank's branches nationwide was named as the official Metro Bank Dog Biscuit.

The established banking institutions' reputation for delivering a poor in-person customer experience left Metro Bank with an open opportunity. Metro took full advantage of the situation to create a revolution in British banking by listening to customers (and their dogs). And it works. In just five years 2,000 Metro Bank employees serve over 500,000 customers across 40 banking locations. The company has risen from a start-up to become one of Britain's leading challenger banks.

Customer Service "Wow!"

Here's another example of great in-person customer service.

After many years of going through travel bag after travel bag, I decided to buy one of higher quality, and after some online research I invested in a Tumi Frequent Traveller bag several years ago. With a price tag of $600, these things are not cheap.

Based on my speaking calendar alone, I calculate that I've put something like a half-million air miles on that Tumi bag since I purchased it. Together, that bag and I have visited at least 25 countries. It clearly shows it has been well used; the scuffs, dirt, and scars on its surface offer a visual chronicle of our adventures around the world.

I didn't have any trouble with the bag for nearly four years, which was much longer than any other bag I've owned. It had already paid for itself. So when the retracting handle broke, I figured it was time for a new one. I wondered if it could be fixed. Probably not, I thought, but it was worth a shot.

Thinking that I'd need to purchase a new Tumi (a half-million air miles is more than "normal wear and tear," isn't it?), I went on a Sunday afternoon to a Tumi retail store in Boston. The salesperson took one look at the bag and said she could fix it by installing a new handle mechanism, "but it would take a few days."

Cool, I thought. "Please do!"

Since I wouldn't be able to return to the store to pick it up, I offered to pay to have it shipped to my home.

She wouldn't hear of it and said they would send it back to me at no cost.

I was amazed that less than 48 hours after I left the bag at the Tumi shop, UPS delivered the repaired bag to my door.

Wow!

The new handle works like a charm, and since then it has probably added another 200,000 air miles to its travel log.

How about that? I went into the store expecting to replace the bag that had served me well for four years. I was planning on spending $600 on a new one. Instead, at no charge, my old one was repaired. Remarkable.

And here I am telling you.

In a world where most companies are only interested in today's transaction, great customer service like that from Tumi is an excellent marketing and sales strategy. Someday when my bag is finally beyond repair, I'll buy another Tumi. I'm a customer for life.

And maybe you will be a Tumi customer, too, after hearing my story.

Or better yet, maybe you'll look at your own company's customer service and imagine how you can turn it into one where people go "Wow!"

First, Educate and Inform Your Customers

The only time customers hear from many organizations is when the organizations send out ridiculous "Your opinion is valuable to us" feedback requests. Some companies, including many hotel chains, send out a survey request after every use of the product. They just ask, ask, ask, ask, ask!

Many customers find this practice highly annoying. It often seems you never hear from a company you do repeat business with except when it wants something back from you. And if you take the trouble to fill out the online form, you never hear back about the survey results or what the company plans to do with them.

There is a much better way.

> Each time you email a customer, you should be providing content of value. You should always be giving more than you are taking in a relationship with a customer.

If companies insist on conducting a survey, it must be real, meaningful research—not just some inane measure of an aspect of the business that results in an internal report that nobody reads, let alone acts upon. And when you do contact your customers, why not offer something of value first?

Why not offer a video link showing how people use the product your customer just purchased? Then ask for opinions.

Why not link to the company blog that talks about common customer issues and how they can be easily solved? Then ask for opinions.

Why not link to the online forums for the service that your customer just signed up for? Then ask for opinions.

Why not tell them, in writing, the answers to the service question you just provided to them over the phone? Then ask for opinions.

The important idea here is to educate and inform your consumers *first* and then ask for a survey to be completed.

Surveys: Your Opportunity to Gather Real Data

Headquartered in Atlanta, Georgia, Jackson Healthcare is among the largest healthcare staffing and technology companies in the United States. It currently serves more than seven million patients in over 1,300 healthcare facilities. For Jackson Healthcare, market research and surveys are an important source of content that is delivered to customers and used in marketing. Research from Jackson Healthcare has been featured on CNN, Fox News, and other national and industry media channels.

"We work with healthcare providers both in direct relationships and by providing referrals, and our research gets used during our work with our clients," says Keith Jennings, vice president of marketing at Jackson Healthcare. The company serves healthcare providers, including physicians, nurses, and other allied health professionals, as well as hospitals and health systems. "Our research and surveys are designed to discover existing unsolved problems in the interaction between providers and healthcare facilities, and any possible opportunities that might resolve them. We gather as much data as possible, and publish reports that shed light on the problems that we see and any trends that we think need to be addressed."

The research is packaged into easy-to-digest reports that are delivered back to the same groups that were surveyed. "We then use the research to kick-start and facilitate conversations on both sides of the table—the providers on one side, and the healthcare facilities on the other," Jennings says. "In the healthcare world, the two groups—clinical and operational— are constantly looking for ways to better engage and influence the other side."

Jackson Healthcare research is designed to provide value for customers who complete the surveys. "It is thought leadership," Jennings says. "Our operating companies have capitalized on the opportunity to connect the research to valuable content they deliver to the two constituents: the providers and healthcare facilities."

Jackson Healthcare worked with one of its operating companies on a national study of physicians to explore why and when they changed the geographical locations of their medical practices. "We examined the decisions physicians face if they are looking to relocate," Jennings says. "We studied whether they are a resident or a veteran physician. When they make a decision to relocate, we wanted to determine the leading factors that influence their thinking, and why they choose a different location to practice medicine. Is geography a major factor? A particular region? How important is the lifestyle that an area offers? Was their spouse a factor? We generated a list of possible trigger points that we then surveyed with physicians and tested with research. This resulted in a report that we shared with both physicians and in-house recruiters in hospitals."

Unlike the vast majority of organizations that carelessly send surveys to customers without thinking about how the request will be received, Jennings says that Jackson Healthcare pays close attention to the survey experience and has developed a four-step process. "Every year we do a Physician Practice Trends survey," he says. "Before we ever reach the deadline to launch the survey, we start a conversation. We send an initial email that says, 'We have a survey coming, but you may not have seen the results of last year's, so here it is.' Those emails help drive expectation and engagement."

Jackson Healthcare's Physician Practice Trends Survey Email #1

From: Sheri Sorrell

Subject: Trends impacting your medical practice

Despite having less autonomy, employed physicians report higher satisfaction than those in private practice. That, among other surprising trends, was what last year's physician practice survey revealed.

These findings were featured in Becker's Hospital Review, Health-Leaders and other leading industry news sources.

This is our fifth consecutive year tracking trends among physician practices and specialties. We look forward to reporting back to you where medical practices like yours are today and how they've changed over the past five years as the ACA has rolled out.

Five years ago, physician outlook was quite pessimistic. Do you think it has improved or remained the same?

This Sunday, we will open this year's physician trends survey. I hope you will participate.

Sheri Sorrell, Director of Market Research

(Note: Active links to each of these news sources were embedded in the email.)

The second step in the process is to send information from the previous year's survey with a request that people complete the current survey. "By the time we finally say, 'It's time to take the survey,' we've tried to answer any questions they might have about why they should participate and what's in it for them," Jennings says. Note that the initial survey emails come from the head of market research. With a competitive survey environment, the data showed that an email coming from her was credible and authoritative.

Jackson Healthcare's Physician Practice Trends Survey Email #2

From: Sheri Sorrell

Subject: Quantifying physician practice trends

Last July, my organization emailed you the findings of our physician practice trends survey.

Among the findings:

- Satisfied physicians were more likely to be employed and between the ages of 25 and 44
- Dissatisfied physicians were more likely to be between the ages of 45 and 66 and own a solo practice
- High overhead, reimbursement cuts and administrative hassles were the primary drivers behind physicians leaving private practice

We conduct this survey each year in an effort give you insights you can use as you lead your medical practice through this transformational time in healthcare.

I hope you will participate. And I look forward to sending you this year's findings.

[Click here] to begin survey

Respectfully,

Sheri Sorrell, Director of Market Research

The third email in the series is a quick invitation to complete the survey from Jackson Healthcare together with a link to a third-party article of interest to potential respondents to get them thinking.

Jackson Healthcare's Physician Practice Trends Survey Email #3

From: Sheri Sorrell

Subject: Last Call—Physician Practice Trends

In a *Forbes* magazine interview last year, Dr. Robert Pearl asked author, Malcolm Gladwell, what topics he should be covering. Gladwell's response: "Help people understand what it is really like to be a physician."

That is exactly what we're trying to do with our practice trends survey. The survey closes this Friday at 5 pm, so you still have time to share your feedback and experiences.

[Click here] to begin survey

In this survey, we're looking at differences between employed and private practice specialties. And we're looking at trends in practice acquisitions, among other areas of interest.

Thank you, in advance, for your participation. If the above link doesn't work for some reason, copy and paste this into your browser: [URL]

Sincerely,

Sheri Sorrell, Director of Market Research

Whether it's survey invitations with related data or offers to check out last year's results, Jennings makes certain that the emails will be welcomed by Jackson Healthcare customers. Once they close the survey, Jennings follows up with a personal thank-you and an offer to participants to be the first to view the findings, ahead of the media.

Jackson Healthcare's Physician Practice Trends Survey Follow-Up

From: Keith Jennings

Subject: Slide Deck—Physician Trends

Here is a recently published 43-slide deck that shares data and trends from various sources on U.S. physicians:

[Image of title slide inserted here]

It's a quick read that covers supply & demand, regulatory impacts, compensation & reimbursement, satisfaction & outlook and practice environment.

Feel free to use these slides in any presentations you'll be giving in the coming months. Here is the URL in case the above link doesn't work: http://www.slideshare.net/JacksonHealthcare/physician-trends-2015.

Sincerely,

Keith Jennings, Jackson Healthcare

In the five years that Jackson Healthcare has done these surveys, the company has evolved the format and media of the final report from a downloadable PDF e-book to SlideShare. And, each year, it publishes a series of articles that tie in to the report. To take a look at some of the content created by Jackson Healthcare, visit these sites:

- Jackson Healthcare physician trends resource center for physicians, hospital executives, and the healthcare media: www.jacksonhealthcare .com/physician-trends

- Jackson Healthcare on SlideShare: www.slideshare.net/jacksonhealth care

Now let's turn to how conducting research about your customers can generate insights that you can use to grow your business.

Using Customer Feedback to Grow Revenue

Organizations have been conducting customer surveys for decades. Until recently, the questions were either asked and answered face-to-face with the survey taker holding a clipboard, conducted over the telephone, or sent and returned through the mail. But with the web, most companies now rely on electronic surveys because they are far cheaper and less time-consuming to implement.

But nearly all organizations using e-surveys are missing a massive opportunity. An electronic survey is by definition providing real-time insights into individual customers, because, when customers hit "send" on their responses, the answers reflect their feelings about the company and product at that precise moment. This intelligence has staggering utility. But because most companies still view surveys through the historical lens of past paper-based survey techniques and apply them to the web, they fail to take advantage of the power to understand customer satisfaction in real time. Instead of reacting to customers in real time, they warehouse their survey results. Instead of treating people as humans, companies aggregate data into rows and columns on a spreadsheet.

Imagine the possibilities of real-time customer feedback! When unhappy customers voice disaffection, the damaged relationships could be repaired by swiftly addressing the problems, thus reducing customer churn. And the possibility of identifying opportunities for growth in comments from delighted customers would mean new sales.

"You keep customers happy, not by doing something different from how you won them in the first place, but by doing exactly the same things," says Guy Letts, founder of CustomerSure, a maker of all-in-one feedback software. "I don't know why the mind-set shifts. You win customers one at a time according to their own needs, you fit the proposition to their needs, you say nice things to them, you listen to them, and you win them over. Then once you've won them over, most companies treat customers differently."

Letts advocates the use of customer feedback to keep more clients and win new business, something that surprisingly few companies actually do. Most companies take hard-won data gleaned from individual customers and dumb it down by averaging it and then putting it into a spreadsheet to be sent to senior executives, most of whom don't even read the resulting report.

The inappropriateness of the way many companies survey their valuable customers is profound. "I like to use the example of a restaurant," Letts says. "It's not appropriate to send a survey to somebody halfway through their meal. What is appropriate in that circumstance is for the waiter to come up when you've just had your meal and say, 'Is everything okay? Was the food okay? Are you happy with how we're looking after you?' To which the answer is either 'Fine, thank you very much' or 'Not so great.' And the waiter graciously replies either 'Good, enjoy the rest of your evening' or 'I'm terribly sorry. Let me fix that for you.' Then they fix it appropriately and give you a round of free drinks or whatever would leave you wanting to come back again."

But the way that most companies survey customers isn't anything like what a good restaurant does. Instead, what's practiced in most companies today would be like having an excellent waiter in a great restaurant serve you a gorgeous two-hour meal and then damage the customer interaction at the very end. "It might be a member of the dishwashing staff standing between you and the exit door with a clipboard and 20 pages of questions with the request, 'Would you mind sparing 20 minutes?' That's what people experience with most company surveys," Letts says.

Before founding CustomerSure, Letts was head of services at Sage Ltd, where he used his experience to transform 10 percent attrition into 20 percent growth. When Letts joined Sage, one of the first things he did was read surveys that had been conducted before he joined the company. "My heart sank as I read them because there was cry after cry for help in these satisfaction surveys," he says. "They had been done the traditional way, which is actually the wrong way: every customer surveyed at once. Not only had nothing been done about these responses; nobody had even read them. There were about 20,000 responses in each survey, and I spent hours reading them. It was heartbreaking. I worked out that six out of ten of the responses represented customers who had left, but had been savable if someone had made the effort."

How to Conduct a Survey That Helps Grow Revenue

Letts decided on a different approach to using surveys. The old surveys wasted a large amount of people's time by asking them to fill out data sheets that were then averaged and used for management reports. Letts's new approach focused on individual customer attitudes toward a company, its products, and its services with the goal of identifying problems and fixing them immediately. He recommends a three-step process to growing revenue by conducting real, meaningful surveys:

1. If you're conducting a survey that allows customers the opportunity to provide your organization with feedback, don't prejudge what they might tell you. The very first thing is to make sure the entire organization understands why you're doing the survey.
2. You have to be geared up to deal with any problem that might present itself. Make sure that others in the organization are prepared to react as customer issues come in.
3. If you decide surveys are right, send them after you've delivered something meaningful to a customer at a time when it would be appropriate for that customer to receive a survey.

"What you see people teach about customers is wrong," Letts says. "The books and consultants typically say: listen, filter, then act. This doesn't work. They say listen by gathering all the responses and then determine the most common themes. Then filter them down by working through several spreadsheets, PowerPoint slide decks, and C-level executive meetings. Because people think they can't possibly do everything, they prioritize and finally end up doing the top three. And the result is so bland that nobody notices any difference."

Instead, Letts advocates changing the commonly accepted model to: listen, act, filter. "Hear from the customers and immediately triage it and deal with anything that needs to be done," he says. "And then after that look for patterns and trends and insights about how the company should be developing, what should be done, what is going right, and where are things going wrong."

Letts says the first step is to make sure that you're ready to respond to customer issues in real time. If not, don't do the survey! "Before you even think about surveys, it's important to make sure that everyone in the company has bought into why you're doing them," he says. "Every individual in the organization has to understand the benefits; otherwise they will be done badly. Very often when the results identify a problem area, someone else will need to be engaged since the person receiving the information or triaging the survey will not be the best person to deal with the issues at hand. It could be anything from 'Oh, by the way, I've changed my address. Can you please update my account details?' to 'I haven't paid my bill because I'm still not happy about something.' It could be absolutely anything."

At most companies, important information like a request to update an address or a cry for help is simply ignored when a customer reports it in a survey. By listening and acting on their problems, you'll impress customers with your responsiveness, and if you deal with the issues quickly you can save customers who were planning to leave.

An annual satisfaction survey is not a good approach. Instead, the best time to send a survey is after you've done something meaningful. "It's best if you have something to pin an experience to," Letts says. "So for an accountant, it's after you've done the tax return. And it is essential to ask relevant questions. Don't ask how old they are or what newspaper they read or how they found out about you. Ask them whether you were good at the things they expect you to be good at. If you're a retailer, did the staff know what they're talking about and advise properly? Did you have the items that they wanted in stock? Were the staff friendly and fast to serve? Since that's pretty much all you want from a shop, just ask those questions."

In a world where most companies send out surveys simply to calculate what percentage of their customers love them, such an approach is radical. Yet the idea that asking customers what they think and fixing problems before people quietly walk away seems such an easy concept. "We have a delightful customer called the Royal Institute of British Architects," Letts says. "They implemented a system that surveyed their customers right after a sale. In a bumpy year, the sales team was walking around with smiles on their faces and all received bonuses. They certainly found that service sells."

While there is no doubt that you can increase revenue by using surveys in this way, Letts offers caution. "It mustn't be cynical," he says. "You can't simply survey customers because you want to uncover sales opportunities. The environment has to be geared up so everyone in the company understands how it fits into the process and how it supports the business objectives. There is no more valuable lesson than hearing what the customers think in their own words."

In the next chapter, we'll expand on the idea of generating instant feedback from customers to look at many different aspects of agile customer support.

8

Agile, Real-Time Social Service

There's no doubt we're living in a real-time world. News updates appear instantly on news sites from media properties like the BBC, CNN, Mashable, and *Wired* magazine. Newspapers around the globe update their sites as news breaks, not just based on the 24-hour daily newspaper printing cycle of the past. Now it's a 24-second news cycle. Or shorter. We communicate to friends, colleagues, and family members instantly through tools like text messaging and Skype as well as via social networks like Facebook, Twitter, and LinkedIn. When was the last time you put pen to paper to communicate to a friend?

If your colleague gets a new job, you learn about it in real time on LinkedIn. If your friend changes his or her status on Facebook to "in a relationship," everyone knows right away (and comments instantly).

Embracing Change

However, most companies are reluctant to embrace this change. Many still operate as if a letter sent overnight via FedEx is the height of speed.

Most organizations favor steady qualities like compliance, caution, and consensus over speedy traits like imagination, initiative, and improvisation. That's the nature of the beast. Big business is designed to move forward according to plan, at a measured and deliberate pace.

I've talked with people all over the world who are wrestling with the challenge, and most are not at all comfortable with adopting a real-time mind-set for dealing with customers. It's not on the corporate agenda or the business school curriculum. And when the notion is put to them, many people dismiss quick response to opportunities or threats as reckless or risky.

What's Expected in the Corporate World

- Respond to customers on your time frame.
- Wait, to make certain.
- Work from checklists dictated by multiyear business plans.
- Measure results quarterly and annually.
- Execute based on a long-term new product launch mentality.
- Organize around multimonth communications campaigns.
- Get permission from your superior.
- Run decisions by your staff.
- Bring in the experts, the agencies, and the lawyers.
- Conduct extensive research.
- Carefully evaluate all the alternatives.

None of this is inherently wrong. Clearly, research, planning, and teamwork are essential. The problem is that speed and agility are too often sacrificed for the sake of process. To overcome that, you need to consciously and proactively adopt a real-time mind-set.

The Real-Time Customer Engagement Mind-Set

Today consumers set the pace. Left to their own devices, they imagine all sorts of things. They take unpredictable initiatives, like starting a blog about your products. They improvise all over the map at high speed. They tweet, and post on Tumblr, and talk about you on review sites.

As I first discussed in my 2011 book (subsequently revised in 2012), *Real-Time Marketing & PR: How to Instantly Engage Your Market, Connect with Customers, and Create Products That Grow Your Business Now*, organizations must rise to this challenge and communicate to their customers in real time. I see definite progress in marketing and public relations functions at companies large and small. Many, but certainly not all, are using agile techniques to engage their marketplace.

Now it is time for customer service to step up and to do the same.

Real-Time Customer Engagement

- Respond to customers on their time frame.
- Act before the window of opportunity vanishes.
- Revise plans as the market changes.
- Measure results today.
- Execute based on what's happening now.
- Empower your people to act.
- Move when the time is right.
- Encourage people to make wise decisions quickly, alone if necessary.
- Make swift inquiries, but be prepared to act.
- Quickly evaluate the alternatives and choose a course of action.
- Get it done and push it out, because it will never be perfect.

Developing a real-time mind-set requires sustained effort: encouraging people to take the initiative, celebrating their success when they go out on a real-time limb, and cutting them slack when they try and fail. None of this is easy.

Let's take a look at a variety of companies that have been successful with agile customer service.

How Boeing Used Real-Time Communications during the 787 Dreamliner Crisis

Imagine that your newly launched product, one that hundreds of millions of people around the world are aware of, suddenly has safety issues forcing the product out of service and disrupting the lives of tens of thousands of people. That's the customer communications challenge Boeing faced when the 787 Dreamliner encountered battery problems in early 2013.

Airlines around the world had been eager to take delivery of the new plane because it was touted as Boeing's most fuel-efficient airliner. But when several 787 Dreamliners experienced onboard fires related to its lithium-ion batteries, the U.S. National Transportation Safety Board (NTSB) and the Japan Transport Safety Board (JTSB), Japan's equivalent organization, launched investigations that prompted the grounding of every commercial 787.

Boeing was quick to take a strategic approach by creating real-time content. Information was freely made available through digital channels and social media to educate and inform constituents around the world.

I had an opportunity to connect with Gary Wicks, who manages much of the digital communications activities for the Boeing Commercial Airplanes unit. He told me how he and his team used real-time content to keep everyone up to date on the situation.

"This was an unprecedented situation for us," Wicks says. "No one expected the airplanes to be grounded. So we quickly had to identify, evaluate, and communicate to key audiences. We asked ourselves, 'Whom should we be addressing?' Our customers, employees, and third-party experts who were being asked to comment on this situation were certainly high on the list. But we also needed to communicate to the flying public and government officials."

Wicks and his team created content to help clarify relevant issues with factual information. For example, a web page about the 787's electrical system included basic information about the airplane's power and details about the 787 systems—in text, print-ready graphics, and video. They used their Twitter feeds, including @Boeing and @BoeingAirplanes, to get the word out.

"Our best content is providing information that only we can provide," Wicks says. "It has to be compelling and informative, but we tried to give a look into the problem that no one else can. We had to keep that in mind when we developed the videos or infographics, because we wanted to make sure this offered a look at what we were doing from our perspective."

Notably, many media outlets took content directly from the Boeing site and used it in their stories. "It was shared widely," he says. "It was picked up by the *Wall Street Journal*, for example. A lot of our content was just taken straight from our site and put into other media like GeekWire and AV Week."

The Boeing team quickly learned that people amplified the #dreamliner story on social media, especially Twitter and Facebook. "There was a great deal of interest and conversation about it," Wicks says. "So we embraced that. We had a story to tell, and we had valuable information to provide that helped clarify the situation. Believe me, there was a lot of misinformation out there."

The Boeing team noticed there were a lot of questions raised via the social channels asking about what the batteries actually do. "We needed to explain the batteries in a manner that is easily sharable and understandable for a wide set of audiences," Wicks says. A page titled *Batteries and Advanced Airplanes* was created for this purpose.

787 Battery Fire Crisis Timeline

- January 7, 2013: After landing and deplaning the passengers and crew, a 787 experiences an auxiliary power unit (APU) battery failure; the U.S. National Transportation Safety Board (NTSB) launches an official investigation.
- January 15, 2013: A 787 experiences a main battery failure during flight; the flight crew diverts and conducts a safe landing; the Japan Transport Safety Board (JTSB) launches an official investigation.
- January 16, 2013: The Federal Aviation Administration (FAA) issues an airworthiness directive suspending commercial operations of the 787 fleet; global regulators follow suit.
- April 26, 2013: The 787 airworthiness directive restricting 787 flights is lifted, clearing the way for 787 flights to resume for airplanes that have been retrofitted.

Once government officials in Japan and the United States deemed the planes airworthy, Boeing ran a live social media chat with Mike Sinnett, 787 chief project engineer, and Captain Heather Ross, flight test pilot. The chat was broadcast as video from Ustream, and viewers could engage via the #787chat hashtag.

"We have a loyal fan base for this airplane," Wicks says. "And we wanted to give them an opportunity to engage directly with us. The great thing about tools like Ustream and live chat is it's so affordable to do these kinds of events, and the technology works. We wanted to take the opportunity to talk about the battery solution but also talk about what's next for this airplane. There were about 5,000 viewers, and the comments on it were really positive."

As I followed the 787 Dreamliner battery crisis story as it unfolded, it was clear that most media, customers, and members of the flying public were giving Boeing a fair listen. Sure, batteries potentially catching fire on your plane is a serious matter, and people were vocal. But because Boeing communicated well, and in real time, the public was also understanding about the glitches that need to be ironed out in any new product launch.

"Even with this unprecedented event, we delivered 65 Dreamliners in 2013," Wicks says. "There are over 100 in service, and the 787 has carried more than 11 million passengers and flown over 95 million miles."

Putting Your Customers First

As long as we are talking about Boeing 787 Dreamliners, I've got another interesting example of real-time customer engagement around 787s, but this one doesn't involve a fire.

Like many people, I'm on hundreds of email lists. I get dozens of customer email messages each day from organizations I support and companies I do business with. I also get a lot of unsolicited emails. You probably do, too. Many of these unwanted messages are so-called graymail—email lists that you technically agreed to opt in for, but are used in ways you don't expect. For example, you buy a shirt at an online retailer. You give your email address in the checkout process. And now you're getting unexpected sales messages every day. Graymail isn't spam because at some point you actually gave permission for that company to send you email. But it abuses the privilege by sending unwanted messages.

Most of the content of graymail is just advertising. You know, things like:

- Ten percent off your entire order!
- Free shipping!
- Two for the price of one!
- Act now while supplies last!
- Available until Friday only!

Very few of the companies that I do business with send me anything of value, especially the six or eight airlines that send me email. The airlines are always bugging me with "sale prices," "special offers," "vacation packages," and other crap. Most airlines just don't understand that someone who travels an average of 150,000 miles a year for business doesn't book travel based on sale prices and special offers.

I was surprised and delighted when American Airlines actually sent me interesting information via email. For a number of years I have been an Executive Platinum American Airlines customer. That represents a great deal of travel and hundreds of thousands of dollars in ticket purchases over the years, making me one of the airline's best individual customers.

The email I got announced American Airlines' plans to acquire 42 new Boeing 787 Dreamliner aircraft. That's actually a big deal because Boeing designed the 787 Dreamliner from the passengers' perspective, thinking that people would book travel based on the plane. That's exactly what I do, and what other frequent travelers do as well. When you're in the air as many hours as I am—about 300 hours a year, nearly two full weeks in a metal tube at 35,000 feet—comfort is the most important thing. It becomes more important than price, special deals, and other things.

The American Airlines email said: "Boeing's Dreamliner aircraft offers a new level of comfort for our passengers. It features improved air and water purification systems, as well as new humidification techniques and lower cabin pressure, which are expected to reduce passenger fatigue. In addition, the 787 advanced engine design provides a quieter operation, with an expected noise footprint 60 percent smaller than other aircraft of similar size, benefiting those in the air as well as those on the ground. The plane's lower overall weight and improved design means we also will reduce our impact on the environment by burning less fuel. The 787 aircraft also has the largest overhead bins in the industry—approximately 30 percent larger than comparable aircraft bins. The large 19-inch windows are designed to make the cabin feel more spacious."

The real-time nature of this email made it work so well. It was sent at the time the airline ordered the planes. American Airlines reached out to me at the precise time when it would have the most impact, before I read about the order in the newspaper or online.

I'm amazed at how often companies send press releases to the media but fail to inform their customers of important news. In this example, American Airlines did send a press release about the new aircraft, but was also smart enough to alert its frequent travelers.

In early 2014 I finally had an opportunity to fly on a 787 when I traveled from my home in Boston to Bangkok for a speaking engagement. No, the plane's batteries didn't catch fire. And yes, the plane offers a wonderful passenger experience.

Customer Service Using Social Media

To learn more about how American Airlines communicates in real time with its customers, I spoke with Jonathan Pierce, director of social communications for the company. Pierce is responsible for defining the company's social strategy and then bringing it to life day-to-day based on an analysis and understanding of customers' comments and what they want from American Airlines. Internally, he works to instill social concepts throughout the different business units with the goal of making social communications a significant aspect of their business, not just a check box on a to-do list.

Because I fly American often, I've been connected to @AmericanAir on Twitter for years. They have 1.3 million followers as I write this, and I have always found them responsive. "We listen to where customer conversation is trending for American; we understood fairly early that about 70 percent to 75 percent of all social mentions for the brand are on Twitter," Pierce says. "We noticed early in its existence that our customers use Twitter for pre-travel and day-of-travel help and support; its short-form text communication is quite appropriate for that kind of transactional customer support. So we focused our customer service on building a very robust solution within Twitter 24/7."

Curiously, Pierce noticed that although people like to use Twitter to communicate with American Airlines before they travel and on the day of travel, after their trip they more often connect on Facebook. This reveals that being active in only one social network is not enough. It also indicates that when staffing support teams, people working with specific social media networks may need differing skill sets. As of this writing, there are 22 people assigned to social customer service at American Airlines. "From an organizational perspective, we consider the type of skills and expertise needed when managing the different teams. Pre-travel and day-of-travel concerns tend to be primarily about reservations. Concerns that arise post-trip tend to lean toward customer relations and after-sales support on Facebook. These groups work together and they sit together, but they just prioritize the channels differently."

On Twitter, Pierce's team actively focuses on real-time customer engagement, and I got to witness this in action. I tweeted a question to @AmericanAir while at Chicago's O'Hare airport and received a reply in less than five minutes. "We've put a lot of our resources into relationships," he says. "The customer service team engages with our clients conversationally, and we hear what our customers want from us: 'What's the status of my upgrade?' or 'What flights are available?' or 'Is my flight on time?' or 'I need a refund.' We look at all of those traditional customer service issues and support. But we also get people asking about our products, the number of seats on a specific aircraft, and the angle of the seats in business class. We get feedback on flight attendants, feedback on agents, questions about pets traveling in the hold, and questions about our policy and procedures. I mean, it literally covers everything related to American Airlines. We try to handle them quickly, and to be able to do that we have to have a lot of connections behind the scenes. We have a very robust information-sharing process so that the person who is handling the issue on Twitter can get the relevant information or the answer to the question very quickly."

While many companies continue to allow glacially slow customer service efforts, Pierce has a definition of real-time support at American Airlines that stands in stark contrast to the norm elsewhere. "Our target is a 15-minute response time 24/7 to every actionable tweet," he says. "An actionable tweet is a genuine customer conversation. (We don't respond to every single tweet, such as someone sharing a press release. There's no need for us to respond to those.) Actual response times depend on many factors, and they can be longer if there is a weather event disrupting travel or when Twitter volume is overwhelming, but overall we are beating our goal. We are at around 11 minutes at the moment. Everyone pays attention to the target, and we have technology to help us manage the target with a ticker that counts down when we are getting close. The team knows that when the ticker goes into the red more than 15 minutes have elapsed, so we know we have to prioritize things differently, or we need to add extra resources to make sure that we are delivering to target and meeting the customers' expectation of us."

Because of the nature of air travel, there are inevitable delays due to weather, aircraft mechanical issues, and whatnot. Sometimes when such circumstances occur, people vent their anger on social networks. "Our strategy is pretty simple," Pierce says. "It's about being responsive and not letting that angry tweet sit out there and gather more anger and more frustration and involve more people. We found that the sooner that we can respond, apologize, improvise, and act on it, the better. We do our best to resolve the issue, or if we can't resolve it we try to make sure that at least the customer knows that we heard them and we are sharing feedback. Our strategy is about efficient, immediate response and empathy and then action where appropriate. People are surprised when we reply and they often say, 'Oh, I wasn't really expecting a response.'"

Many people are astonished when @AmericanAir tweets back in a few minutes, Pierce says. "They say, 'I just needed to vent.' In which case we respond, 'Thanks, and know that we are here for you.' I think people like that."

Occasionally a more serious issue surfaces through social media that might require escalation within American Airlines. "We will capture it, follow up internally, and share it with the appropriate department, and if required there will be investigation," Pierce says. "We will encourage the customer to create a customer relations file, which is the formal process required by the U.S. Department of Transportation. We help facilitate that and make sure to speed that process through to resolution to make sure the customer is happy."

There are certainly similarities in the skills and experience required to do telephone-based customer service and for interacting with customers on social media. However, in comparison, the biggest difference is the public nature of conversations on social networks. Only the people on the telephone know how that interaction went down. However, a public tweet can be read by anybody on the planet with an Internet connection. So the skills required for success in social customer service are quite specific.

"We look for people who have both a very positive outlook and can be quick," Pierce says. "Because they are going to live and breathe social, they need to have that right outlook on life. Anyone doing social is put into a position where what they write not only is directed to the customer but also becomes the public face of the company brand, which is a tall order. Every tweet is being analyzed for typos and for grammar. The tweet could be used in a customer relations file. The media could pick up on it. In addition, to be successful, the company's social people need to have a general handle about what's happening in the news, what's happening in current affairs, and what's happening in celebrity gossip and sports, because that all gets talked about on social networks."

Vodafone Egypt Proves Social Customer Service Works Worldwide

In recent years I have delivered talks in more than 40 countries and on all seven continents. Frequently in my live presentations people express skepticism about doing real-time customer service via social tools such as Facebook and Twitter. They want to know if the way American Airlines handles real-time social customer service would work in their country as well. While the tools may vary—in some countries local social networks are more important than global ones—there is no doubt that in almost every country social networks are an important way to communicate with customers.

When I was in Cairo, Egypt, and in Doha, Qatar, to lead social media marketing masterclasses in late 2013, I had an opportunity to meet with many businesspeople who are using real-time engagement and social media effectively to reach and communicate with customers in the Middle Eastern markets.

In particular, Vodafone Egypt has been very active and successful in its efforts to use Twitter and Facebook for real-time customer service. I learned the details from Ahmed Sabry, CEO of IT Vision, a Cairo-based digital marketing agency working with Vodafone Egypt.

With eight million Facebook likes, Vodafone Egypt has the largest presence on Facebook in the Middle East. On Twitter, the company counts well over 1.4 million followers at @VodafoneEgypt.

According to Sabry, the company employs 25 social media specialists organized into teams who focus exclusively on social media. Besides Facebook and Twitter, they are also active in networks like Instagram and Foursquare. Each team specializes in one network, and they operate 24/7. Team members follow what's being said about the company and, if required, they respond immediately. In true real-time fashion, anyone who makes a customer service query via one of the networks gets an instant response.

Partly through its excellent social media customer support, Vodafone Egypt has grown to become the leading mobile operator in Egypt in both revenue share and its customer base, which numbers more than 36 million.

While it is impossible to make a definitive correlation between the company's growth and its social customer support, it isn't surprising to me that the company with the best real-time engagement is also the one with the largest market share.

Vodafone Egypt also uses social media for crisis communications. Talking about crisis communications in a country that has recently witnessed a revolution, operates under curfews, and experiences daily protests may seem rather odd. But people draw a distinction between what's going on politically in the country—a series of seemingly constant crises—and what is happening with the companies they do business with.

This became an issue for Vodafone Egypt when in 2011 the company ran a *Shokran* ("Thank you" in Arabic) campaign during the month of Ramadan. The social media campaign encouraged people to show their appreciation to someone they wanted to thank. Vodafone Egypt promised to retweet messages using the hashtag #VodafoneShokran and measure who received the most votes.

When supporters of former president Hosni Mubarak voted him to the top of the list, suddenly a fun social game became political and turned into a crisis. The social media team flagged the issue, and very quickly executives decided that Mubarak's name needed to be removed. People vented on Twitter using the hashtag, but it could have been worse if the company hadn't acted quickly.

In fact, according to Sabry, Vodafone Egypt faces a social crisis nearly every month. But using real-time monitoring tools, they know immediately what's going on and they can deal with it right away. And once they engage, they monitor the situation to determine if mentions are increasing or decreasing.

Executives of large organizations often ask me whether real-time customer engagement via social networks is really effective. With eight million Facebook fans, real-time engagement at Vodafone Egypt is a decisive contributor to the company's position as the number one mobile phone provider in the marketplace. With concrete examples such as this, the answer is yes: Real-time social customer engagement works all over the world.

People Want to Do Business with Other People

Do you remember the last time you called a toll-free number and were routed through phone-tree hell ("Press 4 for customer support; press 5 for sales") and then had to wait on hold? How did that make you feel?

Or consider the websites you've visited recently. How many were dull and uninspiring and didn't answer any of your questions? Did it feel like these organizations cared about you?

Of course not.

People want to do business with other people. We're human, and we crave interaction with people who know us and respond as individuals. That's why the real-time customer service techniques practiced by Vodafone Egypt, Boeing, and American Airlines work so well. These companies interact with people on a personal level. The representatives are hired for their social skills and traits like empathy. And they understand context before they act.

When you communicate with customers in an agile and human way, you build a relationship with people much like you would if you met them in person.

When customer service communications and online content seem created by some nameless, faceless corporate entity, it doesn't entice us, and often it alienates. And as a result we're just not interested in doing business with that company.

We all want to do business with other humans. We want to know there's a living, breathing person behind the communications. And we want reassurance that those humans on the other side understand and want to help us.

There's no secret to building great customer service. The answer is to be human.

In this chapter so far, we've looked at three huge companies: Boeing, American Airlines, and Vodafone Egypt. These organizations have 20 or more people dedicated full-time to agile, real-time social customer service.

Now we turn our attention to much smaller organizations as well as independent practitioners to see how they communicate in today's social, networked world.

The Value of Personal Communications

In our modern world of web interfaces, online purchases made easy with a few clicks, pre-populated order forms, and social media share buttons, it's easy to interface with dozens or even hundreds of companies and never have an encounter with a human.

Maybe that's why when somebody does reach out to us personally, we notice. A human interaction can be delightful.

I booked a speaking engagement in Quebec City, Canada, and since it is a lovely six-hour drive from our home near Boston, my wife and I decided to go together and enjoy a few days in beautiful Old Quebec.

Prior to our journey, we researched restaurants on TripAdvisor and other services and made several dinner bookings using online booking engines Open Table at one place and Bookenda at another.

As I usually do, I added a short message in my booking form at each place, something like: "We are looking forward to dining with you!"

Whenever I make an online restaurant booking through a service like Open Table or a hotel reservation through an online interface, I add a personal message. I'm imagining that if there is a person at the other end who is processing a bunch of reservations, I want mine to stand out just a little and perhaps brighten that person's day.

In perhaps 100 restaurant online bookings I've made, I've never had anybody respond to my notes. Until now!

> Humanize in order to delight your customers.

Marcela at Restaurant Saint-Amour replied to my reservation via Bookenda with this: "So do we! Until then, have a lovely week monsieur Scott! Marcela"

This was so unique and unexpected that I immediately shared it with my wife. And during my presentation in Quebec City, I shared it with the audience. We agreed that Marcela's personal reply made us even more excited to dine at Restaurant Saint-Amour. Marcela humanized the restaurant in a way that a hundred other restaurants failed to do when given the opportunity.

And it took just a moment.

When we finally walked into Restaurant Saint-Amour with positive vibes already established, we were hoping that Marcela would be there to greet us because I felt like we already knew one another. While she wasn't working that night, the staff were wonderful and we had a fantastic meal.

Oh, and the rock band Metallica was at the table next to us! They had a show the next night in Quebec City. For a music geek like me, that was fun.

What small function at your organization can humanize in order to delight your customers? It seems so easy, right? Just communicate as a human would. However, that just doesn't happen with most organizations. To illustrate this point, I'm going to focus on the industry that in my personal experience is among the worst at customer service—the healthcare industry.

Lost in Clinical Gobbledygook

Would you want people in this organization to take care of you or someone you love?

> We have assembled surgical and clinical expertise second to none, have a state-of-the-art trauma center, developed sophisticated minimally invasive techniques, and called on innovative training and technology to ensure the highest level of patient safety and quality of care. These clinical initiatives, a thriving research enterprise and an unparalleled [famous university]-affiliated medical education program all enable [Hospital Z] to fulfill our mission.

When I read this world-class, cutting-edge hospital gobbledygook I don't imagine the people working at this hospital as having a great bedside manner. How you communicate with your customers is important. Humans don't speak in what I call gobbledygook, the vaguely important-sounding big words and industry jargon contained in the preceding paragraph.

Can you imagine using this language when you speak to someone in person?

The way you communicate with customers is meant to build a relationship with them. You need to understand your audience and use the words and phrases that they use.

This is particularly true when you're a doctor and you're communicating with a patient. After all, confusion in meaning could lead to serious medical issues.

Terrible Healthcare Customer Service

In my experience as a patient and as a family member of patients, I'd have to say that the healthcare industry has the absolute worst customer service imaginable. It's crazy! If I need to make an appointment with my primary care physician, I can't do it online. I *must* call the doctor's office "during normal business hours," which is a three-hour window in the morning and a three-hour window in the afternoon, weekdays only. No, you cannot call the office before 9:00 a.m. No, you can't call when they are on a lunch break.

And when you do call, there's no way you can actually speak with the doctor. All they will do is grant an appointment.

And don't even get me started about service after an appointment. Typically, the doctor gives you a prescription and sends you on your way with very little information. Sure, you can read the 10-page medicalese that comes with the pills, but that's not helpful. Answers to my questions like "Can I exercise when I take this medication?" aren't included because there are so many warnings that the various government agencies require.

I recall a few years ago when I injured my leg and needed to go to physical therapy. The therapist wanted me to do exercises at home between sessions. So how did he help me to learn the exercises? Well, he demonstrated once, had me do them once, and then gave me a one-page handout that was a series of terrible stick figure drawings of a person doing the exercises. The photocopy itself was awful quality, probably a hundredth-generation reproduction. Got a question about the exercise? Tough. You have to wait until the next appointment to ask.

I'm not sure why healthcare treats its customers so badly. Is it because doctors, with their fancy degrees, are so revered that we patients can't insist on better service? Is it something related to the American healthcare system that removes from doctors any incentive to take care of people properly? I'm not sure of the underlying reasons, but there is no doubt that in my case, the experience has been horrible.

But it doesn't have to be this way. Next, I'll introduce you to several doctors who are pioneering great customer service in healthcare. We will meet an emergency room physician who uses video to provide patients with information they need upon discharge from the hospital, a pediatrician who uses social networks to communicate with her patients and their families, and a clinical psychologist who cares deeply about patient communications.

Healthier Patients through Video Customer Service in Healthcare

According to a report issued by the Center for Information Therapy, five minutes afterward patients remember only half the information conveyed to them during a healthcare consultation. This disconnect between doctors and patients means a huge customer service problem in healthcare.

"Clinicians assume patients understand the terminology we are using with them about their diagnosis and plans for treatment, and clinicians also assume their patients' understanding and cognition can occur very rapidly. These are two very incorrect assumptions," says Kate Burke, MD, an emergency physician at Milford Regional Medical Center in Massachusetts. She also serves as president of Orion Emergency Services, a group practice employing 22 physicians, and holds a clinical associate professorship at the University of Massachusetts Medical School. "Patients are not in our heads as we rifle through our differential diagnoses of what's wrong with them, nor do they have the training, background, or vocabulary that we spent a long time learning. It is not acceptable to think that patients can remember things as rapidly as we verbally deliver information to them, especially if we are also used to talking to other healthcare professionals who also share our knowledge. This results in a real communication gap between what clinicians believe they have communicated clearly to patients, and what the patients understand about what the clinicians were trying to tell them."

Dr. Burke became interested in this disconnect through personal experience with an orthopedic injury she suffered while skiing. She struggled to recall exactly how to do her physical therapy exercises at home. Then she had an idea: On the next visit to her therapist, she took her video camera, asking him to record her correctly performing her exercises in his office so she could remember exactly how to do each movement at home.

"It was a real 'aha' moment for me as a doctor," Dr. Burke says. "I thought, 'Wow, this is unbelievable. I can play my own rerun to revisit my physical therapy sessions and store them on my computer. I can have all of the content that was shared with me from three and four years ago to use regularly and routinely, not requiring me to go back to the provider.'"

Since that experience as a patient, Dr. Burke has introduced video in her own practice, shooting clips for patients at the end of an emergency room visit, explaining the treatment and what to do upon returning home. And she has become involved with the Center for Information Therapy in Washington, D.C., whose sole focus as a not-for-profit organization is working to close the gap so that patients will remember more than 50 percent of what a clinician was trying to communicate. "This led me to trying to figure out a way to share HIPAA-compliant videos with patients in a more scalable fashion," Dr. Burke says. "Video shot during a healthcare consultation can help patients recall important information and instructions later. It's a game changer and will become the standard for ongoing physical care and in other areas of healthcare, too." (The U.S. Health Insurance Portability and Accountability Act [HIPAA] protects the privacy of individually identifiable health information, and sets the national standards for security of electronic health information.)

This communication disconnect between doctors and patients is a hidden problem because doctors are expected to communicate well, and patients are usually too intimidated to speak up about things they don't understand. Together, these issues lead to a terrible customer service problem in healthcare delivery.

"We are talking about communication, basic routine skills that everybody assumes a clinician who goes into healthcare possesses, whether a doctor, therapist, or nurse," says Dr. Burke. "But communication skills are not necessarily inherent in every individual who works in medicine. But it is a skill that can be amplified and taught. And now we all have the ability to capture critical information in the simplest of ways, by using technology at our fingertips: our smartphones."

Dr. Burke films herself discussing the patient's condition and treatment near the end of the emergency room visit. Depending on the situation, she might film the patient. Sometimes she films a member of the patient's family who is involved in care or assistance, such as learning the motions to safely lift someone who needs help being moved. Or she might film herself talking directly into the camera as she gives details about how to take medicine or what foods to avoid. She then shares the information via Postwire Health, a web-based, HIPAA-compliant patient engagement tool used to create a private, customer-friendly place for each patient. She may share articles and links to other content on the Postwire private page, too.

"We all have iPhones or Androids, so clinicians have the ability to capture and share information that's critical and curated to a particular patient," Dr. Burke says. Patients already have the tools required to view the content, simply by firing up their computer or tablet. "It can be shared literally within seconds and integrated into a clinical encounter. I've shared my idea with many different clinicians, and it's now part of my fourth-year elective course, Best Practices in Communication. I have seen it integrated into the medical school curriculum. When I discuss this concept with students, their response is, 'Yeah, of course we would do that.' I have seen an amazing growth in its acceptance."

Dr. Burke describes the problems faced by those who receive a cancer diagnosis. It's a very difficult time for patients and their families as they come to grips with the nature of their disease. Many do a great deal of research on their own. "There are many confusing opportunities for patients relative to cancer care," she says. "Patients have all these questions and learn how important it is to get different opinions. But how, as a patient, can you keep track of this? How can you remember in detail the experts' nuanced suggestions given during a visit? Clinicians can help by curating the content. They can help direct each patient to really good sources that are germane to that patient."

Additionally, patients and their families benefit from sharing these videos, links, and supporting information on a personal site. "This is a very powerful way to take care of a human being," Dr. Burke observes. "And by sharing, equalization and transparency are much more likely to take place. We can stamp out confusion or misunderstanding very early during in the doctor–patient relationship."

The tools required to do this sort of information sharing are fairly simple to implement, yet can significantly increase patient satisfaction. All that's needed are a smartphone camera and a secure online place to store information.

You don't need to be a physician to employ this beneficial approach to detailed customer service. Individually intended content curation and video customer service can work in any business. In this example, just substitute the word *customer* for *patient* to understand how it might apply to your business.

"Medical technology and digitized information storage are evolving at an exponential rate," Dr. Burke says. "Several years ago there were many clinicians who could not imagine using an electronic medical record, but that's routine now. It's incumbent upon physicians to improve how we communicate with patients, facilitate the retention of information we want them to carry forth in their recovery process, and share with their families. Once you admit there is a problem with how we communicate and how much information patients remember from that communication, then you can move on to finding solutions. One wonderful way to do it is by leveraging technology. For me, this is incredibly exciting because finally we are going to address the problem of patients either being unable to understand or failing to retain the information they are provided."

People are naturally reluctant to change the way they work with customers, and doctors are no different. However, making a radical change in how we communicate is not difficult. All that's required is eliminating a fear of the unknown and learning a new routine. Sure, the first few weeks might involve a learning curve. But after that, there should be no additional effort required to communicate with customers in a way they will appreciate.

Making Clients Feel More Connected

Peggy Kriss, PhD, is a clinical psychologist in Newton, Massachusetts, and like Dr. Burke she provides each of her psychotherapy clients with a Postwire Health resource page where she shares videos and other content.

"On their pages might be personalized relaxation breathing practice, or mindfulness videos, or a video clip of the summary of one of our sessions," Dr. Kriss says. She also provides psychoeducational resources such as helpful websites, articles, blogs, referral links, and even motivational photos.

"One client was nervous about upcoming elective surgery and asked me during a session to add a video for her page that included a reminder of all the benefits that would result if she did in fact have the surgery," Dr. Kriss says. "She watched that video many times before actually making her decision. We actually made two videos: one with my voice, summarizing her choices, and then later, an interactive video with the two of us discussing the advantages. She thought she would not want to hear her own voice, but she actually came up with the idea in a later session after concluding that it would be important for her to hear herself saying the words."

Each client's personal page allows the client to communicate with Dr. Kriss, and includes a notification that records whenever the client accesses information on the page. "Some of my clients refer to this page daily," she says. "This might happen if they are having a particularly hard week. Others just engaged in the therapy find the resources very helpful, and have integrated the use of the page into their self-care routine. The notifications I get when they look at the page are very useful to see how engaged they are. So when they are back in the session I already have data to explore with them."

Dr. Kriss believes this way of communicating with her clients both structures and supports them. They have something they can turn to that gives them a road map toward feeling better. "Clients feel they are not alone," she says. "They feel more connected to me and to the therapy process. And since the page can be shared with others, it is an awesome way to communicate with family members, caregivers, and other healthcare providers."

Making Healthcare Personal

Natasha Burgert, MD, a full-time primary care pediatrician at Pediatric Associates in Kansas City, Missouri, has a passion for educating families.

She does this in unique ways through her blog and in social media. However, like Dr. Burke, she is another physician who noticed that people weren't retaining the information she shared on visits, in particular the parents of her patients. "The clinic space is not a good learning space," she says. "It's an information gathering space, but it's not conducive to learning."

Dr. Burgert uses her @doctornatasha Twitter feed, her Facebook page, and her *KC Kids Doc* blog to share information with parents, the teenagers she serves, and the community at large. Like Dr. Burke, she sees tremendous value in delivering follow-up information via social tools. "If you ask me why your child gets a fever, what you need to do about it, what are the myths, and what are the facts, that will prompt a long discussion. And quite frankly you are going to understand only about 10 to 20 percent of what I say," she explains. "So I deliberately don't answer those questions during a visit. I'll say, 'Here are three blog posts that I wrote that are going to explain all that you want to know. When your kid gets a fever, go back to it and look again; that's the time that you are going to learn.' I specifically won't answer certain questions that I have written about, because I just don't believe that's time well spent. It's especially hard to retain verbal information if your kids are distracting you during an office visit. You may be worried about their fear of getting a shot that day. Maybe they're not feeling well."

Dr. Burgert's *KC Kids Doc* blog allows her to deliver important health information but with her personal spin and in real time. Because she's seeing patients every day, the content is derived from her experience in the office. "The Academy of Pediatrics site and WebMD are wonderful places for consumer health information, but sometimes the information doesn't turn over quickly enough to be practical. So that's why I started my blog," she says. "The blogging is to respond to specific things that I was seeing in my day-to-day practice. This covers topics important to families that I was often asked about and provides opinions and direction that weren't necessarily found on the larger health information sites."

For example, some teenage girls asked Dr. Burgert about "thigh gap." So she asked the teens a number of questions and learned that the girls were trying to achieve a valued gap between their thighs when standing with their ankles touching. Girls who didn't display a visible gap were given diet tips and exercise routines by their peers so as to create one. Dr. Burgert was horrified. She did some research and noticed there was very little written using the phrase *thigh gap*. But she realized she was seeing an early trend and quickly wrote a blog post entitled "Thigh Gap: The Newer and Disturbing

Trend in Body Awareness" to get the word out to girls and their parents that this is not a healthy choice. The post provides tips about how parents should to talk to their children about a healthy body image and details of early warning signs of an eating disorder.

"My blog, Facebook, and Twitter are a bit of real life," Dr. Burgert says. "It's my opinion, although I try to support my comments with as much evidence-based literature as I can. I think that's the beauty of having a place where you can speak your mind as a physician. We have these amazing conversations with families that I think are really valuable and need to be shared. The teenagers I see in my practice are very open with me about their concerns and the issues they are dealing with. I hope I can alleviate the anxiety of other teens and possibly prevent them having similar troubles. Without this platform I couldn't share my advice as widely as I do. Parents enjoy the fact that they can turn to one trusted place and know it will have both the research evidence and my opinion."

Dr. Burgert typically creates content for her blog and then shares links via Facebook and Twitter. But she gets the information to parents in any way they are comfortable. "Our community is very technologically savvy, so many people will just look it up," she says. "But my job is to offer as many ways to get the information as possible. If someone needs a particular piece of information, I will just text or email the link. I have bit.ly short codes for all of them. I can write them down. And I have QR codes that I pop onto my computer screen when I am doing my electronic medical record, so they can just scan it on-screen with a QR reader. For those who don't want all that electronic stuff, I have paper copies. It is my patients' choice how they get that information."

As Dr. Burgert was explaining all this to me, I was struck by the huge contrast between how she and Dr. Burke give information to patients and how my physical therapist gave me the old photocopy of the stick figure cartoon diagram.

In addition to providing information to patients and parents following a visit, Dr. Burgert also anticipates what people may need prior to a visit.

"If I know that you are going to see me about a specific issue, I can guess what your questions will be," she says. "I can preempt that visit by giving you answers to those preliminary questions, so when we come together we can talk about how those answers are specifically relevant to your family, and not just dispense general information that you can get anywhere. I develop a plan and specifically ask questions about what may be unique to your family."

Beyond the value of her blog and the social presence it provides to individual patients and their families, Dr. Burgert says there is a sales aspect to what she is doing as well. "It goes beyond information distribution," she says. "It's actually a relationship-building tool and a valued place for families seeking advice and who are trying to make the best decisions for their kids."

She has also seen lots of evidence that her blog posts are shared via social media and discussed among parents in her community, resulting in a raised awareness of her practice. "That's how my brand is marketed and how people find the clinic. They bring in their families because they heard about us on the soccer field," she says. "I can track how my posts are being shared through Facebook and where they are getting linked."

While the agile service she provides to families and the community serves to bring in new patients, she sees a much larger role for her efforts. "A lot of people ask why I started doing the blog, but I think the bigger and more revealing question is 'Why do you keep doing it?'" she says. "Medicine is changing, and the manner in which patients make health decisions is changing as well. As a pediatrician who went to school for a long time, I want to be able to use my knowledge and use my training effectively. There are new ways to distribute the knowledge that I have learned, so I keep doing it because it provides such great value within the community. That's an amazing feeling for a physician: to realize that you are improving on what's already an amazing career by trying something new."

Dr. Burgert continues, "Parents come in and tell me they were really, really worried about a particular medical issue. It was causing them to lose sleep. But then they tell me, 'Luckily, I knew I could turn to your Facebook page, and there I got a lot of reassurance and calm, and then I could rest well.' I'm often told by parents, 'There is so much information out there, but I want to know what you think.' They have already chosen me as their pediatrician. They trust me. Now they just want to know what I think so they don't have to worry about doing all of this research themselves."

Customers and Business Growth

Throughout this chapter, we have looked at a variety of organizations and how they interact with their customers in an agile way. The proactive approach to customer service—anticipating needs and being available around the clock, like Vodafone Egypt and American Airlines—means people are more likely to use your business next time. When your doctor keeps in touch with you throughout the year by providing valuable information via social networks, you tell your friends about it. There can be little doubt from the examples cited here that agile customer support results in happier customers, and that, in turn, leads to business growth. Happy customers keep coming back to you for repeat business.

"You're not doing your job if you don't pay attention to me all year and then call me 30 days before the contract is due to expire to check in about the renewal," says Cliff Pollan, CEO of Postwire. Postwire Health is the personal sharing platform used by Dr. Kate Burke and Dr. Peggy Kriss to share videos and other content with their patients. "You're going to lose the most valuable customers you have. The easiest dollar is always to save the customer you have. The second easiest is to sell more to the customers you currently have. And the most difficult is getting new customers."

Pollan believes that sending information to existing customers about once a week is the right frequency. This keeps you and your organization in their minds. But you need to send information of value, such as what Dr. Burgert shares with patients throughout the year via social media, and what American Airlines sent me about the new 787 Dreamliner aircraft via email.

"Ideally, you are giving customers added value every week—something that will help them," Pollan says. "It could be a tip on how to use the product. It could be an interesting blog post. A company called StandUpPouches creates a page for each customer. The business has grown more than 25 percent each year because the company created a place to share information with its customers. New information is added all the time, which is placed in context for each customer. This enables StandUpPouches to maintain a good back-and-forth dialogue. Added information also creates additional sales for its product, which translates into orders to different departments, as well as referral business. Should a key person working for one of StandUpPouches' accounts leave that company, the history is retained for the next person who comes into the job, meaning StandUpPouches is more likely to keep the account."

Implementing Agile Customer Service

The more people you have in an organization, the tougher it is to communicate in real time. In a command-and-control environment where no action can be taken without authority, without consultation, and without due process, any individual who shows initiative can expect to be squashed.

The challenge is to develop a new balance that empowers employee initiative but offers real-time guidance when it's needed—like a hotline to the higher authority.

Some companies are making substantial progress at this, and we've looked at some examples. One good indicator is whether employees are allowed to do real-time social networking on the job. If your company blocks access to Facebook or Twitter, you do not work for a business with a real-time mind-set.

Companies with a real-time mind-set allow decision making as far down the ladder as possible. Frontline service reps are given the authority to decide how best to deal with customer issues. In a real-time corporate culture everyone is recognized as a responsible adult.

If you're the leader and you want to cultivate a real-time mind-set throughout your organization, tear down the command-and-control mentality. Recognize your employees as responsible adults. Empower them to take the initiative.

9

The Social You

I arrive in Bangkok very late in the evening in the midst of one of the most serious crises Thailand has ever faced. It's early 2014 and protesters looking to overthrow the government have set up barriers at major intersections in the city, seriously disrupting travel and throwing the metropolis into chaos. By the time my driver approaches the area near Siam Square where my hotel is located, it is nearly 1:00 in the morning. And the road is blocked by protesters.

We do a U-turn and drive 10 minutes to avoid the demonstration and get a little closer to the hotel this time. But there is another blockade. Old tires are piled high in the street. Plastic tape has been used to construct makeshift fencing. A number of checkpoints have been set up by the protesters, and those in charge tell my driver he can't go any farther. He turns to look at me in the backseat. It's my move.

"Thanks," I say, and I get out. As I lift my bag from the trunk, the driver apologizes. The protesters stand by watching. He did the best he could under the unusual circumstances, so I give him a nice tip.

I'll have to go the rest of the way on my own. I understand the hotel is several hundred meters away, but I can't see it. And it's after midnight in a city whose government has declared a state of emergency. The U.S. Department of State has issued a warning to Americans who are considering visiting.

But I'm not scared, and I begin to walk.

Leading up to my keynote speech at the Spark Conference, I had been in touch frequently with the event organizers about the rapidly evolving political situation in Bangkok. At one point about a week before the event, we all thought it would be canceled due to the ongoing protests, but they decided to hold it anyway. Even though many of my friends told me not to go to Bangkok—some even said I was crazy to go—I decided that if the conference was still on, I'd be there.

I monitored the State Department website and checked mainstream media sources like the BBC and *New York Times*. But I wasn't worried. The reason I decided to board the plane and make the trip, and the reason I felt fairly calm walking to the hotel, was because I had been following @RichardBarrow on Twitter. Barrow is a full-time independent travel blogger based in Thailand, and he had been tweeting constant updates about the situation in Bangkok.

When the World's Attention Turns to Your Expertise

As the news traveled around the world that protesters were blocking traffic in Bangkok, Barrow realized this was a perfect opportunity to report the real situation in the country. He would act as eyes and ears on the ground for travelers, expats, and the media. Barrow broadcast in real time on an hourly basis as the situation evolved.

One of the most important news stories in the world was exactly in Barrow's area of expertise! And he took advantage of the situation, being agile, getting information firsthand, and reporting to his customers and the public. Being at the center of an important story meant that he had a huge opportunity to significantly boost his personal brand.

"I started tweeting back in February 2010 when there were protests in Bangkok," Barrow told me. "I had just bought my first smartphone, and one of my first tweets was about a protest march into Bangkok. I tweeted pictures and live updates about this march and its effect on the traffic." Over the days, weeks, and months that followed, Barrow visited the rally sites and did live updates from each area. At this time, Twitter was an important information source for expats and tourists. Most of the news coming out of Bangkok was mainly in Thai. So, besides his own eyewitness accounts, Barrow also translated updates from the Thai media. This was when he first started to get a large following.

As the news of the latest protests was unfolding and I was considering my journey to Bangkok, I knew that mainstream news about the protests would be distorted in several ways. It's often the case when a political situation is developing that local news accounts translated into English reflect either a pro-government or a pro-protester bias. The international media often focus on the worst aspects during such events, so I was wary of sensational or distorted media reports. I was also aware that many stories in the international press were not firsthand reports, so they couldn't really be trusted.

That's why Barrow was my primary source. He was in the city, and he understood travel. He created a real-time Bangkok Protests Map that kept tourists informed about the areas to avoid. It was also referenced in many international media stories. Even the local *Bangkok Post* pointed to it.

"The new protests are a bit different," Barrow said at the time of my trip. "The protests have been taking place simultaneously at multiple locations around Bangkok. In addition, they were mobile. Many more Thai media people are on Twitter these days, so I was able to set up a digital office. I collected all the various reports, decided which were reliable, translated the best into English, and then sent them out to my followers. I also received many live reports from citizen journalists (expats and tourists), which I then redistributed to my followers. Every now and then, I would also visit the rally sites on my bicycle to compose live Twitter updates."

What fascinated me about this story was how anybody could suddenly become situated at the absolute center of the world's attention. It's like a mega version of newsjacking except you've already got a following for that particular expertise. It is a perfect opportunity to greatly expand your influence—if you're quick and willing to work hard.

Barrow armed himself with technology to report in real time. He even used a small drone aircraft, which he brought with him to rally sites on his bike, to get aerial shots of protests.

"Technology has improved a lot compared to the 2010 protests," Barrow told me. "Battery life was the main problem back then. Now we have battery packs that keep us going for several days. This time I also have a DSLR camera with WiFi, so I can zoom in easily and have the pictures uploaded live to Twitter. And with the availability of 3G, we can upload pictures and video to social media far more easily. But, at some of the main rally sites, so many protesters are uploading selfies to Facebook that the network can occasionally slow to a crawl. When I send my remote quadcopter above the streets, I get images that provide good crowd estimates, and the pictures can be sent live on social media. All of my new equipment fits into my backpack, and I can still be mobile and cycle between protest sites."

Barrow's updates have captured the attention of the world's media. Reporters around the globe, including CNN, *The Telegraph*, the *Huffington Post*, the *New York Times*, and many others, follow him and use his updates in their stories.

"Twitter has been invaluable for Bangkok's expats and tourists. It provides access to instant updates on the situation from people around the city," Barrow said. "We no longer have to rely on the traditional news media to tell us what is going on. We are organizing it ourselves now."

Barrow's fantastic coverage, and the Spark Conference organizers' assurances that it was safe, removed any worries I might have had about walking to my hotel. I reached the security checkpoint and thanked the guard as he examined my bags and let me pass.

I could have canceled the trip. I could have stayed home. I could have disappointed the thousand attendees of the Spark Conference by not showing up. I could have let fear control me. But Barrow and social networking got me to Bangkok.

Sooner or later the world will be interested in your area of expertise.

> When news breaks about a subject that you know intimately, you have an amazing opportunity to seize the moment in real time and share your knowledge with the world.

If you're agile like Barrow, you can become the global source about what's really happening. And that means for years to come you'll be seen as trustworthy and reliable, just as Barrow is viewed as an authority about what's really happening in the streets of Bangkok and elsewhere in Thailand. It will be a huge part of your personal brand.

Barrow succeeded because he was already social. He had experience blogging, was on Twitter, and had posted videos. And because he jumped at an opportunity that presented itself, he delivered incredibly valuable information to customers who already relied on his travel advice about Thailand.

You can do the same in your marketplace. By becoming active on social networks, you will be more successful. If you're an entrepreneur, you need to be social. If you're a sales representative, you need to be social. If you work in a customer services position, you need to be social. If you run a company, you need to make certain that your employees become social.

In this chapter, we'll look at some other people who have found personal success through social networks, and I'll share what you need to do to follow in their path.

Getting Social

Earlier in this book, I shared stories about organizations around the world that have built businesses by focusing on agile sales and real-time customer service. So far, we've mainly focused on the businesses—how American Airlines and Vodafone Egypt service customers through social networks like Facebook and Twitter, or how agile sales strategies drive success at Quark Expeditions and Basement Systems.

Now it's time to turn to you.

To make the new rules of sales and service part of your world, you must change your mind-set. You'll need to understand your buyers, rather than just talking about your products and services. You'll need to be aware of what's going on in the real-time news and on social networks. You'll need to create content and publish it on the web, and sometimes you'll need to do it urgently to be successful. On social networks, two-way communication is required, not just the typical broadcast approach that most people are used to. These habits and techniques do not come naturally to entrepreneurs, salespeople, or customer service representatives steeped in more traditional ways.

I've talked with people all over the world who are struggling to adapt to these new rules. The process often starts when someone realizes how severely the conventional old methods can handicap their business and career. But since you've read this far in the book, you know that already.

Sometimes people tell me they fear being overwhelmed. There is just too much involved with all this social stuff, too many new and unfamiliar ideas. But here's the good news: You can adapt to the new rules gradually. I don't expect you to stop doing what you've been doing for a decade and do only new things. No, rather you can implement these ideas in bits and pieces! You can focus on Twitter first, perhaps, and then turn to creating videos and posting them to YouTube.

> There's no better calling card than a virtual one.

Once you start to develop your personal brand on social media, you're taking the first step toward building an asset that can help you for the rest of your life. Really! In this chapter I'll introduce you to people like Summer Land, who got a book deal because of her personal brand, and Smit Patel, whose social media participation scored him an internship in Silicon Valley. If you build your social media presence now, you'll have an advantage the next time you need to do a job search or when you're ready to start a new business.

Why Social Networking Is Like Exercise

The second most common question I get asked at my talks is: "How do you find the time to do all this social networking stuff?" People want to know how to find the time to blog, tweet, produce videos, and create valuable online content. (The number one question I get during Q&A is: "What is the return on investment [ROI] of social networking?" But that's another story.)

I've found that finding the time to participate in social media is much like exercise; you need to make it an important part of your life. If it is important to you, you don't even think about it anymore. It just is.

You have a choice. You can choose to exercise regularly in order to stay fit. The most effective way is when exercise becomes part of your routine. Some people like fitness clubs. Others enjoy running outdoors or dancing or kickboxing. But in all cases, success comes from making it an important part of your daily life.

I like to mix it up. Some days I practice yoga, and other days I lift weights. I also do good old push-ups, pull-ups, and sit-ups. Once a week I swim a mile and a half. I always get up early, around 4:00 most mornings, and do much of my training in the family room while watching recordings of the late-night television shows from the evening before. I don't even think about finding the time, because it's a very important part of my life.

The situation is no different with participating in social networks and creating online content—it becomes part of your life. In my case, I do about 100 blog posts a year and maybe 20 videos. I comment on hundreds of blogs.

Most years I write a free e-book. And I'm on forums, chat rooms, Instagram, Foursquare, Twitter, Facebook, LinkedIn, and others.

Many people are surprised when I say that I probably spend about six hours a week on social media—about the same amount of time I spend exercising. I don't even think about it. It's important, so I do it. And I can't really say how I fit it in. It's mainly in microbursts of one or five minutes throughout the day.

I recommend that you don't even try to find the time to create content and participate in social media. You'll fail, just like trying to find the time to exercise leads to failure and wasted money on health club memberships.

Instead, make exercise and social media important parts of your life. If you still cannot fit exercise and social media into your life, cut out television completely. You will be amazed at how much time you will free up!

People You Know

Why even bother with your personal brand? Some people tell me they just don't want to get active on social networks. Even after I tell stories like those found in this book, they're still skeptical about whether a blog, YouTube channel, LinkedIn profile, or Twitter feed can help them.

You need a presence on social networks because we all prefer to do business with people we know. When somebody can instantly find out a little about you on a social network or perhaps read your thoughts in a blog post you wrote, then you're not a complete stranger.

If you have great content, people will find you and interact with you. And this will drive familiarity. As people do their research, they will find others with expertise in the subject they are interested in—much as I did when I was planning my visit to Bangkok. You develop a virtual relationship with those who deliver valuable information—just like Richard Barrow does for those visiting Thailand. That relationship means you're already on the road to making a sale, getting a job, starting a business, or helping a customer succeed.

You're Already Online

Go to your favorite search engine and enter your name together with the name of your current employer. If you've recently left your job, Google your name and that of your most recent employer. If you're a student, then try it with your name and the name of your school.

This is what many people do to learn more about you. Employers Google people who apply for jobs. Buyers Google the salesperson they're assigned. If you're seeking funding for your start-up, there's no doubt that venture capitalists will Google you. Heck, many people study Google results before agreeing to a first date!

Whatever comes up is your personal brand. If you're publishing great content online, then congratulations, because you've got a great personal brand! If you're publishing nothing, then you're leaving your personal brand to others who create content about you (like that arrest record from a wild night when you were in college). And if you're publishing lousy information on the web, then you're creating a lousy personal brand.

No matter what business you're in or what job function you have, you need to take control of your personal brand by jumping into social media.

The Sharing More Than Selling Rule

When I speak with people at conferences, they most frequently ask me exactly how to use social networking feeds such as Twitter, Instagram, LinkedIn, and Facebook to communicate effectively as a sales tool. While most people recognize that social networks are a great place to share content, to interact with others, and to listen in on what's happening, they also sense that social networks can be a way to get the word out about themselves and their businesses as well.

While there is no right or wrong when it comes to content creation and sharing (as you've learned throughout this book), as I review people's business-related social streams I find way too much selling going on. Too many companies are shouting into the social world.

> **Most people, especially those new to a social network, don't share and engage enough. They're too busy selling.**

Therefore, I suggest a guideline may be helpful as a way to think about how you can use the various social networks to educate and inform, and yes, also to sell. I'd suggest you should be doing 85 percent sharing and engaging, 10 percent publishing original content, and only 5 percent or less about what you are trying to promote.

Do 85 Percent Sharing and Engaging

Sharing and engaging include such things as commenting on someone else's blog or Facebook post, quoting a tweet and adding your take, or responding to somebody who has said something that interests you. You can also share an interesting blog post or news report with your network.

I'd say you should be doing this with at least 85 percent of your social interactions, but it could be much more. Since sharing is the easiest aspect of social networking, it shouldn't take much for you to do more of it.

Make 10 Percent Original Content

I'd recommend that one out of 10 of your social interactions be publishing something original. You can share a photo you shot, write a blog post, compose a tweet about something that interests your marketplace, or publish a video. The more helpful this content is to your buyer personas, the better.

Many people worry about social networks as a tool of business because they think that everything they do will have to be new content. But I suggest only 10 percent needs to be!

Only 5 Percent or Less Should Be a Promotion about What You Do

One out of 20 interactions (or fewer) can be something that you want to promote to your audience. This is when you can share a new product your company offers, a special discount for social followers, or other content of a promotional nature.

Most people sell way too much, and as such their social feeds don't have much interaction. People just don't want to be sold to. However, if you are helpful, engaging, and responsive on your social feeds, then you build an audience of people who want to hear from you and who will be receptive to learning more about what you and your organization do.

Social media is about engagement. Sure, it is also a tool for selling, but you need to educate and inform more than you sell.

Building a Fan Base One Download at a Time

When the Electronic Dance Music (EDM) artist Pretty Lights dropped his new album *A Color Map of the Sun* in 2013, customers could purchase it from online downloading services, web retailers, or record outlets. But another way to get it cost nothing: He gave it away free at his site.

Here's what Pretty Lights said that morning. "*A Color Map of the Sun* has now officially been released! If you can, I encourage you to purchase a copy of the album digitally in iTunes or physically through Pretty Lights at prettylightsmusic.com, or at a local record store, or download it at no cost below. Thank you to everyone who has supported PL by purchasing a copy of this record. I hope it is enjoyed!!! To see how this unique album was created, watch 'The Making of' documentary."

So why make it available for nothing? To gain exposure and build a fan base, of course! If I recommended it, you probably wouldn't go out and buy the album. If you heard a track in a dance club, you probably wouldn't buy the album. But you just might take a chance to download it for free and give it a listen. (And you should.)

And then maybe, like me, you'd end up buying a ticket to one of his live shows. I caught Pretty Lights in Baltimore, and it was a fun show with excellent music, interesting people, and a great light show.

And then maybe you'd become a fan and talk Pretty Lights up on social media like I did.

All because of a free download.

But it's not just EDM artists who can use this technique to generate attention. You can too. And you can achieve your goals as a result. Now we'll take a closer look at how you can enhance your own online presence.

Don't Hide in the Shadows

I'm amazed when someone writes a terrific blog, has a great Twitter feed, or has a wonderful presence on a social networking site, but fails to effectively say who they are. Don't they want to stand out from the crowd? Your blog's "about" page, your Twitter bio, your LinkedIn profile, and the other places you interact are great opportunities to say who you are. This is an essential element of personal branding. Don't ignore the opportunity to tell the world about yourself.

As a way to introduce this important concept, let's turn our attention to your Twitter profile. While each social network is different, the concepts of personal branding are similar and can be carried over from one network to another.

Most Twitter profiles don't say enough, and most have lousy design. While that's fine if you're just communicating with friends, if you're using your Twitter feed for your business, you need to pay attention. When you first set up your Twitter account, you have choices. And after you've set up the account, you can make these changes to any aspect of your profile at any time (except your Twitter ID—that's fixed, so be careful what you choose).

Twitter ID: (Mine is @dmscott.) Choose an appropriate ID. Try to have a Twitter ID that resembles your name so when people see you pop up in their feed they know who you are. Because there are hundreds of millions of people on Twitter, you are unlikely to get your first choice (or second or third for that matter), so you might need to add a number to the letters. Try to avoid cute Twitter IDs, like @KittyCatGurl21, or those referencing your hobbies, such as @SurferDude246, unless your hobby is also your business.

Name: (Mine is David Meerman Scott.) Use your real name. Don't just default to your user ID, which so many people seem to do. And don't just use a nickname like Pookie. You can put your nickname in quotation marks inside your real name if you want to. If you really care about your personal brand, you'll want people to know who you really are.

Location: (Mine is Boston, MA.) Use the town or nearest city that makes sense for you. While I actually live in one of the Boston suburbs, my business is global so I use Boston as my location. Saying something cute like "Earth" or "somewhere in Canada" turns people off who don't know you. Besides, the location is a good way to make local contacts.

Web: (My URL is www.davidmeermanscott.com.) If you have a blog or site, put the URL here. Or maybe your profile on a company website makes sense for you. This should be somewhere people can go to learn more about you. If you don't have a blog or site, I recommend that you create a public Google profile (profiles.google.com) with your contact information, and link to that. You can also leave the web link blank if you want, but that says to people that you don't want to be contacted or have people learn more about you.

Bio: As I write this, mine is "Marketing & Sales Strategist, keynote speaker, and bestselling author of 9 books including *The New Rules of Marketing & PR* and *Newsjacking*." This is where you say something about yourself. You get only 160 characters. As a component of personal branding, this is a critical section. Don't leave it blank. And don't make a mini-resume from a laundry list of attributes like this: "father, husband, surfer, economics major, world traveler, marketer, and rock star wannabe." (I confess, that would be my list.) I see this sort of thing all the time, and it is not good for personal branding because you don't really focus on your particular expertise. Try to be descriptive. And try to be specific.

Background image: Twitter provides an opportunity to add a background image to your Twitter page. The default background is much like PowerPoint when it is first opened—it's a default. Twitter has some choices, but many people use them, so you will not be unique. Shoot a custom photo to really shine. I use a close-up image of a nifty old typewriter keyboard. It's my personal brand on Twitter.

Header image: Your personal brand on Twitter can also include a header photo for your profile, which serves as a background for your bio. A header photo is a great way to show your personal brand, but don't try to sell. Many salespeople add an advertising message to this real estate, but I think that's a mistake and recommend resisting this tendency. Adding your messages or heavy-handed branding detracts. Sure, I could have used an image of, say, all my book covers for my banner. Instead I chose an image I really like of me onstage at a speaking gig. Your header photo will show up on your Twitter web page as well as on mobile devices.

Make it public: If you are using Twitter for your business, it's important to not protect your tweets. When you sign up for Twitter, you have the option to keep your tweets public (the default account setting, which is what I recommend) or to protect your tweets. Accounts with protected tweets require manual approval of each and every person who may view the account's tweets—not a good idea if you want to promote your personal brand.

These choices are really easy to set up, but they're very important for your personal brand. If you are on Twitter, take the time to make some changes today.

The same ideas apply on other social networking sites like Facebook and LinkedIn, so don't forget to consider carefully your personal branding on those sites as well.

You Are Not a Cat

If you care about your personal brand, you should use a representative photo of you on social networks. If you don't upload a photo, you'll just be assigned the default by the social network, which makes it appear as if you are hiding. The default on LinkedIn is a creepy sort of shadow image of a person, and the default on Twitter is the image of an egg. The photo you choose to represent you says a great deal about who you are as an individual. (Are you an egg?)

Some people use a cartoon avatar to represent themselves. While that's okay for some, I do think it communicates that the person doesn't like his or her real self for some reason. I definitely urge you to avoid using stand-ins for your photo. I don't think you should use your company logo instead of your photo on your personal social networks. I also suggest that you avoid the random images that many people seem to favor. You know, things like their cat. Or Bart Simpson. Or a snowboard. If you use these sorts of images rather than your photo, you're limiting what you want people to think of you.

Photos appear very tiny on many social networks—like a postage stamp—so use a close-up. If you use a full view of yourself, then you will appear like a stick figure. Remember that your photo conveys a very important first impression when people see your profile for the first time.

There are many choices when it comes to a photo to use. You can use a casual shot taken by a friend. This is a great option for many people. But there are many different approaches, and each says something important about you. Are you in a casual setting, such as at a restaurant? Or someplace more formal, like an office? What are you wearing? A hat? Is it a casual shot of you taken on a vacation with a beer in your hand? Or a formal head-and-shoulders shot in business attire taken by a professional photographer? Smile, or no smile? How close do you crop?

While there is no absolute right or wrong about photos in social media, do keep in mind that each of these choices says a great deal about you.

Building a Following

I have more than 120,000 Twitter followers, and many people ask me the secret to building such a following.

> The secret to building a following on social networks is that there is no secret. You must participate.

To reach more than 100,000 followers, you need to do 10,000 things to improve your personal brand, and each of the small things you do, on average, needs to gain you a dozen or so new followers. (Unless you are someone who is already famous like Howard Stern. He had 200,000 followers a few weeks after he jumped on Twitter. He now has 1.65 million followers.)

I started my @dmscott Twitter feed with zero followers in early 2008. When I started, I was a newbie just like everyone else. But slowly I added a few followers here and a few followers there. I'd notice that when I tweeted something that was shared widely, I got a bunch of new followers. When I deliver a talk at a live event, I put my Twitter ID on all my slides and I always get new followers. But each time it's only a few new people. Getting a large following just takes time.

Here is what I've done to drive followers since I joined Twitter in March 2008:

- Sent 15,268 tweets
- Written 835 blog posts
- Published six books
- Released seven free e-books
- Delivered 336 in-person talks in 31 different countries and on all seven continents
- Spoken on (wild guess) 120 webinars
- Been a guest on (another guess) 500 podcasts and radio shows

- Sat for something like 300 interviews with print and broadcast media
- Been in roughly 325 videos uploaded to my YouTube channel, my Vimeo channel, and other people's channels
- Hung out at (probably) 50 tweetups and other informal gatherings
- Engaged thousands of people via social networks, email, telephone, over coffee, and while sharing a pint of beer
- Gotten retweeted by Howard Stern once!
- Asked President Obama a question on a Twitter chat once which he answered live on television!
- Interviewed the CEO of General Motors once!
- Shared the stage with Cyndi Lauper once!
- Had a private dinner with President Fernandez of the Dominican Republic in his palace to discuss social media once!
- Appeared on MSNBC to discuss my favorite band, the Grateful Dead, once!

I say these things not to brag, but rather to point out that a strong social following takes time to develop.

But once you do have followers, be it 100 or 100,000, you have an enormously important asset that will help you in your career and in your business.

Tweeting Yourself into a Job

Smit Patel, a student at Suffolk University double majoring in information systems and marketing, has accomplished more before he can legally drink in his home state of Massachusetts than most businesspeople do in a decade. Patel has relied on social networking to land prestigious internships at companies in Silicon Valley and in Boston. He's also the co-founder of SayHelloThere, an online tool to create video resumes, and was named a "Boston student entrepreneur to keep your eye on" by BostInno.

"Most of my peers and my friends don't have an online presence," Patel says. "A few use Twitter, but they're just tweeting personal stuff. They rely on either their school's career center or family connections to get internships, and most of them tell me how much they hate being an intern since they learn very little information except the location of the office copy machine. The most important thing they need is an online presence, but most don't have one."

Using his @thesmitpatel Twitter feed, Patel actively interacts with people who interest him. "I tweet a lot about marketing start-ups," he says. "Currently, I'm interested in 'inbound Me generation' customer acquisitions, so I engage with a lot of people and brands to see what I can learn from them. I follow influencers in the fields of marketing and start-ups. When reaching out to them I say, 'Hey, I follow you on Twitter' or 'We just had a Twitter conversation last week, so I just thought I'd email you.'"

When people discover they are mentioned in a tweet written by someone they don't know, most will check out the author's Twitter profile and scan a few recent tweets to learn a little about this person. With Twitter's limit of only 160 characters for a bio (plus location and website link), brevity is required.

Patel's Twitter bio reads: "Co-Founder @sayhellothere—the easiest way to create video resumes. Believe in the power of marketing, hustle and millennials. And, I love onions. Boston. smitpatel.com." Many people also check out the number of Twitter followers someone has; Patel has more than 2,000 followers, a very respectable number for anyone, let alone a university student. His powerful personal brand on Twitter and other social networks means that the people he tweets pay attention.

Not long ago Patel decided he wanted to intern at a company in Silicon Valley during the summer. Rather than plastering companies with CVs like everybody else, he simply used his established social network. "The founder of Flightfox, a company I worked for during the summer of 2012, referred me to the founder of ScriptRock," Patel says. "They checked out my blog and my online presence, and then they reached out to me to say that they wanted me to intern at their company. I went out to Silicon Valley in the summer of 2013 to work there."

Patel says he learned about personal branding and social networks on his own because there was nothing at the school career center or in his classes to prepare him. "I'm taking a couple of marketing classes and haven't learned anything about this," he says. "Kids my age are paying a lot of money for a university education and they're not learning the things that will get them hired."

It's not just university students looking for a plum internship who can make use of an excellent personal brand on the social networks. Entrepreneurs, business owners, salespeople, and customer service representatives all need to pay attention to how the world sees them.

Inbound Job Search

I've been fired three times during my career and I'm damn proud of it. The most recent time I lost my job was in 2002 because the company was acquired and my new bosses decided that I didn't have a future in the combined organization.

So what did I do when I was out on the street? I did what everybody does when faced with such a situation—I updated my CV. I put all the stuff that I thought was important into a Microsoft Word document and I sent it around to people I knew. I was doing outbound marketing to try to find a job in 2002 and it was brutal. I had to interrupt my friends. I had to interrupt my parents' friends. I had to interrupt my friends' friends and say, "I'm looking for a job, so please look at my resume and send it to anybody who you think might be interested in me."

Fortunately, back in 2002 instead of finding a traditional job, I became an independent marketing and sales strategist and since then have had a blast. I feel like I've never worked a day since 2002.

Fast forward to today. I see people doing the exact same thing I was doing in 2002; however, they are looking for jobs mostly using social networks, especially LinkedIn. People I haven't spoken with for a really long time finally reach out to me on LinkedIn and want to connect. I reply, "Cool, haven't heard from you in ages. What's going on?" and when they say, "I'm looking for a job," I think, "Gee, why didn't you reach out to me a really long time ago?" LinkedIn and email are great tools, but the way most people use them to find a job is all about interruption. They contact people when they want something rather than when they have something.

> You have to stop thinking like an advertiser of a product and start thinking like a publisher of information.

If you're looking for a new job, create information that people want. Create an online presence that people are eager to consume. Establish a virtual front door that people will happily link to—one that employers will find. The new rules of finding a job require you to share your knowledge and expertise with a world that is looking for what you have to offer.

There is such a huge opportunity. Instead of just going social when you need something, you should already be publishing really great content, whether it's blog posts or YouTube videos or tweets. If you get it out there and show us who you are, people will be eager to hire you! Hiring managers will find you when they are looking for somebody with your skills and expertise. If you do find yourself on the job market, you're already networking with people, so all you need to do is say you're looking for a new gig and send links to your blog or Twitter feed. These will show that you're doing interesting things and would be valuable for an organization to hire. If you decide to go out on your own and start your own company, your social network will serve as your calling card for anybody that you're trying to reach.

Achieving Your Dreams

Having a strong presence in social media helps in all kinds of ways, not just finding a new job. Your personal brand is one of your most valuable assets and can help you sell anything.

I met Summer Land at a speaking gig in Australia. She's a writer who wanted a major publisher to take on her memoir, and she sought out my advice. I've heard this request before—hundreds of times. Many people want to know how to get published, and, because I've written 10 of my own books and have produced seven others, they quiz me about what it takes.

My first hardcover book was self-published. Obviously there are many routes to publish your work, and working with a major publisher is not the only way. You can self-publish in either the printed book or the e-book format, or you can go with a small publisher, a university press, or a major international publisher. I've published using all of these routes. Clearly there are many ways to get your work into the marketplace.

Since Land wanted a major publishing house to release her memoir, I gave her the steps to get a book deal. While many people want to talk about it, very few people want to know the difficult truth of what it takes to get a book contract: hard work. Very few people are also willing to make the effort. I estimate less than 1 percent of the people I speak to about this are willing to do the hard work required to get published by a well-known publisher.

Here is a greatly simplified version of the four steps required, which I shared with Land.

I must already assume you can write and are a good storyteller.

1. You must publish yourself first. Unless you are already famous and want to write your memoirs—being an ex-president of the United States wouldn't be bad—no publisher will take you on. You need to publish your work yourself in a blog or an e-book that you give away so you can introduce people to your work.
2. You have to build an audience. You need to get your stuff out there and get people interested. Your platform might be through social networking, blogs, or traditional ways such as appearing on television. This takes a lot of hard work.
3. You get your fans to help you. You create content that's worthy of being shared. You figure out clever ways to get your fans to spread the word for you.
4. Then you take your success to publishers. Believe me, if you've built an audience of people who love your work and share it and you can show that success, publishers will be eager to work with you and to cut a book deal.

Lisa Genova followed this route. She used social media to turn *Still Alice*, a book she published herself, into a deal for just over half a million dollars with Simon & Schuster. She made that edition into a *New York Times* bestseller and *Still Alice* was made into a film for which Julianne Moore won the Academy Award for best actress and Genova joined her on the red carpet, all through social networking.

I got my first book deal with John Wiley & Sons because I wrote a free e-book that I published on my blog. *The New Rules of PR* had 50,000 downloads in the first month.

I gave Land this advice and figured I'd never hear from her again. I was wrong. Land launched a site to support her writing efforts. It's well designed and showcases her nicely. She blogs regularly. She wrote a free e-book that she published on her site. She built momentum by creating a Facebook event to promote the e-book launch among her friends, which 1,124 people attended. Then she used social media to engage her readers and grow her audience of followers. And doing all this transformed her personal brand.

This led directly to a book deal from Hardie Grant Books, an Australian publisher. Just two years after giving Land my advice, I was reading her hardcover book, *Summerlandish: Do as I Say, Not as I Did*, a hilarious memoir of a 25-year-old "average American girl" growing up in Gainesville, Florida, the outspoken and outrageous child of an alternative single mom.

"Because I am incredibly impatient and like for things to happen overnight, I didn't want to send the standard query letter and wait," Land says. "I decided to release an e-book to drum up a following and hopefully have publishers come to me. I gave it away for free, no email required."

Land says that although a lot of people did download her e-book, she didn't gain thousands of Twitter followers or Facebook fans, and publishers weren't knocking down her door. "I did, however, gain a steady readership of my blog and I got a call from an agency in Los Angeles who were interested in the TV rights to my future book," she says. "This was amazing, but I didn't want to lose sight of my first goal, which was to publish my book."

Land attended the Sydney Writers' Festival. "At their event, 'So You Think You Can Write,' I decided to pitch my book to a panel of publishers who were there to provide constructive criticism," she says. "When I pitched, I didn't just tell them what it was about. I explained who would buy it. I also told them about my download numbers. Luckily for me, they said really positive things!"

As soon as the event was over, she was approached by an editor from Hardie Grant. They went through the typical author–publisher dance, which resulted in a contract, and a year later the book on the shelves.

"It was important for me to remember what I ultimately wanted to achieve from my book," Land says. "My main goal of writing my memoir, *Summerlandish*, was to make people laugh, and provoke the reaction, 'Me too!' I share stories from my life that are awkward, embarrassing, outlandish, and sometimes mortifying. However, I believe everyone can relate to it. No one escaped childhood unscathed, and I think we're all getting over our miserable high school years one glass of wine at a time. If this book can make someone laugh while on vacation or on their morning commute, I'll be forever happy. I think by exploring and articulating the things that most people are afraid to talk about, we will feel better about ourselves."

Land's book certainly made me laugh. And it did something else as well. It contributed toward my own personal fulfillment. My work is largely motivated by a desire to help others achieve their dreams, even if only in a small way; it's one of the most rewarding aspects about what I do for a living. All I do is provide an idea, or a spark, or a little motivation to those who read my books or my blog, or hear me speak. Then those people do the hard work required to market and sell their business or their idea. When I learn that Land or someone else has achieved success as a result of something I suggested, it makes my day (or my week).

It's great that Land attended one of my talks in Sydney, Australia, a few years ago. It's terrific that she approached me to get some ideas about how to get her book in front of publishers. But more than most people, Land actually took the advice and made a success. She did the hard work. She achieved her dreams.

So can you. And your personal brand on the social networks is a critical component.

Manage Your Fear

As I travel the world evangelizing the ideas of real-time sales and service and how you can become more social to achieve your dreams, I hear from people that the biggest barrier is fear. Most people don't actually admit to me that they are fearful of embarking on this new path, but I can tell based on what they choose to tell me as well as their body language when doing so. Frequently people make excuses about why they can't get social and go real time. But what's really at work is fear.

We all face fear in our professional and personal lives. Fear of the strange, of the new, of the untested. We fear bucking the trend and going against the accepted. It's a natural human response.

To truly achieve greatness in the form of personal fulfillment, you must act. That might mean you are a pioneer, a rebel, an instigator. You may need to challenge the status quo and make a difference in the world.

Yes, you might fail. You could even fail spectacularly.

But a fear of failure is not a reason to sit in front of the television all evening instead of working on that project that's burning away in your gut. You need to make a decision right now to engage in social networks and real-time communications. You need to commit to make it happen.

When you are reluctant, instead of not starting at all or quitting before you give it a chance, manage your fear. Analyze your hesitancy. Why are you fearful?

The Many Manifestations of Fear

- Fear of looking silly
- Fear that if you put yourself out there, acting on your dream, people will say negative things about you
- Fear that if you don't have an MBA or whatever degree is deemed important to the gatekeepers in your world, you don't have the qualification to act

- Fear that makes you sell your products and services in the way that you've always done (like cold calling)
- Fear that giving away your best content for free won't benefit you
- Fear that your competitors know more than you do, resulting in you copying their moves
- Fear that something won't work in your industry, or your geography, or your company, or with your customers

You need to develop a new mind-set. I've talked with people all over the world who are struggling. They tell me the road to success often starts with understanding just how severely conventional methods can handicap your business, your career, and your personal life.

What a World We Live In!

That device in your pocket? What was science fiction just a few years ago is science fact today!

How incredible that you can instantly create a video stream on a service like Periscope and reach thousands of interested people who pay attention to what you are broadcasting. At no cost!

Or you can have a two-way video conversation with a potential customer on the other side of the planet with a service like Skype. For free!

Your mobile device is much more powerful than what the creators of *The Jetsons* imagined.

Each of us has the ability to reach almost any human on the planet in real time. You can publish content—a blog post, video, infographic, photo—for free to reach potential customers who will be eager to do business with you.

Getting attention a few decades ago was hard work.

> Now is the best time to grow a business in human history.

We're living in a time when we can reach the world directly. There is a tremendous opportunity right now to reach people by publishing great stuff that brands us as leaders. Now we can create videos, tell stories, interact with people, and develop interesting information that people want to consume and that they are eager to share with their friends, families, and colleagues.

There's a new world—are you part of it?

If not now, when?

Now is a terrific time to start. It is not too late. If you've got something to say, then say it.

What are you waiting for?

You are in charge of your own success.

Now it's your turn. You can do it. It doesn't matter what line of work you're in or what group of buyers you're trying to reach or what you want to accomplish.

If you're like many people I meet, you have colleagues or family members who will argue with you. They will say you're not up to it or your ideas won't work.

But you know they're wrong, because you've managed your fear. Go on. Get out there and make it happen!

Oh, and when you achieve a success similar to those I profile in this book, please let me know. I'm always looking for new examples to share!

Now that we've looked at a few people who have achieved success by getting social and I've shared my thoughts on how you can do the same, let's move on to how your entire organization can communicate in real time and participate in social media to grow business and keep customers happy.

10 Your Social Company

Y ou've read in these pages how organizations communicate with customers to drive agile sales responses and implement real-time customer service. In this chapter we will explore how companies can integrate social communications tools into their business and their employees' daily work. At smaller organizations or newly founded start-ups, designing and instituting the new system happens fairly smoothly. They avoid the problems associated with entrenched processes, systems, and the established corporate mind-sets that hinder older and larger organizations. If you're starting with the new rules of sales and service, your business will operate far more easily if you can avoid dealing with "we don't do it that way" baggage.

But what if you're inside a large, established, successful organization with existing strategies and tactics? How do you build agile social selling and customer communications into your business?

Building the Social Selling Process into a Large Organization

Matt Petitjean is vice president of marketing at ADP, Inc., a large provider of business processing, payroll systems, and cloud-based solutions to employers around the world. Besides marketing, Petitjean is also responsible for social selling at ADP. "My charter is enabling the sales force with social tools and techniques," he says. "We have a big funnel to generate sales leads, and no matter where you interact with the prospect—a trade show, a brand advertisement, a web search, or social media—our efforts are all coordinated, centered, and focused on helping move these contacts through the funnel."

ADP is a large and successful company with more than 5,000 salespeople located around the world. This makes it a challenge for Petitjean to implement strategies that might appear to involve additional work for the salespeople and their managers. Social media savvy and experience are among the most valued skills when hiring candidates for new rep positions. This previous experience can be easily augmented with in-house rep training. Veteran salespeople and their managers, however, need to be educated to understand how social media can benefit them and help them sell more efficiently. "To be successful, you train people in a way that makes this a part of their job," he says. "It doesn't become a choice of 'Do I do social, or do I do something else?' They need to ask, 'How do I work this into my selling process?' and 'How can I then augment my selling process with these social techniques?'"

Petitjean says there are four important components to the social selling process. He articulates his strategy throughout the organization using this four-part model: tools, communications, training, and measurement.

The first quadrant is the tools. "This could be tools within LinkedIn to help salespeople see who they are connected to," he explains. "We tell them, 'If you're going to have a phone conversation, a sales pitch, or an executive overview session with someone, look at their LinkedIn profile first; it's a very simple thing to do.' We suggest they look at their company's LinkedIn profile as well, to better understand the hot topics they're dealing with."

Besides social networks like Twitter and LinkedIn, other tools help with more specific sales tasks, such as keeping track of trigger events. As an example, Petitjean offers this scenario: "If I sold payroll to a customer, and that person changed jobs from Company A to Company B, I would want to send a note to that person saying, 'Hey, I just saw that you moved companies. I'm not sure who you're using for payroll, but if there's anything I can do, please feel free to reach out to me.'" A trigger event could be a company going public or acquiring another firm. Or it could be a company being acquired. Finding those trigger events in social media tends to be easy. Many of the social tools used by ADP are free, and many salespeople were already using some of them, especially LinkedIn. However, other tools, such as those from the Salesforce.com network—for example, Radian6 and Buddy Media—are also either used centrally by ADP or purchased and deployed to the salespeople.

ADP also uses a social media database that includes a large collection of content ready to be used by its salespeople. "We provide legally approved, marketing-approved tweets, LinkedIn updates, status updates, success stories, things like that. These are available in a database that is segmented to align with our sales population," Petitjean says. "So if you're selling large solutions to enterprise-size companies, you use different types of social media nuggets than if you're in small business sales, or if you're selling insurance, or if you're selling retirement."

The second quadrant in the ADP social selling strategy is communications. Petitjean communicates to thousands of salespeople, providing ready-to-use content. Because he is in charge of both social selling at ADP as well as marketing, he can align the content with the way that people sell. "We make it really, really easy," he says. "A rep can just retweet what we say. You know it's approved, and you're helping the brand because you amplify the message. That's the whole point. We have 5,000 or 6,000 salespeople; they should help us amplify the marketing message, just like they help the brand every time they hand someone a business card or show up with a printed piece. You can do the same thing with social, so don't feel compelled to write your own content; feel free to share what we're sharing."

The third quadrant is training the ADP sales teams so they are able to make use of the company-provided social tools and content. "Training ranges from introductory uses and boot camp training to certifications," Petitjean says. Some training is delivered in person and can be customized, while other sessions are delivered via the web. Training basics start with setting up a Twitter profile, finding things to tweet, and suggestions for using LinkedIn more effectively. They also provide information about why salespeople should be active on social networks and the long-term benefits for sales.

Petitjean says the way they suggest sharing content can also serve to train salespeople. "We explain the tools and tips and new things that are out there," he says. "We show them a blog article about innovation and how to share it. Or we suggest they send a tweet with a link to the article."

The final quadrant in the ADP social selling model is measuring and monitoring. While the marketing team pays close attention to what's being said about the company as it affects the overall brand, it's important to monitor agile sales strategies. "If a rep had some very, very positive interaction with a number of clients, I might want to contact someone to say, 'Hey, John Miller just shared this really great piece of content, and he's getting lots of engagement,'" Petitjean suggests. "It informs what kind of content we should be delivering to the sales force, but it also indicates how other people may want to interact with their clients."

The team also monitors public social networks for things that might negatively impact ADP. "After we started monitoring, we had to ask ourselves what happens when something goes wrong," Petitjean says. "So we built escalation and playbook processes. A one-off comment by one salesperson, whether it's a picture or a video or even just a text to a link, has the potential to do damage to the brand." An important aspect of monitoring the public social feeds of employees is a governance policy that was created to define what's appropriate to say on social networks and what's not. The governance team includes people representing products, sales, service, human resources (HR), legal, and global security.

The ADP social selling model had been used for two years before I had an opportunity to speak with Matt Petitjean, so they've had an opportunity to measure the results. "We've looked at a group of sales associates who used social, versus a control group who didn't," Petitjean says. "It was fair; we didn't stack the deck to include only the star performers in social media. We also compared these results to the ADP sales organization as a whole. Using key performance indicators important to ADP—which are the same indicators any sales force would reference—we found that the group that incorporated social media in their work consistently outperformed the control group, as well as the sales organization as a whole."

Rolling out social selling to a sales organization of more than 5,000 professionals isn't easy, yet Petitjean's measurable success at ADP shows that if you have a plan and there's commitment throughout the organization, you can be more successful with social selling.

Hiring for Social Success

The old model of a successful salesperson was somebody who was very diligent at dialing for dollars. That person had to be tenacious and able to tolerate many people saying "no" (some with rudeness). With the new approaches of consultative selling, agile sales, and real-time engagement, sales managers need to look for a new set of skills when hiring salespeople.

"Our best people get on the phones and build trust as step one," says HubSpot's Mark Roberge, who has hired hundreds of salespeople. "And there's a range of ways one can build trust. A good doctor builds trust when you walk into his office. You see his diploma on the wall, and if he's skilled he immediately gives you his complete attention. A salesperson can build trust from having a great LinkedIn profile, asking smart questions, making observations about the business, or giving someone a free information tip. And once the salesperson has the client's trust, the next step is to figure out what's going through the client's head, what's their strategy, what are their priorities, what are their goals. It's much more about diagnosing and prescribing and much less about pitching and closing."

So when hiring salespeople, what do you look for in order to differentiate those who act like good doctors? "A couple of decades ago, it was someone who was just smart enough to be able to memorize the 10-page sales playbook and display the aggressiveness of a varsity football captain. This was someone who could get pummeled to the ground 10 times but never failed to get up, and worked tirelessly to make it happen," Roberge says. "We've moved away from that. I've had management consultants come onboard as salespeople. I've had MBAs come onboard. I've had engineers come onboard. They have a higher degree of business acumen. They have a quicker learning curve. They have a higher level of intelligence. And they can come near the status of a consultant or advisor with the buyers that they are speaking to."

The other significant attributes of a successful salesperson are social media skills and an existing network of contacts. A hiring manager in 1980 might have asked sales candidates about their Rolodexes and how many people they knew in the sales territory. Now the hiring manager can check out the potential employee on LinkedIn and Twitter, and can see if the person maintains a blog or has a YouTube channel. These personal branding attributes are important in today's selling because they are essential sales tools, and because they are the things a potential buyer will look at when a salesperson makes contact. So if you're hiring salespeople or customer service staff, it's very easy to instantly gauge job candidates' connections before they are invited in for an interview.

Greg Alexander from Sales Benchmark Index says a person's network of online contacts is a new set of competencies that should be considered during the hiring process. He calls this someone's social personal branding: the ability to create and perpetuate a digital brand that portrays expertise. "If you are a salesperson trying to open up a new account, expect the decision maker at that potential new client to Google you before the initial appointment. What's your online brand? Previously you didn't have to care about that. Why? The way you made a first impression years ago was you wore a blue suit, white shirt, and red tie; you shined your shoes, brushed your teeth, and combed your hair, and you had a shave. You had a firm handshake, and you looked somebody in their eyes, and this made your first impression. That first impression today now happens online. What's your equivalent of all that? It's a LinkedIn profile typically. That's a new competency."

Because of that new competency, Roberge and Alexander advocate that organizations clearly define that making a great first impression online should be a requirement when hiring salespeople. What social personal branding attributes should you research before considering someone for a position? Depending on the type of company, you should consider LinkedIn connections, Twitter followers, content creation via social platforms like blogs and YouTube, and more. If you run an existing sales team, you might benchmark a prospective new employee's social personal brand against the salespeople who have achieved the greatest success through social selling.

"Years ago," Alexander reflects, "when being interviewed for a sales position, the candidate would say, 'I've been in this territory for 10 years, and I've called on this account, that account, and that account.' But there was really no way for the interviewer to verify that. Today a sales manager just goes to the person's LinkedIn network and looks over their connections and checks out their social personal branding."

Alexander says social personal branding is so critical today because of the nature of sales referrals. Because of this, it is essential to hire people with the largest potential referral networks already in place.

"Think about the old ways we used to generate referrals," Alexander says. "You would go to a trade show, you would meet somebody, and you would swap business cards. But that offline activity didn't scale, because if you hand me your business card, I just know you. Once that activity gets moved online through a network like LinkedIn, then when you hand me your business card, we connect online too and I now know how to connect to everybody that you know. I can peek into your network. That takes a single connection and turns it into thousands of connections. Yes, I could be irresponsible and abuse that privilege, or I can be respectful and use that to my advantage. There's a phrase that we use called 'social debt.' This means, if I am a valuable resource for a prospect, and I give and give and give, at some point I'm going to have earned the right to ask for a favor. I might say, 'Hey, Joe, I noticed in your network that you know Mike Smith, who works at this company. We do work for companies like that. Mike might be experiencing these problems. We have expertise in these areas, and we would like to meet him. Would you be kind enough to provide an introduction?' That's social referral generation. That's a whole new set of skills required by salespeople. The organizations that are doing that well are producing phenomenal sales results."

As critical new skills become important in the new social selling model, you need to ensure you're hiring the right people. Over time, you might need to consider if your existing people are right for the new realities. Are they able to adapt? What about the team that manages the salespeople? Are your sales leaders the right people to carry your company forward?

Sales Managers Must Adapt, Too

In my past roles as a marketing executive at a handful of different companies, I interacted on a daily basis with sales managers up to the vice president level. All of these people had been successful individual contributors early in their careers. Because they had met their sales quotas and were among top producers, they were promoted into junior management positions as player/coaches, and then the ones who did well at this level were promoted to director and then VP level, where they managed a few dozen to hundreds of people in their sales teams. I recall that sales managers spent a great deal of time managing the metrics of the people in their teams, with data showing how many cold calls were made, how many leads were followed up on, and the number of meetings booked, all of which were predictive of sales success.

Just like individual salespeople now require new competencies that build social personal branding, sales managers and senior sales leaders must learn new skills and manage a new set of metrics. Managers must realize that when salespeople are interacting on Twitter or updating their LinkedIn profiles, this activity is more likely to contribute toward eventual sales than cold-calling a buyer. At some organizations, using social networking services during work hours is banned. This is ridiculous, of course. But even in those organizations where it isn't an outright policy violation, many sales managers don't allow time for social networking or give credit to the people who use social media effectively to build business.

"A sales manager's job is the same today as it was throughout the history of sales management," says Greg Alexander. "They have to be an effective coach, and their job is to make the salespeople more successful. What has changed is how they coach and what resources the salesperson is given. For example, if I'm a sales manager and I want my team to use something like social selling, I have to teach my salespeople how to create content on networks like LinkedIn. I have to teach them about content that will nurture leads and how to syndicate it across their social connections. Years ago I used to teach them how to make a cold call. It's completely different now."

This new sales management approach must be understood and encouraged all the way to the top of an organization. Alexander says it's still rare to find sales managers who are good at managing to the new social selling reality, but he lays the blame on senior management. "There are a lot of sales managers that are way behind the curve," he says. "I'm sympathetic, because it's difficult when companies are still measuring them using old-school metrics and holding them accountable to yesterday's business process execution. I talk to a lot of them in the course of my business, and while many of them tell me they want to use social selling, it's difficult to find the time because their company requires them to do countless other things that consume 100 percent of their capacity."

As you implement social selling, carry out real-time customer service, and develop into an agile company, make sure that the people up at the top of the organization understand what's required. You'll need to ensure that your management team is operating to the right metrics to drive success in this new world.

Training for Social Success

A salesperson's social personal brand is his or her most important asset, and the ability to communicate and show empathy on social networks is a critical skill for customer service representatives. Yet it is still rare that corporate training for salespeople and customer service staff includes courses on social networking. This needs to change.

If your salespeople are communicating only through traditional channels, you need to start by showing them that social channels can be far more successful. A LinkedIn network, for example, becomes their personal database. Once they have a connection, they have been granted permission and a very personal communication channel is now open to that person. With traditional sales, the telephone and email are the primary way to reach out to a buyer. But with people receiving hundreds of emails a day, it is tough if not impossible to break through. And today, phone calls go directly into voicemail or are screened by support staff. If I send an email, it's now email number 321 in somebody's inbox that day. But if I reach out to a connection on LinkedIn, mine might be one of a tiny handful of messages and it will be looked at. That's a whole new competency that can be taught—both the strategies and the tactics. Salespeople need to be trained on how to expand their reach, and how to make themselves attractive to other executives so that other executives will want them in their network. It's a new skill.

Managers need to build time into people's daily routines to allow them to participate in social media and cultivate their personal brands online. "Take one less hour of cold-calling," says HubSpot's Mark Roberge. "Take one less hour of going out to that networking event, and spend that hour in social media. Spend that hour on those blogs, commenting, visiting the LinkedIn groups, and running your own blog, and see which one yields more."

At HubSpot, training on social media is an important aspect of sales-people's introduction to the company. "Every single salesperson that goes through HubSpot sales training creates their own blog. They all amass a Twitter following of at least a hundred people. The business owners that they speak to say, 'You're the fourth person who's called me. Why should I talk to you?' That's when the HubSpot salesperson suggests they do a Google search on a topic of relevance, which includes either a blog they wrote or a piece that makes reference to them. They can then say, 'That's me right there,' and it immediately positions them as an expert. They have quickly leaped into a consultative doctor–patient type of relationship."

The same thing is true for training customer service representatives: You need to build social networking into your training programs. For example, new staff members in the social customer service role at American Airlines are put through a rigorous training program. "We work with them on everything from grammar and written style, to knowledge about the brand, to understanding context clues on social media, and when to get involved and when not to," says Jonathan Pierce, director of social communications for American Airlines. "After training, and before someone can work the public channel, we go into a practical mentored situation for a couple of weeks. And when they finally work the public channel, they undergo a period of quality control and monitoring. We make an important investment in training. It's essential when you start to scale social, as it's a very important part of your strategy."

A New Kind of Company

Putting the ideas of this book to work at your organization means you're creating a new kind of company, one that is agile and one that is social. It doesn't matter if you're running your own single-person company, or a small business of a few dozen people, or a major enterprise with hundreds of thousands of employees—the ideas are the same and the nature of the required change is similar.

GutCheck has developed a powerful niche as a web solution that enables people to conduct detailed online research in less time than usual, sometimes within hours. Because GutCheck sells to a savvy audience of people looking for agile market research, the way GutCheck sells and services clients must be aligned to this new reality of speed. Traditional sales and service techniques just don't cut it when buyers are operating in real time.

"We think of the education we provide buyers online as architecture," says Matt Warta, the co-founder and CEO of GutCheck. GutCheck also delivers content within the sales process that shows buyers why it is valuable for them to use the GutCheck service to do quicker and more affordable research. "Based on what they are doing on our site, we know if they're at that high level where they're interested in on-demand communities, or if they are interested in the next two layers down. When we interact with them, we are very knowledgeable about what level they're at."

Warta says that his analysis shows that when a buyer signs up for something on the GutCheck site—for instance checking out a webinar or asking to speak to a salesperson—the buyer is about 70 percent toward closing a deal. Armed with the knowledge of what information a buyer has already seen on the site, the salesperson then goes into agile, real-time sales mode, frequently via social networks. The salesperson targets that individual buyer with just the right outreach at just the right time.

"If we see a prospect looking exclusively at our higher-level content on our site, then when we contact them we're going to talk about saving time, doing things quicker, and how GutCheck's services enable them to be successful in their position and advance their career," Warta says. "But if we discover someone is consuming a lot of our content about how agile market research enables the product innovation process, then we'll talk to them on a completely different track and discuss a more iterative approach to doing consumer research."

In a world where most sales processes are generic and each potential customer is sold to in the same way, the concept of understanding each individual buyer based on what content they have already consumed is revolutionary. It's a fundamental theme of the new rules of sales and service.

If you know how this process works, your salespeople can close more business by being less aggressive. Warta says that it is important to know when to just let the buyer absorb the information. "We understand that when people are in certain phases of the buying process, we should just leave them alone. We let them get comfortable. If we contact them too early they might think we're too Big Brother-ish. We hire people who have intellectual agility and can go where the customer is leading them."

Warta and his team use a similar content-centric service approach to support the customer's journey. "Once an account is closed and they've done business with us, we have a team we call our Online Research Strategists, and they are the primary interface with our clients," says Warta. "When we understand how they are using our platform, and what kind of everyday challenges they are facing in their jobs, we can create content around that. Once we've interacted with them on both the sales and services layers, we can then go back and say, 'How are you guys handling your product innovation process today? How are you guys handling your marketing and communication testing process?' We might say, 'We know that you guys have eight initiatives this year where you're going to go through this product innovation process.' Or, 'You're going to go through this marketing and communications process soon. Let's sit down, understand your plans for the year, and see where this on-demand capability can really help you out.'"

Agile, real-time sales and the provision of online content throughout the customer journey continue to drive business. When you lead with content that can influence sales, you're letting the buyers do the work of educating themselves about your products and services. "The great thing about selling this way is that it's very efficient," Warta says. "It's efficient from the perspectives of time and capital. Instead of having 50 salespeople running around spreading our message, we rely on content to do that."

You can achieve the same success.

Your Sales and Service Ecosystem

Growing up in Fairfield County, Connecticut, I knew that many of my parents' friends worked at the nearby IBM world headquarters. Back in the

1970s, IBM was known around town for excellent sales training and for the uniform its salesmen wore: dark blue or gray suit, a shirt "of any color as long as it is white," a subtle tie, and black shoes. In the decades when "nobody gets fired for buying IBM," the highly trained, identical-looking IBM salesmen were in charge of the relationship with buyers. They controlled the information and they dictated the terms.

Today, IBM has adapted by doing much more than ditching the corporate dress code. The company has thrived more than a century after its founding by making social business a part of everything it does. The company was among the first to encourage employees to participate on social networks nearly a decade ago. This was codified in the IBM Social Computing Guidelines, a document first released in spring 2005. The guidelines, which are freely available to anyone on the IBM site, cover online collaboration via blogs, wikis, social networks, virtual worlds, and social media. IBM has empowered team members to become social employees and build their personal brands by sharing content on a daily basis. As a result, most are active on Twitter, and tens of thousands publish their own blogs.

"You've got to develop that relationship online versus just in person; that's what social is all about," says Sandy Carter, general manager for ecosystem development and a social business evangelist at IBM. (Carter has also written a book on the subject, *Get Bold: Using Social Media to Create a New Type of Social Business*.) "Social selling is the ability to build your social graph and be connected socially as a seller—to attract, engage, and connect. It's about knowing your prospects and your clients. For example, I recently went to meet with a very important CEO, and before we met I looked at his Facebook profile and I called up his LinkedIn page. I found out that this particular person really likes art, so I invited him to a private showing at our little IBM art gallery. One of the things that caused him to come and hear more about our products was that connection to art. I think more and more sellers are going to have to be more P2P—person-to-person—not just B2B or B2C. They need to sell to people as people, not as a company."

Another aspect of traditional selling that has been cast aside at IBM is the notion of a predictable sales funnel with its perfectly defined steps during which salespeople lead buyers to the point of close. "At IBM it is a continuous funnel versus a funnel that moves progressively down," Carter says. "If you think about any marketing course, you start by identifying a lead and you progress it through the funnel. In the new world it's a set of little tornadoes. You might connect with someone and you engage with them. There's more continuous contact and working toward long-term relationships that make a difference versus a traditional set of lead management capability. So, to me, that means you've got to change the way you do things."

Carter offers the National Football League as an example of how this works. Indeed the NFL is the most successful professional sports league in North America. "With the NFL, the event of the year is the Super Bowl," she says. "But instead of generating leads culminating in an event like the Super Bowl—which is what a lot of companies still do—NFL marketing and engagement are like a set of little tornadoes. For example, fantasy football keeps fans engaged all year. Before the Super Bowl they do pre-parties all over the United States, not just in the Super Bowl city. They start things nine months in advance to connect with their buyers—the fans—and they do this in lots of different ways. It's a great example of a continuous campaign, which I think is required in the new social world."

IBM has made social not just the way it sells today; it has implemented social business throughout the entire organization. It has developed applications that IBMers use every day to solve problems for customers. For example, there's an IBM mobile app that enables IBMers around the world to connect to people inside the company as they work on customer projects. "It's used as the ecosystem inside of IBM to find the right expert," Carter says. "The expertise could be very broad, like who's the best mobile expert in Canada? Or it could be very specific, like who knows J2EE new rule number 12? It helps you instantly to find that person, socially, based on their expertise. Using all the social tools, we rate that person's expertise, how they've been tagged, their Klout rating, and how many people have recommended them. We're building a social ecosystem on mobile that helps you sell."

Your Turn

Just like IBM, your organization needs to build social business into all aspects of your sales efforts to buyers and how you service existing customers. But it takes time. IBM has been working at it for 10 years. If you haven't started already, you've got to start now.

I've found that managing fear is one of the best starting points. People are naturally wary of things they don't understand, and engaging with your marketplace using the new tools might provoke some anxiety in you or in others in your company.

There might be resistance at the top. You'll need to be an agent of change to implement some of these ideas, and that's a challenging position to be in, but one that can pay off with great personal and company-wide success.

You can do it.

It doesn't matter what marketplace you're in or what group of buyers you're trying to reach. You can master the new rules of sales and service and build powerful relationships with your buyers and your customers. So get out there!

Acknowledgments

First, a disclosure: Because I do advisory work, run seminars, and do paid speaking gigs in the world that I write about, there are inevitable conflicts. I have friends in some of the organizations that I discuss in this book, on my blog, and on the speaking circuit, and I have run seminars for or advised several of the companies mentioned in the book.

The spark for *The New Rules of Sales and Service* came during a discussion with HubSpot CEO Brian Halligan over afternoon beers at a nice sunny spot one summer afternoon. Thank you, Brian, for your help in crystalizing my thinking. And for the beers.

Alan Andres read every word of an early draft of this book, and his sound advice and practical suggestions made it much better.

John R. Harris provided valuable early input into the structure. Andrew Davis and Rich Jurek offered suggestions when I was stuck.

Tony D'Amelio, who manages my speaking activities, is always a font of valuable advice, and his fingerprints are in these pages. Matt Anderson, Carin Kalt, Carolyn Monaco, Jenny Taylor, Hilary Kline, and Shanna Wheeler work with Tony and are amazingly helpful to me.

At John Wiley & Sons, my publisher Matt Holt and my editor Shannon Vargo have steered me through the publishing business with wit and wisdom. We've now done seven books together! Also at Wiley, thanks to Elizabeth Gildea, Melissa Connors, Peter Knapp, Deborah Schindlar, and Sadhika Salariya for their help and support.

And especially, thank you to my wife, Yukari, and daughter, Allison, for supporting my work and understanding when I am under deadline or away from home speaking in some far-flung part of the world.

About the Author

Photo by Bruce Rogovin, rogovin.com

David Meerman Scott is an internationally acclaimed marketing and sales strategist whose books and blog are must-reads for professionals seeking to generate attention in ways that grow their business. David's advice and insights help people, products, and organizations stand out, get noticed, and capture hearts and minds. He is author or co-author of 10 books—three are international bestsellers. *The New Rules of Marketing & PR*, now in its fifth edition, has been translated into 28 languages and is used as a text in hundreds of universities and business schools worldwide. It is a modern business classic with over 350,000 copies sold so far. David is also the author of *Real-Time Marketing & PR* (a *Wall Street Journal* bestseller) and a co-author of *Marketing the Moon* and *Marketing Lessons from the Grateful Dead*.

A graduate of Kenyon College, David has lived in New York, Tokyo, Boston, and Hong Kong. He is a marketer in residence and on the board of advisors of HubSpot, and on the board of advisors of ExpertFile, Visible-Gains, and GutCheck. He also advises nonprofits and is on the advisory board of the Grateful Dead Archive at the University of California at Santa Cruz, and is a member of the digital media advisory board of HeadCount.

Check out his blog at www.WebInkNow.com, follow him on Twitter at @dmscott, or download his free iPhone or iPad application.

Index

Have David Meerman Scott Speak at Your Next Event!

Photo by Rajiv Sankarlall at Tony Robbins Business Mastery, January 19, 2016.

As a speaker, David's high-energy presentations are a treat for the senses. He's informative, entertaining, and inspiring. That he has spoken on all seven continents and in more than 40 countries to audiences of the most respected firms, organizations, and associations underscores the value he brings to audiences. David's keynotes and master classes are an urgent call to action. Real time is the mind-set for the future—and content rules! His tailored presentations delve deeply—offering strategies and tactics that help audiences seize the initiative, open new channels, and grow their business.

Top firms have engaged David to present at events and meetings, among them: Cisco Systems, Hewlett-Packard, PricewaterhouseCoopers, GenRe,

SAP, Microsoft, McCormick, Dow Jones, Nestlé Purina, Jackson Healthcare, Omnicom, Ford Motor Company, Century 21, National Geographic, Abbott Medical Devices, and the New York Islanders. He has delivered keynotes at conferences and expos, including the Self Storage Association, NASDAQ Stock Market, the Government of Ontario, U.S. Air Force, National Investor Relations Institute, Entrepreneurs Organization, International Health Forum, Credit Union National Association, Giant Screen Theater Association, Realtors® Conference, National Agri-Marketing Association, Belize Tourism Industry Association, and many, many more.

All of David's presentations are a combination of three things: education, entertainment, and motivation.

Visit www.DMS.live to see videos of David in action or for information on booking him to speak at your event.